Policy, Power and Order

Policy, Power and Order
The Persistence of Economic Problems in Capitalist States

KERRY SCHOTT

Yale University Press
New Haven and London
1984

Designed by Caroline Williamson.
Set in Compugraphic Baskerville
by Red Lion Setters, Holborn, London.
Printed in Great Britain by Pitman Press Ltd, Bath.

Library of Congress Catalog Card Number 84-40187
ISBN 0-300-03237-4

Contents

Acknowledgements

Since a great deal of the material in this book covers areas in the social sciences that are typically ignored by the economics discipline, and with which I was thus unfamiliar, I had much to learn, and I owe a considerable debt to 'non-economists'. These scholars were most patient and encouraging to a learner in their midst, and to John Goldthorpe, Walter Korpi, David Cameron, Miles Kahler and Bob Gilpin I give thanks.

Among economists I would like to thank Tony Atkinson who encouraged my interest in economic theories of the state and who read and commented on an early draft of this book. Paul Bowles also commented on all the manuscript and left me feeling I had much to learn. Laurence Harris, Ben Fine and George Catephores read the section on Marxist theories of the state and their critical comments were most useful though not always attended to in the way they would have wished. Deborah Mabbett and Tim Hazeldine also read several sections and drew my attention to unclear argument and wording which I have tried to amend. Finally among economists I must give great thanks to Victoria Chick who read several chapters and who discussed my argument with me as it developed.

I began writing this book in the fall term of 1980 when I was a visitor at the Woodrow Wilson School at Princeton University. It would be difficult to imagine a better place in which to work, and to those who made that visit possible I give thanks. University College, London University, gave me leave from my teaching duties at that time. The actual production of the book was assisted by the typing of Maria Correa, Elizabeth Dew, Sue Field Reid, Diana Simmons, Pam Doolin, Sue Curtis and Ann Robinson. My cohabitees and friends endured the usual tiresome rigours of associating with an author, and to Linn Cameron, Jennifer Earle, Russell Hay and especially Sophie Watson I acknowledge this particular debt. Finally to John Nicoll and Caroline Williamson of Yale University Press my thanks for their editing, and for their good humour with a person who almost never met their deadlines.

1 Introduction

The winds must come from somewhere when they blow,
There must be a reason why the leaves decay;
Time will say nothing but I told you so.

Auden, 'If I Could Tell You'

Background

My particular concern with economic policy and economic theories of the state first came from my experience as an economist working within government. In the latter half of 1975 I was fortunate enough to be employed by the Australian government as an economic advisor in the now defunct Priorities Review Staff. This small group was originally set up by the government to examine longer-term policy issues and priorities. This role was envisaged as a supplement to the shorter term policy concerns of existing government departments, which in their day-to-day running tended to give longer-term issues less attention than it was felt they deserved.

In reality what happened within the Priorities Review Staff was that longer-term policy was examined but shorter-term demands were also placed upon it from time to time by the Prime Minister's Department. This seemed to occur particularly when conflict over policy was evident. This conflict was either between different government departments or between the Cabinet and government departments. Either different arms of the public service had different views on policy recommendations, or government politicians had different views from the civil service. There were also occasions when both kinds of conflicts occurred simultaneously.

These differences over policy are of course part of the normal functioning of government, but my training as a macroeconomist had

1

not prepared me to pay heed to the way in which policy was eventually formulated within government. This political input into economic policy outcomes did not only come from the ideological concerns of the governing party via its cabinet but also from the interactions between government departments and indeed from political influences originating outside these state institutions. Through this daily experience of the interactions between politics and economics it became obvious to me that economists needed to pay more attention to these interactions than they typically do in their textbook models. My explorations in this field led naturally to the literature on economic theories of the state. These theories, which were new to me at that time, are attempts to explain the actual economic behaviour of a state. Unlike a typical economic policy model these theories are not asking what a state ought to do; they are simply trying to understand what a state actually does.

In thinking about these economic theories of the state I concurrently read some history and in doing so I was struck by the fact that the one overriding concern of any state was its desire to maintain social and economic stability or order. Indeed it makes no sense to speak of a state once order has broken down and governance has ceased. Hence whatever the actual actions of a state it seemed to me that these must, at a very fundamental level, be concerned with maintaining order.

Now this state quest for social and economic order appeared to be curiously neglected in the economic theories of the state I examined. Typically order is either implicitly assumed and hence entirely ignored; or alternatively order is explicitly taken as given and its persistence is explained by state behaviour. In the latter approach, common among Marxist economists, the ongoing stability of capitalist society is due to state intervention, but this order is usually assumed to be reached without too much difficulty on the part of the state.

But is stability really so easy for a state in democratic developed countries to maintain? What are the characteristics of the economic and social system within which we live and work and are these conducive to social and economic stability or not? In considering these questions it became clear that the economic systems of the developed countries have changed gradually but dramatically over this century. In particular, in all developed countries we now have a very large public sector and money wages and price movements are sticky in a downward direction. Both these changes are especially apparent since World War II and both are relatively new developments.

These changes appear to be related to an increase in the power of the working class. As unionization increased this century so too did the influence and control of workers over their money wages. In turn, increasingly concentrated industries and firms were capable of passing these increased money wage costs on to consumers in the form of price increases. The downward stickiness of prices and wages, common in all developed countries, appears to be at least partly related to the increase in unionization of the workforce.

The labour force has also increased its strength and influence in the political arena. The introduction of universal suffrage this century is associated with a not surprising increase in the vote for broadly left-of-centre political parties in all countries except the United States. Where these parties have governed for prolonged periods and had a substantial presence in the Cabinet it is clear that public expenditure has been higher out of GDP than in other comparable nations.

We thus now appear to be living in an economic society where the power resources of the working class have increased. These power resources cover developments such as increased unionization and the rise of political parties that attempt to represent working-class interests. It is through resources of this type that power can be exercised. These social and political developments are associated with the observed economic changes already noted. Wage and price movements are sticky downwards and the public sector has grown dramatically. Furthermore this conjuncture of events is now coincident, and perhaps causally connected, with difficulties in economic management. In the 1970s and early 1980s the developed economies have performed significantly worse than in the two decades following World War II. Economic growth has been slower, inflation has been a serious problem, and unemployment has reached levels that were unthinkable in the 1950s and 1960s. And these economic problems, as I write in 1983, appear to be extraordinarily persistent. Different economic policies to remedy the situation have been tried in different countries, and at different times in the same countries, but the ongoing frustration with economic policy, and with the theories behind it, continues in the minds of all but the most dogmatic.

For the first time in developed countries an economic crisis is associated with a social and political situation where the working class has more power resources at its command than at any previous time. During the 1950s and 1960s this working-class strength was coincident with a successful economy; and in periods of economic crisis in previous history the workforce were not so strong. Hence this conjuncture of economic crisis and a strong workforce is quite unprecedented.

This is not to argue that the workforce is necessarily the strongest group in society. It is simply to suggest that it is now stronger than in previous historic periods. And this increased relative strength on the part of the workers has important implications for state economic behaviour. In maintaining both social and economic stability the state is now in a new and interesting position, and this may be one reason why

3

current economic problems are so persistent. Economic policies to remedy the dismal economic situation may be ineffectual if they are applied because of social changes in our societies; or economic policies may be judged simply as non-operational because of the social conflict they would engender if they were applied. The state, in developed democratic countries, may be groping for a solution to its economic problems, but to find this solution is difficult or even impossible. Stability and order must be upheld and any economic policy that conflicts with this goal is either severely constrained or not on the agenda.

This type of interaction between the polity and the economy is the subject of this study. On one level this book is a plea to economists to begin seriously the task of integrating social and political arrangements and practice into the body of economic theory. This is not a job to be left to sociologists and political theorists; they have done some excellent work in this field but economists have a contribution to offer which only they are equipped to make. For too long this sort of work has been classified as 'not economics' and avoided like the plague by many of my colleagues. But economic policy analysis is only useful when it can be applied, and this means we must understand the sort of society in which we are operating. Indeed if we do not seek this understanding we are in danger of working on policies that will never be applied or of applying theories in inappropriate situations. It is well to keep in mind the salutary experience of Emperor Franz Joseph of Austria who worked diligently on his papers every day from four in the morning until noon while his empire disintegrated about him.

Outline of the Book

As a necessary step in resolving the economic difficulties facing the developed countries we must first understand the problem. The economic explanations of the dismal economic performance of the 1970s are briefly examined in the next chapter. There I focus on neo-Keynesian and neoclassical theory and argue that both approaches lead to policy prescriptions that can in practice be quite ineffectual. The ability to solve domestic macroeconomic problems depends on both the application of policy and the responsiveness of the economy. The appropriate policy must be chosen, but if society is not responsive to this policy for some elusive reason, the policy will not be effective.

For neoclassical policy to be effective in the present climate it is clear that a reduction in the money supply and in government expenditure must be accompanied by a fall in prices and the real wage. If real wages and prices do not fall in response to this deflationary policy the end result will simply be reduced output and employment.

With a neo-Keynesian policy the recommended way to deal with an economic slowdown is to have an expansionary policy. But with an expansionary fiscal and monetary policy there is a real danger that runaway inflation in prices and money wages could result. To deal with this contingency the Keynesians usually link their expansion to an incomes policy, and should this be successful the expansion will not generate inflation. However experience suggests that if an incomes policy cannot be implemented than an expansion will generate inflation.

Hence the policy effectiveness of both the Keynesians and the neoclassicals depends critically on the response of the economy. For the Keynesians an incomes policy is vital in order to restrain inflation; for the neoclassicals both prices and real wages must fall. These considerations immediately lead to two questions. First, which is the appropriate policy strategy to pursue? Second, will the economy respond appropriately?

Now in choosing the appropriate policy strategy we must decide which theory is the most applicable to the society we are examining. We know that in microeconomics it makes no sense to apply a perfect competition model to a monopolistic market. In macroeconomics one hopes we would similarly choose to reject a theory of policy if it was not appropriate to the given situation. In this sense a theory is rejected not because it is wrong but because it is inappropriate. In Chapter 3 it is argued that neoclassical theory is inappropriate in the light of the changes indicated above. The workforce now has sufficient strength to stop real wages falling, and should this policy be applied it will be ineffective. This increasing strength on the part of the working class also has implications for Keynesian policy strategies and specifically for whether or not a successful incomes policy can be implemented.

It is suggested, on the basis of public choice theories, that where social groups have evolved that are encompassing there is every reason to expect that an incomes policy will work. An encompassing group is one that includes virtually all individuals or interested parties. It is not fragmented into smaller groups with diverse goals. The aim of any group is to achieve benefits for all its members and where this group encompasses all society the outcome is more likely to be in the broad social interest. Where, on the other hand, groups are fragmented, the benefit to a group is more narrowly defined and less in line with the wider social interest. Thus in a country like Britain where the union movement is strong but fragmented there is little reason, on public choice grounds, to expect an incomes policy to hold. On the other hand in a country like Sweden or Austria where the union movement is strong and approximates an encompassing group we might expect an incomes

5

policy to work effectively and in the wider social interests of all workers.

This argument is investigated in some detail in Chapter 4 where the domestic economic performance of eighteen OECD countries is examined. There are quite clear links between political arrangements and economic outcomes which tend to support the previous argument. Low inflation and low unemployment tend to be associated with liberal corporatism. Under modern corporatist arrangements encompassing groups, typically labour and business leaders, meet together and decide economic policy with the state in a mediating role. As an interest mediator the role of the state is crucial, and its aim of avoiding conflict and achieving economic stability is quite overt.

This interaction between politics and economics is completely missing in the most familiar economic analysis of policy. The framework within which most economic policy is discussed is considered in Chapter 5. Here it is argued that this basic policy model is logically inconsistent and naive. The assumption that agents within the state sector act in the public interest conflicts with the assumption that agents in the private sector behave in their own self-interest. Since a public sector worker is also a private sector consumer this set of behavioural assumptions involves an assumed schizophrenia on the part of some individuals. While they are at home they are self-interested; but once they are at work in the public service they rather oddly act in the public interest.

Also this model assumes an omnipotent state which operates in a socially stable private and public sector. There is no possibility of a breakdown in governance in this model, and the maintenance of order is quite simply assumed.

Now since this model is used to give advice to governments it addresses what the state ought to be doing and not what the state is doing. However even within its own terms this framework for analyzing economic policy suffers from severe shortcomings. The next two chapters, Chapters 6 and 7, turn to economic theories that seek to explain actual state economic behaviour.

Within these economic theories of the state there are two quite distinct approaches. The first assumes that individual agents in the public sector, be they politicians or bureaucrats, act to pursue their own self-interest, and conduct economic policy in line with this self-seeking code of conduct. There could be constraints on this behaviour but nevertheless the outcome of it is most unlikely to be in the public interest.

The second approach to understanding state economic behaviour is derived from Marxist economics. The prolonged stability of capitalism was something of an enigma to Marxist theorists who, on the basis of their theory of capitalist production, might have expected a crisis in capitalism accompanied by social conflict. In the event of a continuing capitalist order these theorists sought to explain this stability by examining the role of the state. They suggested that capitalist order prevailed because the state evolved institutional forms and functions that maintained this social system. The state, in capitalist society, acted to preserve the system and it was essentially these state actions, including its economic policy, that enabled capitalism to prevail. This line of theory also of course implies that economic policy is not directed at public interest objectives. It is determined by the requirements of capitalist production, including the maintenance of social relations which serve capitalism.

But both the Marxist and more mainstream economic theories of the state tend to overlook the difficulties a state may face in achieving stability and order. The first type of state theory, based on the pursuit of individual self-interest, assumes stability and order within both the private and public sectors. No attention at all is paid to the maintenance of this order in society. Order is simply and implicitly taken for granted. In Marxist theories of the state on the other hand, the focus is on explaining why there is an existing and rather long-lived order. But the problem here is that because the observed order is being explained in these theories, little attention was placed on the difficulties that might appear in the actual maintenance of this order. Because Marxist theories were trying to explain order, they tended to take its existence for granted. These Marxist theorists observed stability, and thus somewhat curiously assumed that it had been achieved by the state without too much trouble.

On the basis of this criticism of both the Marxist and mainstream economic theories of the state this study then goes on to consider the problem of order. Chapter 8 begins with a discussion of the existing economic literature on this topic. This treatment is essentially an economic analysis of the Hobbesian problem: how can order be obtained given a crude state of prevailing anarchy? The main argument in this chapter is that present-day society does not spring from a starting point of anarchy. If it did the economic analysis in this chapter would be of more interest. But looking at the evolution of democracy from feudalism suggests that the power distribution within society changes over time and that we can best understand this by examining the relative power of different groups in society.

This discussion relates back to the work on power in Chapter 3 where the power resources of the workers are examined in some detail. On this basis Chapters 9 and 10 then attempt to analyze how order may be established when power is distributed across groups, specifically workers and capitalists. The first approach in Chapter 9 is static but it does show that if workers become more powerful then this change in power must be accommodated if order is to prevail. Various economic implications of this are discussed and the strategies that a state might be expected to pursue are explored.

However for insight into the different growth and investment performances of the developed countries, we must look to dynamic analysis. In Chapter 10, a simply dynamic model of capitalism is developed to investigate these matters. Both the power of the labour force and the particular economic situation affect whether or not consensus around economic policy is likely and attainable. In view of this model the social and economic quiescence of the 1950s and 1960s can be explained and the difficulties now confronting present-day economic management can be at least partly understood. The final chapter summarizes this argument and concludes that our current economic problems could persist for a very long time. The reasons for this are not only economic; nor are they simply caused by a crisis in economic theory. The problem is both economic and political. Only when these two issues are considered together can we hope to understand the modern economy. While no grand new theory is offered here it is hoped that the start made will be sufficient to persuade other economists to join in the development of a new political economy.

2 A Shortcoming of Domestic Macroeconomic Analysis

The generally accepted view teaches
That there was no excuse,
Though in the light of recent researches
Many would find the cause

In a not uncommon form of terror;
Others still more astute,
Point to the possibilities of error
At the very start.

Auden, 'Let History Be My Judge'

Introduction

In this chapter I argue that both neo-Keynesian and neoclassical analyses of the macroeconomy suffer from a common shortcoming. I begin by discussing the bare elements of both these theories and point out that in practice both can lead to policies that can be quite ineffectual in coping with the problems that are now facing the developed economies. The effectiveness of economic policy depends on the responsiveness of the economy in which this policy is applied, and if the economy, for some elusive reason, remains unresponsive to policy actions then the policy fails. I then proceed to suggest that macroeconomic theory must be adapted to take account of changes that have occurred in the society to which it is applied. This part of the chapter is methodological and it sets the stage for an examination of some changes in the developed economies that are examined in some detail in Chapter 3. The focus of our attention in macroeconomic theory must be switched to pay heed to these changes and unless this occurs our understanding of the present macroeconomic situation is severely limited.

Macroeconomic Theory and Present Problems

The switch from economic prosperity in the 1950s and 1960s to the slow-down and inflation of the 1970s has caused something of a trauma in economic policy analysis. Those of us who learned economics during the 1960s were told, quite mistakenly as it transpired, that the age-old problems of large cyclical swings in economic activity had been solved. The dismal experiences of the depression in the 1930s were never to be repeated and the sad photographs of large queues of unemployed people taken during that cyclical downswing were merely a matter of past history.

Keynesian economics had triumphed and in the process the business cycle had been tamed. Minor recessions and booms would be experienced but larger-scale economic upheavals were, we were taught, a thing of the past. Being an economist was to be a delight, guiding the now apparently fairly stable economic system from one minor hiccup to another, all the time avoiding deeper cyclical swings with ease. Living standards throughout the 1950s and 1960s rose, and as economists we congratulated ourselves on our social usefulness and success.

This may be something of a caricature, but since the late 1960s dramatic economic upheavals, which became particularly manifest in the 1970s, have changed this satisfied mood. Economics really is a dismal science after all, as we search for policies to restore full employment, stable prices and growth. At present this quest for policy solutions is dominated by the ongoing debate between neo-Keynesians and neo-classical economists. This dialogue is accompanied by severe critiques of the theory used on both sides of the debate and details of this critique are well reviewed in Bell and Kristol (eds.) (1981). Here the details of this largely theoretical criticism need not detain us since I wish only to point out a severe shortcoming that is shared by the neo-Keynesians and the neoclassicals. The nature of this shortcoming is obvious if we consider an over-simplified version of each theory (Scharpf, 1983).

Neo-Keynesians attribute the economic slowdown of the 1970s simply to the deficit in aggregate demand in industrialized countries. This demand deficit occurred because of rises in commodity prices and notably the oil price shocks of 1973 and 1979. These price rises were not sufficiently compensated by a recycling of 'petro-dollars' or by expansionary fiscal and monetary policies in the deficit countries. Because of this decline in aggregate demand, caused especially by the outflow of petro-dollars, economic growth fell and unemployment increased. The cost push effect of oil price rises simultaneously led to inflation and together with the decline in demand we experienced the stagnation of the last decade. In this scenario there was a bunching of unfortunate and largely exogenous events which were unlikely to occur again.

The policy recommendations that follow from this simple view of events are straightforward. The recession should be attacked by a mix of monetary and fiscal expansion to restore aggregate demand to its full-employment level. If this increase in demand is accompanied by wage and price rises in the presence of unemployment then some form of wage and price control must also be implemented. These wage and price rises that imply a need for incomes policies are caused by the power of labour and by economic concentration in industry and these pressures must somehow be curbed, if only temporarily. In this scenario those countries that have performed relatively well will be those that have followed expansionary fiscal and monetary policies while at the same time managing to achieve wage and price stability via some form of controls.

For neoclassical economists, on the other hand, the interpretation of events is somewhat different. The commodity price rises and oil price shocks are changes which can lead to quick market adjustments. These adjustments however will be hampered by government intervention and attempts to manipulate aggregate demand. In particular such intervention will prevent real wages falling in a recession, and this is especially true when the power of labour is strong. This union strength along with government intervention means that in a recession real wages will not fall. As a result labour markets will not clear and there will not be a return to full employment.

It is also argued that growth is hampered by high minimum wages, the increasing financial burden of the welfare state and the non-productive public sector, and by a rising number of restrictive regulations and bureaucratic controls imposed on market actors.

This view of events leads to policy recommendations in stark opposition to those of the neo-Keynesians. Unemployment should be attacked by decreasing real wages and inflation should be attacked by restrictive monetary and fiscal policies. This would encourage growth by lowering taxes and decreasing the financial burden of the state sector. In addition deregulation and a lessening of bureaucratic controls would assist growth. On the basis of these policy recommendations those countries that have been most successful economically will be those that have seen restrictive monetary and fiscal policies along with various supply-side policies of deregulation.

Now both these theories suffer from a rather similar difficulty. Within the terms of both theories, if wages and prices are not responsive, either to controls or to market forces, then there is a big problem. For the neo-Keynesians, if wages and prices cannot be controlled somehow an increase in demand will generate inflation. The increase in demand might make some contribution to growth and employment but

11

the contrary effect of runaway inflation will cause this expansionary Keynesian policy to fail. It is this fear that has caused writers like Modigliani (1977) to remark that the design of policies to control wages and prices is 'the greatest challenge presently confronting those interested in stabilization'.

The neoclassicals' problem is not in fact dissimilar. It is clear in their paradigm that if the money supply is limited and fiscal expenditure is cut back without an accompanying fall in prices and real wages, the end result must be reduced output and employment (Gordon, 1981). For their policy to be successful, prices and real wages must be responsive to restrictionary monetary and fiscal policies. If this is not the case, the end result of these restrictive policies will simply be further recession. Thus for both these schools of economists the weakness in their theories lies in the potential responsiveness of wages and prices to either cuts or increases in demand. If wages and prices do not fall in the face of restrictive neoclassical policies or if they cannot be controlled in the face of expansionary Keynesian policies both sets of economic policy recommendations are effectively useless.

While this problem is often conveniently ignored in the higher reaches of abstract theory, it does receive some attention from economists who are concerned more directly with policy. Typically the neo-Keynesians have shown their awareness of the situation by formulating various incomes policy schemes. On the neoclassical front the concern with deregulation policies and various proposals to cut back government intervention are often directly related to their aim of achieving more perfectly functioning markets. These endeavours are quite clearly based on the common fear, held by both neo-Keynesian and neoclassical economists, that their policies will not work unless the economy responds satisfactorily.

Now if we were to try and use either of these theories to explain the different economic experiences of different countries during the 1970s this common shortcoming in both theories really becomes obvious. As we will see later, the economic experience of the developed nations during the 1970s has been mixed. While all the countries that we consider have fared worse since 1970 than they did in the 1950s and 1960s, there is also a considerable variance in economic performance across nations. Put bluntly, some countries have done better than others.

Now since countries have different resource endowments and to some extent are at different stages of development we would of course expect some differences in economic growth and unemployment levels. However the differences we do observe also appear to be related to the economic responsiveness of particular countries. Some nations, a neo-Keynesian would simply argue, have been more successful with their incomes policy than others. On the other hand, where neoclassical policy has not appeared to be successful the neoclassicals would suggest that it is at least in part because of market imperfections that must be removed.

These sorts of arguments that might be offered to explain at least some of the cross-national differences in economic performance are terribly limited. If the economic policies pursued vary in their practical consequences across nations, economists can simply blame this variance on institutional causes. For the neo-Keynesians if their expansion is not effective it is simply because the society in question will not conduct a suitable incomes policy. On the other hand, for the neoclassicals the cause of any policy failures lies in the existing market institutions and the incapacity of society to remove market imperfections.

But this line of reasoning in both the neo-Keynesian and neoclassical schools simply begs questions that cannot be ignored by the economics discipline if we are to understand the current economic situation more comprehensively. Why do some countries appear to find it difficult, to the point of impossibility, to implement an incomes policy? And why have some countries been more successful with incomes policies? Also why, if neoclassical theory is accepted, are markets apparently so unresponsive.

These important questions lurk behind most macroeconomic policy analysis but they are rarely directly confronted. We thus have a situation in macroeconomic theory where policy recommendations, whether Keynesian or neoclassical, may not work because the economy is for some 'social' reason simply not responsive. Domestic economic management can conceptually be divided into two steps — the recognition of policy and the responsiveness of the economy to it (Kindleberger, 1970, p.66). In present macroeconomics the focus is on what the correct policy ought to be, and virtually no attention is paid to the social response that this policy will generate. If one chooses Keynesian policy and this is 'correct', it will be useless unless prices and wages respond favourably. On the other hand if one chooses neoclassical policy and this is 'correct', it too will be useless within its own terms unless real wages and prices fall. If society lacks whatever elusive ingredients are needed for successful price and wage responses, the chosen policy will quite simply not function even if it does happen to be correctly chosen in a technical economic sense.

This argument suggests that present domestic macroeconomic problems may not simply be the result of pursuing incorrect economic policies — though this is of course important. Current economic performance also results from the responsiveness of society to economic policy, and some countries may have performed better because they were more responsive to policy for some reason. Their inflation, unemployment and growth records are not simply the result of their chosen economic policy but also a consequence of the way in which this policy was accepted or indeed opposed within that society.

A Note on Methodology

This lack of attention paid to the responsiveness of a society to economic policy is one consequence of the act of theorizing. Any theory is simply a tool of analysis, and to be an effective tool it must simplify and cut down. Attention must be focussed on those issues that we perceive to be important, and at the same time we must ignore those issues that we think are unimportant. This is the only way we can deal with a complex reality. As Hicks (1976, p.208) has argued, 'we must work, if we are to work effectively, in some sort of blinkers'.

Now the art of theorizing lies in making appropriate choices about what issues to highlight and what issues to ignore. In economics this appropriate choice is not a straightforward one, and it is this delicacy that makes economic theory more of an art than a science. As Hicks (1976) has written, the facts that we study are neither permanent nor repeatable. They change incessantly and without repetition. This implies that our theories, as tools of analysis, must also adapt to these changing circumstances. In a changing world a theory which forces attention on the right issues at one time may illumine the wrong issues at another time. There cannot be an economic theory that will do for us everything we want all the time.

Because of this, the choice of theory is a 'horses for courses' situation. We may choose one theoretical approach at one time and another approach at another time. The theory of perfect competition may be a useful tool of analysis in some specific market, but if this market becomes monopolistic our choice of theory to apply must of course alter if our understanding is to be enhanced. In this sense a theory might be rejected not because it is wrong, in some technical sense, but simply because it is inappropriate.

In the context of macroeconomic analysis there does seem to be a need to focus attention on the responsiveness of society to economic policy. If we do not do so our understanding of present macroeconomic outcomes in developed countries is limited. Furthermore, once we have illumined this issue we then need to consider what theory, as a tool of analysis, is most appropriate. As a prelude to this consideration we must first identify changes in the world that appear to be important.

What is the particular situation that our theory is being applied to? In other words what is the course like that we are choosing the horse to run on? Does the theory from which our economic policy recommendations flow fit the situation we are studying? It is to these questions that I turn in the next chapter. It transpires that there have been dramatic changes in the society in which macroeconomic analysis is applied, and after identifying these changes I argue that current neo-Keynesian and neo-classical theories are inappropriate as tools of analysis for developing policy recommendations. I eventually proceed to develop an approach which appears more pertinent. But first let us examine some changes in society that may be relevant.

3   Changes in the Distribution of Power

You need not hear what orders he is giving
to know if someone has authority.

Auden, 'Sext'

Introduction

In applications of economic theory it is usual to consider the situation in
which the theory is being applied. It makes no sense to apply monopoly
theory to a perfectly competitive market. In deciding on the appropriate theory to use, the applied economist, often quite unconsciously,
first considers the existing situation. This consideration implicitly
includes some assessment of the power distribution prevailing. If there is
some dominating agent in a market this influences the choice of theory.
If there are no agents more powerful than others this would imply a different choice of model. In microeconomic applications this is quite well
understood, but in macroeconomics little attention has been paid to the
distribution of power in society and what this means for economic
analysis.

In this chapter I consider this issue and discuss the power distribution in the developed economies. I argue that there have been dramatic changes in this power distribution and that these changes are of
consequence for both the application of macroeconomic analysis and
the choice of an appropriate theory. The rather slippery concept of
power is discussed before an empirical assessment of changes in power is
made. The implications of these changes in the power distribution for
economic analysis are then explored.

The Concept of Power

Power is a notoriously difficult concept to define but political theorists have suggested various ways in which power might be considered. For Dahl (1957), power is revealed if an individual can get someone else to do something they would not otherwise do. This power might be both actual, in that it intuitively exists, or it might be exercised, in that it is revealed in actual action. In studies using this idea of power, influence is regarded as much the same thing as power; and in observing behaviour this power is manifest in who actually makes decisions or who wins the vote to make decisions. There is an observable conflict of interests, and the most powerful person or group is the one which subsequently makes the decisions.

This is rather straightforward, but Bacharach and Baratz (1970) have argued that power is more complex than this. Power is certainly reflected in who makes decisions at times of conflict; but it is also reflected in the fact that these decisions are actually on a public agenda in the first place. The extent to which a group or an individual can get an issue debated reflects power. Some groups and individuals are so lacking in power that their concerns never even get on the agenda. Thus the fact that unemployment is seen as an economic concern reflects an increase in the power of the unemployed. When unemployment was not considered an economic concern, as in the nineteenth century, the unemployed were a less powerful group than they now are. This is not to imply that the unemployed are more powerful than other groups but simply that they are now more powerful than they were, say, a century ago.

More recently Lukes (1974) has expanded the concept of power further. He considers that a group or individual is powerful if it can manipulate society in such a way as to keep potential conflict latent. In this sense the conflict is never observed, because some groups or individuals are sufficiently powerful to keep the potential conflict latent. Thus in the days when unemployment was not considered to be an economic concern some group was powerful enough to keep it off the economic agenda. The latent conflict between this powerful group and the unemployed was never observed, though the forms of manipulation used to keep the potential item from the agenda were apparent. One item in this manipulation was the use of that economic theory which suggested that unemployment was a temporary disequilibrium situation which would soon disappear. If this was the case there was no need to put unemployment on the agenda of economic concerns.

Thus if we are to identify the power distribution in society and any changes within it we can, on the basis of this discussion, look for three signs of power. First, what group is making decisions, and has this group changed? Second, what are the items that are on the agenda of concern, and have these changed? If they have what do they signify

17

about power changes between groups? Finally what latent conflicts never surface, and what power distribution does this imply? Answers to these questions would tell us something of the prevailing power distribution in society and how it has changed. Given this information we might then proceed to examine the implications of this power distribution on economic policy and the economy more generally.

Pluralism, Marxism and Corporatism

To identify the distribution of power in Western society we must first decide what groups or individuals may possess power. In an empirical study where should we begin to look for power? Now there are basically three alternative answers to this question, and the choice of answer depends on whether you choose to work in a pluralist, Marxist or corporatist conception of society. For pluralists like Dahl (1957) and Rostow (1960), power in modern society is widely diffused among individuals or many rather small interest groups. There is a multiplicity of power bases and no particularly distinct lines of conflict. Pluralist writers suggest that the conflict between labour and capital that dominated early industrialization has broken down because workers have become more geographically and socially mobile. Any present conflicts in Western society are not based around a pattern that involves a few large groups; instead power is spread diffusely and its distribution tends to be rather stable across many small interest groups.

Marxist writers have consistently challenged this position, and the bulk of this criticism, as we will discuss later, has been in the Leninist tradition. For these writers, the basic power conflict in society is between the working class and the capitalists who dominate through their ownership of the means of production. Every person and group in society depends on the output of this production, either directly or indirectly, and this gives capitalists a dominating role. Government and the state reflect the concern for capitalist productive success and the state always acts on behalf of the capitalist class. The significance of democracy and of the composition of the elected government tend to be granted little major significance and Jessop (1979), following Lenin, refers to parliamentary democracy as 'the best possible shell' for capitalism. In this approach two basic conflict groups are identified, workers and capitalists; moreover the relative distribution of power between them is assumed to be stable. Capitalists always dominate.

This Marxist-Leninist alternative to pluralism has more recently been joined by a corporatist attack on the pluralist theme. These corporatist writers, whose views span almost the complete spectrum from pluralism to Marxism, have studied ways in which conflicting interests are organized in developed countries (Schmitter and Lehmbruch (eds), 1979, and Lehmbruch and Schmitter (eds), 1982). The basic point made is that interest organizations in countries where corporatist arrangements are practised are few in number and these groups are closely related to the organization of the state. There are many theoretically identified forms of corporatism but what is generally understood is that in certain developed industrial countries we can observe three major interest groups. In modern conceptions of corporatism, organized labour, an organized employer group and a social democratic form of government together articulate their concerns at a tripartite level and decide on actions. These three groups, it is argued, are the important and powerful actors in society.

Hence in examining power we can choose the pluralist assumption that the power distribution in society is diffuse and across many small groups; or, alternatively, we can follow the Marxist-Leninist tradition and assume that power is distributed between capital and labour with the dominant position being adopted by capital; or, finally we could assume that power is distributed across three groups: organized labour, organized capital, and a form of elected government that acts as both an interest mediator and perhaps as an independent actor in some way.

In my treatment of power distribution here I choose to follow a corporatist line and specifically the work of Korpi (1983) who begins with class groups as a point of departure. He regards the working class as subordinate to the capitalist class, but in contrast to the Marxist-Leninist tradition he hypothesizes that 'through political and union organizations the working class can decrease its disadvantage in power resources in relation to capital' (Korpi, 1983, p.14). The advantage of this approach is that it admits that the relative power of the working class can vary across time and between countries. The wage-earning group are always relatively disadvantaged vis à vis capital because they depend on capitalist production for their livelihood, either directly or indirectly. Employers hire labour, and their control over physical capital and the human capital they acquire in the labour market always places them in a relatively powerful position in capitalist society. However the working class, through various strategies, can strengthen its position, and its relative degree of inferiority to capital can alter at particular times and in particular places. This conception of changes in power is far more fluid than that pemitted in Marxist-Leninist treatments of power, and it turns out to be analytically fruitful.

The particular strategies that workers have pursued to better their power position include collective bargaining and the organizing of political parties. Both strategies can potentially promote workers' interests in capitalist democracies and form structural bases from which further actions can be contemplated. The acceptance of unions and the rights of workers to organize, the introduction of universal suffrage and the formation of left-of-centre political parties can all be considered as historic working-class gains. These developments add to the power of wage-earners by enabling them to develop institutions through which they can articulate their concerns. As these institutions develop, wage-earners can then get their interests put on the agenda of social concern and to an extent have their demands voiced and met.

However, the position of wage-earners as a group in capitalist society must always be assessed in comparison with business interests. The power position of business in society is affected by many factors, including the degree of concentration of private ownership in the economy and the extent to which the economy is dependent on export industries. The extent and nature of business interest organizations is also clearly relevant, as are the alliances which business interests form with political parties. However, in historical perspective it can be argued that the greatest changes that have recently occurred in the power distribution are those that have affected wage-earners. There have been changes in the power position of business interests but these have not been sufficient to halt the rise in the relative increase in power accruing to wage-earners. On the basis of this proposition the relative power distribution in developed countries can be examined by limiting ourselves to changes in the power resources of wage earners.

Of course pluralists will object to this choice of analysis because of its stress on class conflict. Writers in a Leninist tradition will also object that suffrage and the organization of political parties are simply a form of co-option that happens to suit capital and basically causes virtually no shift in the distribution of power. Many economists will probably object that in any case this is not economics and is of no concern to them. To all these groups of potential dissenters I can only recommend that they assess the evidence that follows.

Assessing the Distribution of Power

We are now in a position to examine changes in the relative power distribution in Western societies. This assessment includes changes both across time and between countries, and we begin with indicators of the mobilization of the working class. In Table 3.1 the changes in the level of unionization in seventeen OECD nations are presented for the period 1900–76. The level of unionization is measured in the usual way as the percentage of union members in the non-agricultural workforce.

The most remarkable feature in this table is the overall increase

Table 3.1: *Union Membership as a Percentage of the Non-Agricultural Workforce: 1900–76*

	Before World War I	Interwar	1946–60	1961–76
Austria	6	43	54	56
Belgium	5	28	42	52
France	7	12	28	19
Ireland	—	15	33	40
Italy	11	19	27	18
Germany	16	46	36	34
Netherlands	16	27	31	33
Switzerland	6	15	25	22
Australia	30	37	52	48
Canada	8	12	25	27
USA	17	25	44	39
Denmark	16	34	48	50
Finland	5	8	30	47
Norway	6	19	47	44
Sweden	11	30	65	76
UK	15	29	43	44
Japan	—	20	26	28

Source: Korpi (1983, p.31).

in unionization between 1900 and 1960. Every country has experienced a long-term increase in the percentage of workers unionized, though there have been some short-term variations in this trend. The most notable of these variations was the sharp decline in union membership in Sweden in 1909, and in Britain in 1926, after unsuccessful general strikes. Also in Finland in 1917 union membership trebled before the Civil War. It is also remarkable that the level of unionization after 1960 has not shifted much in any country except Sweden and Finland, where it has risen, and Italy and France, where it has fallen.

There are also clearly some big differences between nations. Australia had a high level of union density rather early, which in part can be associated with the compulsory arbitration system that prevailed there and which enabled workers by law to register their organizations. In the post-1945 period, the United States, Canada, Switzerland, France, Italy and Japan all stand out as relatively low on the union density scale. On the other hand Austria, Belgium, Denmark, Sweden and Australia appear to have highly unionized workforces.

To an extent the strength of this particular mobilization depends on whether or not there are splits in the union movement. In several countries these union splits have been on religious grounds, and this has been particularly the case in Catholic countries; France, Italy and

Belgium all fall into this category. The unions in the Netherlands and Switzerland are also split on religious grounds and in Austria and Germany this was the case before 1939. In the USA and Canada the union movement was split on craft versus industrial lines from 1936 to 1955, and in Japan and Finland the unions are split on a political basis. On the other hand unions have been unified in a single confederation in Ireland, Australia, New Zealand, Denmark, Norway and Sweden during this century.

The other major indicators of working class mobilization are in the political arena. First, the relatively recent introduction of universal suffrage is worth noting. By the end of World War I universal *male* suffrage had been introduced in most developed countries except Japan, though in many countries the vote was not extended to females for many years after. The extension of democracy to cover all males and females, irrespective of their wealth or social position, was of course a long historic struggle in most countries and the years in which full democracy was attained are set out in Table 3.2.

Table 3.2: Year of Establishment of Democracy

Country	First attainment of democracy	Male democracy (if prior)	Reversal (excluding foreign occupation)	Beginning of present-day democracy
Australia	(1903)			
Austria	1918			
Belgium	1948	1919		
Canada	(1920)		1931	(1945)
Denmark	1915			
Finland	(1919)			1944
France	1946	1884		
Germany	1919		1933 (1956)	1949 (1968)
Italy	1946	(1919)	[1922]	1946
Japan	1952			
Netherlands	1919	1917		
New Zealand	1907			
Norway	1915	1898		
Sweden	1918			
Switzerland	1971	*c.* 1880	([1940])	([1944])
UK	1928	1918		
USA	*c.* 1970			

Source: Therborn (1977).

Brackets denote qualifications, square brackets a process of reversal or re-establishment of male democracy.

Some of the dates in Table 3.2 require some clarification. The introduction of suffrage in Australia at a federal level in 1903 was applicable only to whites, and the local aborigine population was not granted a federal vote until 1962. In Canada property qualifications were used to restrict the franchise until 1920 when universal white suffrage was introduced for federal elections. Up until the end of World War II various Canadian provinces also excluded non-white voters, and the Communist Party was prohibited in 1940 for some years. In Finland the Communist Party was also excluded in the 1919 legislation and it was only after World War II that this restriction was lifted.

In Germany present-day democracy followed the fall of the Third Reich and the end of the Allied occupation. However the Communist Party was banned in 1956 and reappeared, under another name, in 1968. Italy did not adopt a fully democratic constitution until 1946 and earlier the male suffrage of 1919 was reversed by the fascists in 1922.

The introduction of universal male suffrage in Switzerland is difficult to date as each canton used different laws and practised a number of exclusion clauses. The Communist Party was banned in 1940, largely in order to accommodate Nazism, but after the war this was reversed. Women did not gain full suffrage in practice in Switzerland until 1971. Finally in the United States the Fifteenth Amendment enfranchized the blacks in the northern states but in the south this Amendment was not effective until the late 1960s, when civil rights demonstrations and activity led to enforcement. The requirements in the USA of advance voter registration also tended to lead to low participation, particularly among the lower social classes. Thus although dating 1970 as the first attainment of democracy in the USA is somewhat surprising, it is the case that the effectiveness of the Fifteenth Amendment was not apparent in the south until around this time.

It is no surprise that the extension of the franchise affected the pattern of the vote for 'left' parties in this century. If we define 'left' parties to comprise reformist socialist or social democratic parties and all other parties to their left, we can examine the share of the left votes in eighteen OECD countries. Splinter parties from social democrats towards the right, some of which are labelled Social Democrat, are excluded from our last definition. The proportion of the valid vote given to left parties is shown in Table 3.3.

This table clearly shows an overall increase in the left share of the vote over this century, though with some variations around this trend. The differences between countries are also striking. In the USA, Canada and Ireland, the share of the left vote is comparatively low and well below the 40 per cent figures in the post-World-War-II period that are recorded in other nations.

Table 3.3:   Left Percentage of Valid Votes in Eighteen OECD Countries, 1900–80

Country	Before World War I	Interwar	1946–60	1961–80
Austria	23	41	48	40
Belgium	23	38	42	40
France	13	32	43	41
Ireland	—	10	12	15
Italy	18	26	35	41
Germany	31	40	34	41
Netherlands	13	25	36	33
Switzerland	16	28	30	28
Australia	37	45	50	47
New Zealand	5	35	48	44
Canada	0	3	13	17
USA	4	5	1	0
Denmark	26	39	45	46
Finland	40	39	48	46
Norway	15	36	52	50
Sweden	13	46	52	51
UK	5	33	48	45
Japan	—	—	32	41

Source: Korpi (1983, p.38).

The vote for left parties tended to peak after World War II, and in the years from 1945 to 1960 the subsequent decline was most marked in Australia, Britain, Denmark, France, Germany and Sweden. In Finland, the Netherlands, Norway, Italy and Japan, the left maintained its relative voting strength over this period. From 1960 to 1980 the left share improved in Italy, Ireland and Germany, though it decreased in Belgium, the Netherlands and Switzerland. In France the left share has tended to go up since the late 1960s, and Japan has experienced an increasing strength in its left political parties.

Now the extent of electoral participation is only one aspect of political strength, and it is the exercise of this political power that is perhaps most pertinent. To get some idea of this, the proportion of seats in each cabinet held by socialist parties is noted. This cabinet share gives some indicator of the working class's ability to exercise political influence. In Sweden and Norway the weighted cabinet share held by the left has been relatively high over the 1946–76 period; in Austria, Denmark, New Zealand, the United Kingdom, Belgium, Australia and Finland there has been only a relatively low presence.

The proportion of time that the left has held this cabinet representation over the 1946–76 period has been high only in Sweden,

Norway, Austria and Switzerland. In the USA, Canada, Japan, France and Australia, the share of time that the left has been represented in cabinet has been short, and in the other eighteen countries this presence has been 'medium'. In France, Finland, Italy and Japan the left parties have been deeply split, and in Norway, Belgium and the Netherlands the left parties are also split but rather less seriously over the 1946–76 period.

All this information yields several remarkable conclusions. First, the increase in the power of the working class over this century is striking in all developed countries. The percentage of the workforce that is unionized has risen remarkably from before World War I and the interwar years; universal suffrage has been established; and in all countries except the United States there has been an astounding increase in the left share of votes in elections after World War I. All these developments imply that because of this increase in power, the interests of wage earners have become more articulated and evident and their influence and power in society has increased. Adam Smith's labourers are clearly no longer agents without considerable representation and influence in developed countries—and this is true for every nation we have examined.

A second remarkable feature is the considerable difference across countries. In Sweden, Austria and Norway we can discern a relatively stronger working class than in other countries on the basis of our indicators. The percentage of unionization is high, the share of left votes is high and the representation of the left in cabinet is strong and of long duration. Furthermore the union movement is not split, and in Norway the split amongst the left parties is only minor. These three countries are relatively strong both in terms of union activity and left political representation when compared to other countries.

In Denmark, New Zealand, the United Kingdom and Belgium, union density is high but the left share of votes is less striking and the left parties have only exercised occasional control in parliament. Belgium is at the bottom of this group in terms of wage-earner power, due to minor splits in its left parties and political and religious cleavages in its union movement.

A third group covers a wider and rather more disparate band of countries. Australia over the 1946–76 period is quite odd, with a high union density and rather high left share of the vote, though only occasional periods of left cabinet representation. Finland, France, Italy and Japan all have medium union densities and left shares of the vote and the presence of the left in cabinet has been sporadic. The strength of the left in all these nations has also been affected by major splits in left parties and splits in the union confederation along political or religious lines.

In Ireland, Canada and the USA the position is more straight-forward. Here the left is relatively weak. Unionization is low and the left vote is hardly relevant, although there has been some left representation in the Irish cabinet.

The final grouping of countries, Germany, the Netherlands and Switzerland, is the most problematic. These countries are all split on religious lines, and Protestants and Catholics are of about equal strength in each. Working-class mobilization has attained low or medium levels but social democratic parties have participated in government rather regularly and for long periods.

This information about comparative country differences has been collated by Korpi (1983) and is presented in Table 3.4. Countries are grouped on the basis of both working-class mobilization and political control of government, and splits within the union movement and left political parties are noted where they are relevant.

Economic Implications

The increasing power position of wage earners in all developed countries over this century is clear on the basis of the evidence presented. Working-class mobilization has increased through rising unionization everywhere and an increase in the left share of electoral votes in all nations except the United States. In many countries these developments have been accompanied by a degree of left-of-centre political control over government. These trends must necessarily lead us to consider whether neoclassical theory in a macroeconomic context is an appropriate tool of analysis in the sense discussed in Chapter 2. This theory presupposes a pluralist conception of society so that no interest group is sufficiently large or influential to interfere systematically in economic policy decisions and outcomes. However, even in the United States and Canada, where unionization is relatively low, we have a situation where around 30 per cent of the workforce are arranged in a collective group of trade unions whose power appears to be substantial.

In practice this would imply that wages and prices might be sticky in a downwards direction so that neoclassically-based policies simply will not be effective as suggested in the previous chapter. Restrictive economic policies will not be accompanied by falling prices and real wages, because of the increased power of the workforce, and as a result these restrictive policies will lead only to recession and rises in unemployment and corporate bankruptcies. If the workforce is sufficiently strong to stop nominal wages from falling in the face of a managed recession, prices will also be unresponsive since wages account for the majority of industrial costs. If wage costs remain sticky, prices will

Table 3.4: *Patterns of Working-Class Mobilization and Political Control in Eighteen Industrial Capitalist Societies 1946–1976**

Pattern	Country	Per cent unionization	Left votes as percentage of electorate	Working-class mobilization	Weighted cabinet share	Proportion of time with left representation in cabinet	Splits within the labour movement: Parties	Unions
High mobilization, stable control	Sweden	71	43	High	High	High	Minor	
	Austria	55	45	High	Medium	High	Minor	.
	Norway	46	41	High	High	High	Minor	
High mobilization, occasional control	Denmark	49	39	High	Medium	Medium		
	New Zealand	42	41	High	Medium	Medium		
	United Kingdom	44	35	High	Medium	Medium		
	Belgium	47	32	High	Medium	Medium	Minor	Political, religious
Medium-high mobilization, low control	Australia	50	44	High	Medium	Low		
	Finland	39	37	Medium	Medium	Medium	Major	Political, religious
	France	25	32	Medium	Low	Low	Major	Political, religious
	Italy	23	34	Medium	Low	Medium	Major	Political, religious
Low mobilization, exclusion	Japan	27	28	Medium	Low	Low	Major	Major
	Ireland	36	9	Low	Low	Medium		
	Canada	26	11	Low	Low	Low		
	United States	27	1	Low	Low	Low		
Low-medium mobilization, partial participation	Germany	35	31	Medium	Low	Medium		
	Netherlands	30	31	Medium	Low	Medium	Minor	Religious
	Switzerland	23	18	Low	Low	High		Religious

* For description of variables, see Korpi (1983, Chapter 3).

behave similarly because firms must cover costs, and this is true whatever the degree of concentration in industry.

Wage and Price Stickiness

In this respect it is interesting to note the behaviour of prices and wages in the United States over this century. Sachs (1980) and Cagan (1975) have both pointed out that price and wage behaviour before and after World War II in the USA has been markedly different. It used to be the case that when there was a cyclical downturn, prices and costs of production would fall, but since World War II in the USA this has not been the case. Mild and deep recessions since 1945 have not been accompanied by falling prices and wages, though in cyclical downturns earlier in the century prices and wages did contract. Apparently prices and wages are now very sticky in the downward direction and this phenomenon marks an historical shift of some consequence. We are now dealing with stagflation and not simply stagnation in a recession.

This relatively new stickiness in wages and prices can be demonstrated by identifying previous periods of contraction in the business cycle and by examining price and wage inflation during each business contraction. Sachs (1980), using US data, identifies several periods of mild, moderate and strong contractions. These cyclical downturns, from a peak to a trough in industrial output, are listed on the left of Table 3.5. We begin with mild contractions in industrial output and the lower changes in price and wage inflation during these downturns after World War II are evident. With moderate and strong contractions this new downward stickiness in wages and prices is even more obvious. In the earlier part of this century a strong or moderate contraction in industrial output was accompanied by severe falls in both wages and prices. However in the moderate contraction of 1957−8 prices and wages fell by only 1·4 per cent; and in the severe recession in 1973−5 both wages and prices in the USA actually increased. Recessions, even when they involve a strong fall in industrial output, apparently are no longer accompanied by falls in prices and wages.

This development implies that neoclassical policies, whose effectiveness depends upon falls in prices and real wages, will not be successful. These neoclassical policies fail because applying this theory in a society where wages and prices are not responsive because of wage-earner power is simply inappropriate. And if neoclassical theory is inappropriate in the United States, its application in other countries, where the workforce is even stronger, is even more inappropriate. Thus we can conclude that the neoclassical approach is quite simply misguided and unsuitable for the macroeconomies of the developed world.

Table 3.5:   *Wage and Price Behaviour During US Business Cycles, 1890–1976*

Peak trough	Percentage change in prices	Percentage change in wages
Mild contractions		
1893–4	−12·9	−12·1
1895–7	−4·4	4·4
1899–1900	−·2	−4·2
1910–11	−12·5	−4·9
1923–4	−6·6	−6·7
1926–7	−1·3	0
1953–4	1·5	−2·1
1960–1	−·5	−1·0
1969–70	·3	·2
Moderate contractions		
1902–4	−5·8	−4·2
1913–14	−3·3	−7·3
1948–9	−13·0	−5·5
1957–8	−1·4	−1·4
Strong contractions		
1907–8	−8·4	−8·4
1918–19	−16·4	−14·8
1920–1	−56·8	−37·4
1973–5	·8	2·9

Source: Sachs (1980).

There may also be other more technical reasons why this theory is incorrect (Desai, 1981), but the argument here suggests that whatever the technical merits of this approach it will in practise be quite ineffectual. Furthermore this ineffectiveness occurs in the United States which is perhaps the one country where neoclassical policy success might be expected to be most likely. This nation has one of the weakest working classes of any developed country, and if prices and wages are sticky there we would also expect this to be the case elsewhere. Hence neoclassical theory and policies for dealing with the present economic situation ought to be abandoned because they are not suitable for the developed economies in which they are applied. These economies are not pluralist and interest groups are sufficiently powerful to stop wages and prices falling.

The only alternative to this conclusion, given the prevailing evidence, is to try and turn back the historical clock to somewhere in the pre-World-War-II period. In policy terms this would amount to legislation and action to weaken the union movement and the political power of the workforce. This course of action is contemplated by some partisan neoclassicals but given the strength of the workforce in all countries such action is unlikely to be successful. It will undoubtedly be resisted, both in the political and labour organization arenas, and the social changes it implies appear to be quite impractical. It is unrealistic to imagine a return to a society where the workers' right to organize collectively is abandoned and where the political influence they exert through universal suffrage and left-of-centre parties is diminished in any major way. Lessening political control by the citizenry at large has been suggested by Niskanen (1975, p.531), for example, who writes, 'Democracy is an instrument, not an ideal . . . A government that serves only the interests of the majority is neither achievable, desirable, nor stable.' Abandoning democracy would undoubtedly diminish the political power of the citizenry and the workforce, but most people in Western nations are unlikely to embrace willingly a non-democratic alternative form of governance. Hence I would argue, at least on pragmatic grounds, that the neoclassical approach must be abandoned. The situation in which such a theory could be successfully applied, even if the theory is correct in some sense, no longer exists, and there is no likelihood that society can be altered to make the application of such a theory appropriate. This is the first implication of the changes in the power distribution in society that we have examined.

The implications of these historic changes in power are also evident in areas apart from the wage responsiveness issue. As the working class has increased its power, it has been gradually more successful in demanding public goods and services and adding its demands to the agenda of social concern.

The Increasing Size of the Public Sector

The phenomenal increase in the size of the public sector is perhaps the most remarkable development in recent economic history. At the beginning of this century public spending amounted to only a very small part of the total national expenditure, and generally public expenditure was less than 10 per cent of the gross national product in most developed countries. The economic activity of the public sector in 1900 was not anywhere near as important as it now is. In many developed nations the public sector now spends close on 50 per cent of the national gross expenditure which by any criteria is a quite amazing increase.

One measure of the growth in the quantitative importance of the public sector is displayed in Diagram 3.1 where the growth of total public spending in the USA and the UK as a proportion of GNP is displayed.

Figure 3.1:   Growth of Total Spending by the Public Sector in the USA and UK as a Percentage of GNP

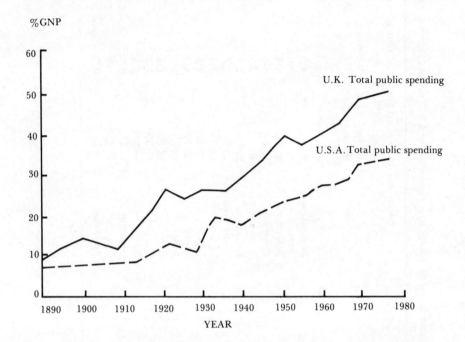

Source: Atkinson and Stiglitz (1980, p.17), where original statistical sources are quoted in full.

This quite astonishing growth in the relative size of the public sector has also occurred in other Western nations and is discussed in some detail in Nutter (1978). Though it is crude to measure the importance of any economic sector simply in terms of its total spending, there can be no doubt that the public sector is now a crucially important part of our economy. This is true of virtually all Western developed countries as Table 3.6 shows.

A significant part of the increase in public expenditure is accounted for by the rise in spending on social security benefits and social assistance grants, as Table 3.6 indicates. However the increase in these welfare-based programmes is generally below the increase in total public expenditures over the 1960−3 to 1977−9 period. The only exception to this observation is the United States, where social security and assistance grants grew by 5·1 per cent compared to an overall growth in total expenditure of 4·7 per cent.

By the end of the 1970s only a minority of the countries were

Table 3.6: The Levels and Increases in Total Government and Social Spending, as a Percentage of GDP, in the 1960s and 1970s[a]

	Total government expenditures % of GDP				Social security benefits and social assistance grants % of GDP		
	Annual average level 1977–9	Increase, 1960–3 to 1970–3	Increase, 1970–3 to 1977–9		Annual average level 1977–8	Increase, 1960–3 to 1970–3	Increase, 1970–3 to 1977–8
Sweden	59·7	13·1	14·4	Netherlands	27·7	8·9	7·0
Netherlands	57·7	11·9	10·2	Sweden	20·1	5·0	6·9
Denmark	51·1	13·8	8·1	Belgium	20·3	3·4	5·6
Norway	51·3	11·3	8·0	Denmark	15·8	4·6	3·5
Ireland	49·0	9·0	9·4	Norway	16·5	6·3	1·4
Belgium	49·2	7·8	10·5	France	22·2	2·8	4·8
Switzerland	40·0	5·9	9·7	Switzerland	10·9	2·6	4·2
Austria	49·0	5·5	8·7	Ireland	12·3	3·8	2·6
Italy	44·8	6·9	6·5	Japan	9·5	1·3	4·4
Germany	46·4	5·1	7·2	USA	10·7	3·0	2·1
Japan	30·5	2·5	9·5	Austria	18·8	1·7	3·0
Finland	39·1	5·0	6·8	UK	12·1	2·3	2·5
Canada	40·3	6·8	3·9	Finland	11·0	1·7	3·0
UK	43·8	5·8	4·1	Italy	16·2	3·5	0·7
France	45·0	2·2	6·5	Germany	16·5	0·6	3·6
Australia	31·7	3·1	5·4	Canada	10·7	1·8	1·9
USA	33·4	3·5	1·2	Australia	9·5	0·2	3·5

[a] Nations are ranked by total increase in 1960–3 to 1977–9

Source: OECD, *National Accounts.*

devoting around 40 per cent or less of their GDP to public expenditure. In this relatively low public spending category were Japan, Australia, Finland, the United States, Switzerland and Canada. At the other end of the spectrum were those nations devoting more than 45 per cent of their GDP to government expenditure. In this high government expenditure group we have Sweden, the Netherlands, Denmark, Norway, Austria, Belgium, Ireland and Germany. Three countries, namely Italy, Britain and France, fall in between these high and low public spending groups.

Now the increases in public spending that have occurred since 1960 have occurred at different times in different countries, though generally the increase in the 1970s is more marked. This data is also shown in Table 3.6. The most striking increase in public expenditure in the later period has been Japan. Though its level of government spending is relatively low, Japan appears to have increased its public expenditure greatly during the 1970s. Another interesting feature of this data is the rather low increase in public spending recorded in the USA both during the 1960s and the 1970s. Given the considerable rhetoric from the present US government about its 'wildly excessive' public spending its performance compared to that of other nations is salutary.

Much of this increase in public spending is devoted to 'welfare' programmes — and specifically social security and assistance. The Netherlands allocates more of its resources to this item than any other country (27 per cent) followed closely by France, Belgium, Sweden and Austria (around 20 per cent). In North America, Australia and Japan the proportion of resources devoted to social security and assistance is considerably less, at around 10 per cent of GDP. The level of expenditure on this item and the increases over the 1960−78 period are also set out in Table 3.6.

The allocation of welfare spending across different programmes varies between countries too, as Table 3.7 reveals. Germany, Denmark and the Netherlands devote more resources to social security and welfare than other nations, and especially more than Japan, Australia and the USA. Britain devotes more to public housing than any other country, and Germany and Denmark allocate more to health. In the education field, Denmark and the Netherlands are high spenders and Japan the lowest, though there is less variance between nations on this item of expenditure than the others in Table 3.7.

These increases in public expenditure are noteworthy in two ways at this stage in my argument. First the increase in public expenditure in all nations over this century is evident and the increasing success of the citizenry and workforce in having its public demands met in this way must surely be associated with the increase in its power in all

33

Table 3.7:   The Spending Effort of Government on Programmes Associated with the 'Welfare State'

	Health	Social security and welfare	Housing and community amenities	Education
		1970–1		
USA	2·1	8·0	0·4	5·6
Japan	3·0	2·9	1·6	3·7
Britain	4·0	9·0	3·0	5·4
Germany	4·5	14·8	1·1	4·3
Italy	4·3	12·6	0·8	4·7
Australia	3·3	4·4	0·3	4·3
Netherlands	n.a.	18·9	n.a.	7·1
		1975–6		
USA	2·6	10·8	0·4	6·3
Japan	4·1	5·6	2·1	4·9
Britain	5·1	10·8	4·3	6·6
Germany	6·6	19·2	1·2	5·3
Italy	5·8	15·3	1·1	5·0
France	5·7	16·1	2·2	5·9
Australia	5·4	7·4	0·6	6·2
Denmark	6·0	18·2	1·7	8·1
Netherlands	n.a.	25·0	n.a.	7·8

Source: Cameron (1982).

developed countries. There are also undoubtedly other factors at work behind this growth in the public sector but the influence of increased power appears to be present.

This point is also supported if we examine the relative size of the public sector in different countries, as seen in Table 3.6, and compare this ranking with the power groupings in Table 3.4. Those nations where working-class mobilization and political control are relatively low (the USA, Canada, Australia, Japan, Finland) tend to have relatively low levels of government expenditure as a percentage of GDP. Ireland is a possible exception to this statement, but the share of public expenditure going on social welfare categories in Ireland is rather low, which might suggest that its public expenditure is directed in favour of other interest groups apart from paid workers.

On the other hand in Sweden, Austria, Norway and Denmark, where working-class power is relatively strong, we observe extremely high total public expenditure out of GDP and high spending on social welfare categories. Thus there does appear to be some connection between power and public expenditure behaviour.

The Increase in Public Sector Concerns

The vast increase in the economic size of the public sector has been accompanied by what we can call an increase in the economic agenda of the state. Modern democratic governments are now concerned with many more issues than their counterparts were at, say, the turn of the century. Most notably modern governments accept at least nominal responsibility for the rate of unemployment. If this is high there is general concern, and both citizens and government seem to feel that the state can and should do something about the problem. In days gone by the unemployed were the concern of charities and possibly 'do-good' sections of the Church, or they were thought to be lazy good-for-nothings who had only themselves to blame for their predicament. Even in the most conservative and reactionary Western countries this attitude to the unemployed is no longer dominant. Whatever the perceived causes of unemployment it is now accepted that the state must provide some grants to assist the unemployed and in all likelihood some form of retraining and help in securing a future job. The unemployed are now undeniably on the economic agenda of the state.

There are many other similar though possibly less dramatic examples of how this economic agenda of the state has grown. Environmental protection laws, planning regulations about building, safety codes of conduct at work, individual health care, public housing, old-age pension schemes and assistance for the handicapped are all now generally deemed to be part of public sector responsibilities. This has not historically always been the case, and each of these issues has over time been added to the business of government. The economic agenda of the state varies from one nation to another and has been added to at different times but it is clear that whatever the specifics of accepted responsibility the economic concerns of the modern democratic state are now vast.

This development has not passed the notice of political analysts, and indeed several have argued that democratic states are now so overloaded by demands that the collapse of democracy may be imminent. The diagnosis of Crozier *et al.* (1975) is that expectations of what governments can and should do are now high but that at the same time the capacity of democratic government to fulfil these expectations has declined markedly. The reason for this decline in government capability is generally linked to the increased economic interdependency of modern society. Industry is dependent on a wide range of government decisions for effective performance and upon the cooperation of large economic interest groups. These interest groups include trades unions and employers' organizations. Lack of co-operation and the incapacity of government to enforce or achieve consensus in society leads to problems of governance and failures in economic policy.

In this scenario private groups increasingly challenge the authority of government (King, 1975), and the 'industrial anarchy' in Britain over the past fifteen years is cited as a symptom. This alleged anarchy has not been curtailed by legislative means (Ionescu, 1975) and the trades unions in particular are suspected of causing the fall of two recent British governments who attempted to curtail their powers through legislation and policy. The Conservative government who lost the 1974 election and the Labour government who lost the 1979 election are listed as examples of governments who tried to challenge trades union power and ultimately lost (Coombes, 1983, p.43).

This argument views society as being particularly vulnerable to the actions of skilled workers who as a group can withdraw labour which cannot be replaced. In an interdependent economy such groups are very powerful, and their refusal to produce goods and services or to accept wage control can quickly lead to an economic crisis. The attempts by government to control inflation merely sharpen the conflict, and consensus in society seems to become more and more difficult to achieve. On this basis several writers have urged that the functions of government must be re-appraised and in particular the agenda of the state must be somehow cut and limited.

In this connection, Usher (1981) has argued that democracy is only viable if government does not partake in the allocation of society's income and wealth. This allocation he suggests must be decided by the market or the capitalist system; once government begins allocating resources amongst groups and individual citizens and companies, consensus is impossible and democracy breaks down. As Schumpeter (1943, p.291) argued, 'the effective range of the political decision should not be extended too far'. If the agenda of the state becomes too vast these analysts expect that democracy will crumble and be replaced by a less democratic form of governance; alternatively the agenda of the state can be cut and democracy preserved.

Whether or not one agrees with this diagnosis it is undeniable that the economic agenda of modern democratic states is much larger than it once was. Furthermore the implications of this for economic policy and state economic behaviour generally are likely to be significant. The increased economic size of the public sector and its increased agenda mean that the economic system we are now dealing with is considerably different from that in the pre-World-War-II period.

So far we have argued that because of the changes in power that we have documented neoclassical theory is inappropriate as a tool of analysis of modern developed economies. Also the changes in power, as well as being related to a downward stickiness in wages and prices, appear to be connected to the increase in public expenditure this century and to what I have termed the increased agenda of the state that is evident in all developed countries.

The final implication of the power issue that I wish to mention relates to the appropriateness or otherwise of neo-Keynesian analysis. I argued in the last chapter that this analysis, in the context of the 1970s, is only effective if a viable incomes policy can be implemented. Now various institutional studies by colleagues in other social sciences have focussed on various 'voluntary' price and wage restraint schemes and on understandings that have been reached in some countries between government, trades unions and employer organizations about macro-economic policy generally and incomes policies specifically. Existing arrangements in various countries suggest that where the system of industrial relations is concentrated and centralized, and where a 'corporatist' pattern of interaction exists between government and major organized economic interest groups, the economy has performed more successfully than in those nations where industrial relations is more decentralized and fragmented. More fragmented forms of interest mediation are associated with less successful economic outcomes (Lehmbruch and Schmitter (eds), 1982, and Schmitter and Lehmbruch (eds), 1979).

In terms of a public choice approach, more familiar to economists, these hypotheses based on specific country studies should be of no great surprise. Olson (1982) has argued that when societies develop encompassing social organizations, that exclude few individuals or groups in society, their behaviour is likely to be more in line with the interests of the entire society. However where interest groups are fragmented and more pluralist, their actions will not be in the interests of the whole society but more directly concerned with their own specific group interests. In this instance Olson suggests that the outcome of group confict and consensus can be so out of line with the broader public interest that national economic problems are exacerbated.

Also where groups are simply not existent at all, and not organized, a public choice approach suggests that achieving an outcome in the total public interest will not be hampered by group pursuits. This would of course approximate the neoclassical view of society and has led Scharpf (1983) to suggest a threefold classification of the organization of economic interests. The non-organized groups classification and the encompassing and integrated groups classification both favour economic performance for different reasons. However the third classification of fragmented or pluralist groups is far from favourable for economic outcomes.

Hence the institutional hypotheses at the macro level are in line with the public choice literature and they also imply one reason why the economic performance of different countries during the 1970s has been different. Furthermore this approach has the potential to throw some light on the very real problems of domestic economic management that have been facing many industrialized countries. If this is so, economists can simply stop blaming poor economic outcomes on the lack of responsiveness in society to their policies and begin to suggest viable working arrangements that might improve their responsiveness. However as we will argue in Chapter 10 this advice is not as simple to arrive at as the institutional studies have so far suggested. The economic situation prevailing at a particular time is more important than has so far been recognized. Nevertheless if these institutional approaches are relevant, they should explain some of the cross-country differences in recent economic performances. Keynesian expansionary policies will have been most successful, it is suggested, in those nations where the workforce has become sufficiently powerful to develop an encompassing and centralized interest group and where this group has acted in concert with a similar business interest under the mediation of a social democratic government. On the other hand expansionary policies will have been less successful where the power of the workforce is evident in a less centralized and more fragmented interest grouping and where left-of-centre political control has not been dominant.

The evidence relating to the different economic performance of nations is presented in the next chapter. Here it is sufficient to note that if this argument about interest mediation is correct then Keynesian analysis and policies are appropriate and successful only in those countries where there is a broad consensus over incomes policies and that this will occur only in certain institutional circumstances. These circumstances are directly related to power, and perhaps surprisingly we might expect Keynesian policies to be most appropriate in countries where the workforce is relatively powerful in terms of mobilization and political control. This issue is explored in some detail in the next chapter.

Summary

We have studied the change in power of the workforce in developed countries over this century. On the basis of this evidence it is argued that the power of the workforce has increased since 1900 and that while business interests are still dominant in capitalist society, the shift in working-class power is not without economic implications.

It appears that the increase in wage earners' power may be related to the post-World-War-II stickiness of wages and prices and also to the increase in public expenditures and in the agenda of state concerns. The power of labour interests is in any case now sufficiently great and cohesive for neoclassical analysis to be inappropriate. Society is not pluralist and I have argued that it is virtually impossible to change it to a pluralist system. Hence neoclassical approaches must be abandoned as analytical tools. Their application to modern macroeconomics is analogous to applying models of perfect competition to oligopolistic market structures.

The increase in power of the workforce is also relevant for neo-Keynesian analysis. It was suggested on the basis of public choice reasoning and institutional studies that a Keynesian expansion would only be effective in societies whose interest groups are centralized and encompassing and where different interests are mediated via corporatist arrangements through social-democratic-style government. In this type of system an incomes policy is perceived as being in the public interest as a whole and the consensus achieved may be more than temporary. On the other hand, in countries where interest groups are more fragmented, a Keynesian expansion is unlikely to be effective because consensus over wage and price restraint will not be forthcoming in any but a temporary fashion. In particular the workforce in these nations is not sufficiently strong to be all-encompassing and wider social concerns will not be its main concern. For this reason an incomes policy or voluntary economic arrangement will fail and the Keynesian expansion in this situation will be ineffectual as wages and prices rise. Only when encompassing groups have formed will Keynesian policy be potentially effective.

4   The Macroeconomic Performance of the Developed Nations

In the Hungry Thirties
boys used to sell their bodies
for a square meal.

In the Affluent Sixties
they still did:
to meet Hire-Purchase Payments.

Auden, 'Economics'

Introduction

In this chapter the macroeconomic record of the developed countries throughout the 1970s is examined and related to the institutional arrangements and power distribution in those countries. When this is done several facts emerge that are surprising in the light of economic theory that ignores the prevailing structures of the macroeconomy. Countries which have experienced relatively low unemployment rates have also experienced low inflation rates; and these nations include those where the working class is most powerful and where consensual arrangements over wage and price restraint have been implemented successfully.

It is also apparent that one of the quid pro quos offered for this wage and price restraint is a high level of government spending which has been increasingly financed through deficits in the public sector. Because of this relationship, where high government spending is part of the consensual arrangement for wage and price restraint, the connection between public sector deficits and inflation is not as it is sometimes hypothesized. There is no evidence, on a comparative country basis, that deficits cause inflation. Indeed increases in deficit financing in the public sector in the 1970s tend to be negatively related to price acceleration. Once we consider the relationship as a bargaining outcome between interest groups this is no surprise.

40

The connection between government expenditure, investment and economic growth is more complex. Economic growth is associated with investment, and in several countries investment has declined despite the presence of wage restraint achieved through consensual arrangements. This decline in investment could be associated with the rise in public expenditure, though the experience across different countries has been varied.

What is fascinating in this recent experience is the link between economic performance and more directly political issues concerned with maintaining consensus in the system. It is this link that I try to make clear in this chapter. The relevance of such a link for domestic economic management is obvious. Where consensus over wage and price constraint is not achieved, Keynesian policies are ineffectual and can only be made effective by somehow gaining consensus. If expansionary policies are pursued in a country without wage and price restraint the outcome is simply runaway inflation. This implies that one of the aims of government must be to reach a consensus between the major interest groups in society if current economic problems are to be attacked through a Keynesian expansionary policy. But as we have already suggested in the last chapter, this aim will be very difficult for some nations to achieve.

The Political Arrangements in Different Countries

Before examining the macroeconomic performance of different countries, which appears to be related to the political arrangements in these countries, it is necessary to be clear about what these functional arrangements are in different nations. For our purposes we do not require lengthy analyses of each country's polity but we do need some underlying understanding of how these countries are governed.

Obviously all the developed countries we are considering are democratic, and as we have seen they all have workforces with varying degrees of mobilization and political control. More specifically it is also possible to differentiate between nations on the basis of their government's political complexion, derived from the share of cabinet seats that left of centre parties held over the period, and whether or not countries pursued governance through corporatism.

Corporatism is a system of regulating conflict between interest groups in society. There is, in European corporatism, a strong social partnership between unions and employers' organizations and a cooperative mode of economic policy formation. Strong corporatism is typically classified to cover those countries where trade unions and employer associations are committed to a social partnership ideology;

where the state, the trade unions and employers' associations co-operate in some economic policy areas; where no authoritarian incomes policy is enacted by the state; and finally where the incidence of blatant and open conflict, for instance in strikes and lockouts, is very low. On this definition of strong corporatism, Austria, Norway, and Sweden are strongly corporatist in their polity.

It is also usual to include Switzerland and Japan in the strong corporatist group, though their form of corporatism is somewhat differ- ent. In the case of Switzerland, characteristics of corporatist intermed- iation are evident though the state is only minimally involved in interest intermediation (Kreisi, 1982). In Japan the style of corporatism is pri- vate and excludes labour, which as we have seen is relatively weak and which is not centralized in a unified body that is officially recognized (Pemfel and Tsunekawa, 1979).

Countries which are classified as weakly corporatist are those where employers and trade unions are not co-operative and where strikes and lockouts are frequent. There may be income policies enacted from above, but these policies are more imposed than consensual as in the British Social Contract of the 1970s. Nations who are weakly corporatist include Australia, Canada, France, Ireland, Italy, the United States, and Britain.

In between the strong corporatist group and the weak corporat- ist groups we have a residual category of medium corporatism. Nations in this grouping include Belgium, Denmark, Finland, Germany and the Netherlands. This classification of countries into strong, medium and weak corporatism is based on the work of Lehmbruch (1977), von Bryme (1977), and Schmitter and Lehmbruch (eds.) (1979).

The political complexion of the government in different nations is usually classified in terms of the representation of parties in cabinet seats. Korpi's (1983) classification for the 1946–76 period, in the last chapter, put Austria, Sweden, Norway and Switzerland into the high left representation group. At the other end of the representation scale we had Australia, France, Japan, Canada, and the USA where left rep- resentation in cabinet was low. In between, with medium representa- tion, were Germany, the Netherlands, Denmark, Britain, Belgium, Finland, Italy and Ireland.

More recent data, covering the period from 1974 to 1978 that has been compiled by Schmidt (1982), shows that in this later period there have been some changes. The left representation in Switzerland has been dominated by right of centre parties and the election of the Australian Labour Party to government for the three years during the 1970s suggests that left representation has recently increased there.

However, drawing all this together in Table 4.1 gives a crude overview of the polity in different developed countries. In this table 'left' simply denotes a high social democratic presence; 'right' denotes very little social democratic or left control of government; and 'balance' is some position between these two extremes of political complexion.

Table 4.1:   Government's Political Complexion and Corporatism

	Corporatism	Government's political complexion
Austria	Strong	Left
Norway	Strong	Left
Sweden	Strong	Left
Japan	Strong	Right
Switzerland	Strong	Balance
Germany	Medium	Balance
Denmark	Medium	Balance
Netherlands	Medium	Balance
Belgium	Medium	Balance
Finland	Medium	Balance
France	Weak	Right
Australia	Weak	Right
Italy	Weak	Right
Ireland	Weak	Right
UK	Weak	Balance
Canada	Weak	Right
USA	Weak	Right

It is interesting that the three nations, Austria, Norway and Sweden, where the working class is relatively most powerful have developed corporatist arrangements. However, consensual arrangements, implied by corporatism, have also been practised in Japan where the working class is rather weak, and in Switzerland. We might expect the gains made by the working class in the bargaining and agreement that corporatism entails to be rather different in these two countries where the position of the workforce is not as strongly established as in Austria, Norway or Sweden. As we have already seen, government expenditure in Japan is relatively low and Switzerland's public expenditure is not high as is the case in Sweden, Norway and Austria.

It is also notable that in those countries where the working class is relatively weak, as discussed in the last chapter, corporatism has not developed, with the exception of Japan. For corporatism to function, encompassing groups, in Olson's sense, are required. An encompassing group does not exclude individuals or specific groups to any major extent. Where unionization is low and the union movement is split and not centralized we clearly do not have an encompassing labour group.

In this latter case groups are fragmented. Nations in this category include France, Italy, Ireland, Canada and the USA. However, let us now turn to the economic performance of all these countries.

Inflation and Unemployment

During the 1970s the developed countries experienced a widespread and savage increase in the rate of unemployment. This increase in unemployment was most marked in Belgium, the UK and Denmark and less severe in Switzerland, Japan and Sweden. Only in Norway and Austria was there virtually no change in the unemployment position in the 1970s though these countries have experienced relatively modest increases in their unemployment rates since 1980. This position is revealed in Table 4.2 which also gives data on labour force increases in each country. The increases in the labour force during the 1970s were not markedly different from earlier changes and this of course indicates that the rise in unemployment was not principally caused by increases in the available workforce. Only in Austria, Sweden, Norway and Switzerland was unemployment at 2 per cent or less of the labour force by the end of

Table 4.2: *The Rate of Unemployment in Western Nations, 1960–80*

	% of total labour force unemployed		Increase in % of total labour force	
	average, 1960–80	average, 1977–80	1960–3 to 1977–80	1970–3 to 1977–80
Ireland	6·3	8·6	3·5	2·7
Canada	5·9	7·8	1·5	1·9
Italy	5·8	7·3	2·4	1·4
USA	5·4	6·4	0·7	1·2
Belgium	3·9	8·3	5·8	5·8
UK	3·8	6·4	3·8	2·9
Australia	3·0	6·0	4·1	3·9
Finland	2·9	6·0	4·6	3·8
France	2·9	5·5	4·1	2·9
Denmark	2·8	7·1	5·2	6·2
Netherlands	2·3	4·7	3·8	2·8
Austria	1·9	1·9	−0·3	0·5
Sweden	1·9	2·0	0·4	−0·3
Norway	1·8	1·8	−0·3	0·2
Germany	1·7	3·6	2·8	2·7
Japan	1·5	2·1	0·7	0·8
Switzerland	0·1	0·4	0·4	0·4

Source: OECD, *National Accounts.*

the 1970s. In Ireland, Canada, Italy, Belgium, Denmark, the UK and the USA, the unemployment rate was over 6 per cent by the end of the 1970s.

This general rise in unemployment was associated with stagflation. Economic growth was slack but price inflation was high. During the 1960s prices gradually accelerated and this experience became particularly acute in many countries during the 1970s. In only five countries, namely Japan, the Netherlands, Austria, Germany and Switzerland, did price inflation moderate during the 1970s. Furthermore the experience of inflation, though widespread, was rather different between nations. In Austria, Germany and Switzerland the inflation rate was below 5 per cent in 1977−80. On the other hand in Italy, the UK and Ireland the level of inflation in the same period was in excess of 13 per cent. Thus although inflation was a common problem in the industrial countries it was far more severe in certain nations. This inflation data is summarized in Table 4.3.

Table 4.3: The Rate of Inflation in Consumer Prices in Western Nations, 1960−80

	Average % change in consumer prices 1977−80	Acceleration in average % change in consumer prices,	
		1960−3 to 1977−80	1970−3 to 1977−80
Italy	16·3	12·1	9·7
UK	13·9	11·2	5·9
Ireland	13·2	9·8	3·9
Denmark	10·8	6·2	3·9
France	10·7	6·6	4·7
Sweden	10·6	7·1	3·8
Australia	9·9	8·2	3·6
USA	9·8	8·5	4·9
Finland	9·8	6·2	3·0
Canada	9·1	8·0	4·4
Norway	8·2	5·5	0·3
Japan	5·9	− 0·2	− 1·6
Belgium	5·7	4·5	0·5
Netherlands	5·3	2·2	− 1·4
Austria	4·8	1·6	− 1·0
Germany	4·0	1·6	− 1·3
Switzerland	2·5	− 0·3	− 3·9

Source: OECD, National Accounts

Now the economic theory behind a crude Phillips curve analysis would suggest that where unemployment rates were high, inflation would be low; and where unemployment rates were low inflation would be relatively high. However, as the data in Figure 4·1 shows, this is surprisingly not the case and almost the direct opposite holds. Those countries (Japan, Switzerland, Austria, Germany, Norway, the Netherlands and Sweden) with average unemployment rates at below 3 per cent over the 1965–81 period also had relatively modest inflation rates. Countries with high inflation over the 1964–81 period also had high unemployment. Italy, Ireland, Britain, the United States, Canada, and to a lesser extent France, all fall in this unfortunate grouping.

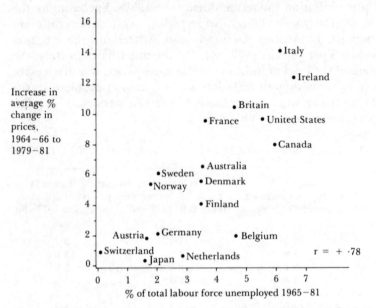

Figure 4·1: The Relation between Inflation and Unemployment in Seventeen Nations: 1965–81
Source: Cameron (1983)

The arrangement of countries in Figure 4·1 indicates that there is a positive relationship (r = ·78) between unemployment and inflation in the industrial countries over the 1964–81 period. Those countries with low average unemployment rates also had relatively low inflation. On the basis of this array of average national performance we can conclude that Italy, Ireland, the UK, the United States, Canada, and to a lesser extent France all form a group of high unemployment, high inflation nations. Preferable outcomes on both the price stability and unemployment fronts were experienced by Switzerland, Japan, Austria, and Germany. In these countries the maintenance of unemployment at or below 2 per cent did not produce enormous price increases—and to an extent this was also the case in Norway and Sweden.

The causes of inflation in the 1970s have been attributed to many factors including fiscal and monetary policies, exchange rate volatility, commodity price rises, oil price rises and wage push. All of these determinants of inflation are important but in explaining the price rises in industrial countries over the 1964–81 period it is remarkable that increases in nominal earnings account for around 94 per cent of the variance in inflation across countries. The relation between changes in nominal earnings and inflation is very close, as Figure 4·2 shows.

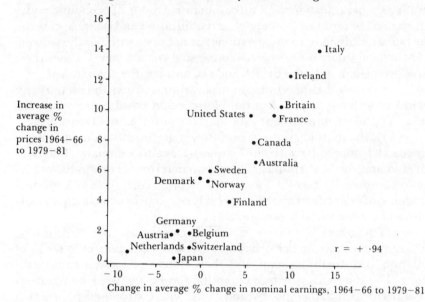

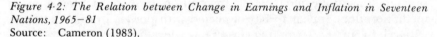

Change in average % change in nominal earnings, 1964–66 to 1979–81

Figure 4·2: The Relation between Change in Earnings and Inflation in Seventeen Nations, 1965–81
Source: Cameron (1983).

National differences in inflation since the mid 1960s reflects 'the difference in the extent to which labour has pushed for, and obtained, larger increases in pay . . . the largest increases usually exceed the rate of increase in prices and thus cause an increase in real earnings' (Cameron, 1983).

Now the grouping of countries in Figure 4·2 is similar to that in Figure 4·1. Italy, Ireland, Britain, France and the USA and Canada all experienced high inflation and high average increases in nominal earnings. On the other hand in Germany, Belgium, Switzerland, Austria, Japan and the Netherlands an average *decrease* in nominal earnings over the 1964–81 period was associated with relatively modest price rises. Labour in these countries experienced a modest fall in their real

47

earnings though as we have seen their unemployment record was relatively good, with Belgium standing as the sole exception.

The varying economic outcomes between nations are quite remarkable. If we begin with the relatively bad performers on the inflation and unemployment front we have (from Figure 4·1) Italy, Ireland, Britain, the USA, Canada, France and Australia. In none of these countries is corporatism, as a system of regulating conflict between groups, practised. There is no strong social partnership between unions and employers' organizations and no co-operative mode of economic policy formation. In terms of working-class mobilization and political control, the labour movement in these nations has not been sufficiently strong to want or to be able to move towards consensual arrangements. When these have been tried, as in the British Social Contract, they have failed.

On the other hand where corporatism is strong and established, as in Switzerland, Japan, Austria, Norway and possibly Germany, the inflation and unemployment rates have been far more favourable.

In the middle group of performers on the inflation and unemployment front we have (from Figure 4·1 again) Denmark, Belgium, Finland and the Netherlands. This group in terms of corporatist organization is typically classified as medium corporatist. This is a residual grouping of countries who are not weakly corporatist or strongly corporatist and their economic outcome is also middling.

Thus there is a rather clear linkage, perhaps not surprisingly, between the economic performance of developed countries in terms of inflation and unemployment and their system of interest intermediation. Those nations which are identified as having weak corporatism have performed rather poorly and those where strong corporatism is practised have done much better. In addition the mode of interest intermediation does appear to be connected with power, in that countries with relatively strong working classes have developed corporatist modes of actions that in turn have led to better economic outcomes. A strong and powerful working class is not however needed for consensual arrangements, as the cases of Switzerland and Japan suggest. But where the working class is highly mobilized and consensual arrangements are not achieved the economic outcome is less satisfactory.

It is also evident that those nations where unemployment and inflation has been most severe are those where the political complexion of government has been classified as to the 'right'. The only exceptions to this statement are Japan and the UK. In Japan a government of 'right' political complexion practised corporatism and achieved wage and price restraint and low levels of unemployment. In the UK a government of 'balanced' complexion was not associated with corporatism and its inflation and unemployment in the 1970s was severe.

In the 'left' government countries of Austria, Sweden and Norway the unemployment rate was relatively low, though in Sweden and Norway price and wage inflation was around 5–6 per cent in the 1965–81 period. Finally in those countries where the political complexion of government was 'balanced' the inflation and unemployment record was relatively middling though in Germany and Switzerland it was relatively good. Both these nations however practised a form of corporatism.

The impact of the complexion of government thus appears to be of importance (Schmidt, 1982; Payne, 1979), though whether or not corporatism is practised appears to be more important (Schmidt, 1982). These two political variables are not unrelated but the impact of political arrangements on inflation and unemployment in the developed countries in the 1970s seems evident.

Government Deficits and Inflation

Government spending has increased over the last two decades as we have already seen in Chapter 3; and those nations where the level of public spending was highest as a percentage of GDP tended to be those where both working-class mobilization and particularly political control was strong. The increase in public expenditures was accompanied by increases in tax revenues in all countries but as Downs (1960) would have expected the increase in revenues did not keep pace with the increase in public expenditure.

Downs (1960) argued that this increase in expenditure over revenue was likely to lead to a decrease in public expenditure, but during the 1970s this did not occur. The growing level of government expenditures in most countries was met by increasing public sector deficits between 1960 and 1979 as is evident in Table 4.4. The only nation which decreased its deficit as a percentage of GDP over the two decades was the United States; and in Norway and Finland where there was a budget surplus in 1977–9 the size of this surplus as a percent of GDP had diminished markedly from earlier periods.

It is obvious from the data in Table 4.4 that by the late 1970s many more nations were in deficit positions and in some cases this deficit was quite high as a percentage of GDP. In Ireland, Italy, Switzerland, Japan, Belgium and the UK the deficit in 1977–9 exceeded 5 per cent of GDP. It is also interesting to note that despite the passion and rhetoric of recent pleas for balanced budgets some countries with dramatic increases in their deficit positions—Japan, Germany and Switzerland—are among the more economically successful (Cameron, 1982).

In terms of political bargaining it has already been suggested

Table 4.4:   Budget Surplus or Deficit of all Government, 1960–79

	% of GDP Total government surplus (+) or deficit (−)			Change in surplus or deficit, as a % of GDP, 1960–3 to 1977–9
	Average 1960–3	Average 1970–3	Average 1977–9	
Japan	2·7	0·6	−5·2	−7·9
Ireland	−3·8	−4·3	−11·6	−7·8
Italy	−2·6	−7·7	−9·3	−6·7
Switzerland	−1·1	−3·4	−6·5	−5·4
Germany	1·8	−0·3	−3·3	−5·1
Denmark	1·8	4·3	−2·4	−4·2
Sweden	2·2	3·4	−1·7	−3·9
Belgium	−1·9	−2·4	−5·7	−3·8
UK	−2·3	−1·5	−5·2	−2·9
Norway	3·2	3·7	0·4	−2·8
Austria	−1·9	0·3	−4·3	−2·4
Netherlands	−0·9	−0·8	−2·9	−2·0
France	−0·2	0·0	−2·2	−2·0
Australia	1·7	1·7	−0·1	−1·8
Finland	2·3	3·9	0·7	−1·6
Canada	−3·0	−0·9	−4·0	−1·0
USA	−1·1	−1·5	−0·9	0·2

Source: OECD, *National Accounts*

that the provision of public goods and services is part of the quid pro quo of economic consensus. If this is so we might expect increasing deficits to be *negatively* related to price acceleration, and Cameron (1982) has shown that this is indeed the case. He examined variations among nations in their size of deficit increase during the two decades after 1960 and compared this to the rate of change in prices. Nations with the largest increase in deficits, as a percentage of GDP, tended to be those in which price acceleration was least rapid. Some nations — namely Ireland and Italy — did have large deficit increases and high inflation increases, but in Germany, Switzerland and Japan, where deficits also increased dramatically, the rise in inflation was relatively modest. Inflation tended to increase less dramatically in countries where left of centre parties governed, and these governments were more successful in getting wage restraint as we have seen. Such governments also increased the so-called social wage by expanding social services and public employment in exchange for wage moderation (Cameron, 1983; Schmidt 1982). Now while there are economic reasons why deficits might not necessarily be connected with inflation, the political quid pro quo of public goods and services in return for wage restraint appears to be important.

Economic Growth

In Table 4·5 the rate of economic growth in seventeen countries is shown. All these nations have experienced a slowdown in growth. In the early 1960s the average growth rate in real GDP was around 5 per cent but by the late 1970s this average had almost halved to 2·7 per cent. Indeed in several countries, notably Sweden, Denmark, Belgium and the UK, the growth rate had fallen to less than 2 per cent per annum by the late 1970s.

Table 4.5:   Rates of Economic Growth in Western Nations, 1960−80

	% Change in 'real' Gross Domestic Product		
	Average, 1960−3	Average, 1977−80	Change in average, 1960−3 to 1977−80
Japan	11·4	5·0	− 6·4
France	6·0	2·7	− 3·3
Switzerland	5·8	2·0	− 3·8
Italy	5·7	3·4	− 2·3
Canada	5·5	2·3	− 3·2
Sweden	5·5	1·1	− 4·3
Denmark	5·5	1·4	− 4·1
Belgium	5·4	1·9	− 3·5
Germany	4·8	3·2	− 1·6
Australia	4·8	2·4	− 2·4
Netherlands	4·8	2·0	− 2·8
Austria	4·7	3·5	− 1·2
Finland	4·7	3·8	− 0·9
Norway	4·7	4·1	− 0·6
Ireland	4·4	3·8	− 0·6
USA	4·3	2·9	− 1·4
UK	3·4	0·9	− 2·5

Source: OECD, National Accounts

The determinants of economic growth are complex but one major factor is the proportion of resources devoted to capital formation.

The percentage of GDP devoted to investment in selected countries is shown in Table 4.6. What is most remarkable about this data is the low proportion of resources devoted to investment in the UK, the United States, Italy, Belgium and Canada over the 1960—79 period. In Switzerland, Austria, Norway and Japan, the allocation of resources to investment was considerably higher. Interestingly this suggests that those countries where strong corporatism was the practice tended to have a high proportion of resources devoted to investment. Nations in this group include Japan, Norway, Austria, Switzerland and Germany with Sweden standing as the corporatist low investor exception. On the other hand, in Italy, Canada, the United States and Britain, the proportion of resources devoted to investment was low and corporatism was not practised. Thus again there appears to be some connection between political arrangements and economic outcomes.

Table 4.6: Gross Fixed Capital Formation as a Percentage of GDP in Western Nations, 1960—79

	Average % of GDP 1960—79	Change 1960—3 to 1970—3	Change 1970—3 to 1977—9
Japan	32·7	3·5	−4·0
Norway	29·6	−0·8	3·9
Austria	26·5	2·1	−2·5
Switzerland	26·4	1·2	−7·7
Finland	26·2	−0·9	−3·0
Australia	24·8	0·1	−2·5
Germany	23·9	0·4	−4·0
Netherlands	23·8	0·4	−3·2
Denmark	23·4	2·8	−2·5
France	22·8	2·4	−2·0
Ireland	22·4	6·9	4·9
Sweden	22·3	−0·7	−2·3
Canada	22·2	0·7	0·8
Belgium	22·1	1·4	−0·5
Italy	20·9	−2·8	−1·6
UK	18·3	2·0	−0·8
USA	17·8	0·4	−0·2

Source: OECD, *National Accounts*

However the change in resources devoted to investment out of GDP during the 1970s is more interesting. In all countries except Ireland, Canada and Norway, the resources devoted to investment fell but the decline was least in the United States, the UK, Italy and Belgium.

Hence, with the exception of Norway, those nations who almost maintained or increased the resources they devoted to investment were *not* strongly corporatist or left in the political complexion of their government. In strong corporatist states the decline in the resources devoted to investment was over 2 per cent during the 1970s (except in Norway) and in Switzerland the fall was a staggering 7·7 per cent as Table 4.6 shows.

This might suggest that during the economic difficulties of the 1970s the consensus achieved through corporatism was leading to concessions to interest groups that did not favour investment. And this occurred whatever the political complexion of the government. In non-corporatist nations, investment held up better than in strongly corporatist states, and for these reasons the decline in growth was most severe in corporatist countries.

Some economists would argue that the particular concession of high public spending crowds out capital formation and retards growth. Now as Desai (1981) has argued, this hypothesis is difficult to test properly but here we can examine the cross-country differences at least in an ad hoc way. It appears that the proportion of GDP invested in each nation in the late 1970s is not correlated with the level of government spending out of the GDP ($r = \cdot 01$). Also the correlation between the increase in public spending from 1960–79 and the decrease in capital formation is very low at $r = \cdot 01$ (Cameron, 1982). However in the 1970s this correlation, between government spending increase and investment decline, rises to $r = \cdot 16$ and this has caused Cameron (1982) to argue that there may be some limits to public expenditure increases.

In Germany, Italy, Switzerland, Sweden and the Netherlands the marked increase in public expenditure in the 1970s was accompanied by a sharp drop in capital formation. In Sweden and the Netherlands, where public expenditure is about 60 per cent of GDP, he suggests that investment has been especially hindered — and with it economic growth. This relationship may or may not be established since there are other interrelated economic factors and relations at work, but in any case most countries are not at this high level of public expenditure. If public expenditure does impede investment and growth, and this remains uncertain, then using the provision of public goods and services as a quid pro quo in interest intermediation has limits. Increased public expenditure may be related to low inflation and unemployment but if it hinders growth there are clearly difficulties in policy management to be faced.

Thus on the basis of the data in Table 4.6 we might conclude that the connection between political arrangements and economic growth does exist but is more complex than the linkages between political arrangements and unemployment and inflation. This might be because public expenditure growth is damping investment but it may also be for some other reason. The correlation between capital formation and public expenditure is not high and while this proves nothing in the way of a lack of causality it does suggest that some caution is in order.

Investment in capitalist economies is undertaken mainly by private firms, and if the entrepreneurs in these firms do not wish to invest for some reason there is no direct mechanism for forcing them to do so. Thus even in countries where corporatism is practised the investment decision remains in the hands of entrepreneurs. Business leaders might promise some investment rate in return for wage moderation but it is more difficult for them to enforce their promise than it is for a centralized and hierarchical trade union structure to enforce wage moderation. This has led the Social Democratic party and the union organization (LO) in Sweden to devise schemes to facilitate capital formation as part of their corporatist arrangement (Meidner, 1980). Under this scheme forced savings by workers are to be channelled into investment and in return workers and unions will gradually increase their control over business enterprises.

Schemes such as this highlight a possible weakness in consensual corporatist management. If investors will not invest, say simply because they dislike the political complexion of government or its high level of expenditure, then corporatism could be associated with low economic growth. And if wage restraint is managed through consensus it is logical to wonder whether it will continue if economic growth remains slack for long periods. In periods of stagnation both private and public consumption are necessarily restrained and the concessions that can be offered for wage restraint diminished.

This line of thought raises the issue of the impact of economic performance on political arrangements. In the political science literature the emphasis has been on the impact of political arrangements on economic outcomes but it is also likely that the state of the economy influences the political arrangements and their ongoing viability. I will address this issue later.

Macroeconomic Performance and Political Arrangements

At this point we can draw together the economic performance of the developed nations during the 1970s. This is summarized in Table 4.7.

In this table a good average growth rate was classified as being over 3 per cent; medium growth was 2−3 per cent; and poor growth was less than 2 per cent. The average inflation rate was deemed good when it was less than 2 per cent; medium in the 2−7 per cent range; and poor when over 7 per cent. The average unemployment rate was taken to be

Table 4.7: Countries Ranked by Economic Performance Criteria and Political Arrangements throughout the Seventies

	Growth rate	Inflation rate	Unemployment rate	Corporatism
Group 1				
Japan	Good	Good	Good	Strong
Austria	Good	Good	Good	Strong
Germany	Good	Good	Good	Medium
Switzerland	Medium	Good	Good	Strong
Norway	Good	Medium	Good	Strong
Group 2				
Netherlands	Medium	Good	Medium	Medium
Finland	Good	Medium	Medium	Medium
Belgium	Medium	Good	Medium	Medium
Sweden	Poor	Medium	Good	Strong
Australia	Medium	Medium	Medium	Weak
Denmark	Poor	Medium	Medium	Medium
France	Medium	Poor	Medium	Weak
Group 3				
Italy	Good	Poor	Poor	Weak
Ireland	Good	Poor	Poor	Weak
USA	Medium	Poor	Poor	Weak
Canada	Medium	Poor	Poor	Weak
UK	Poor	Poor	Poor	Weak

good when it was less than 2 per cent of the workforce; medium when it was 2−4·5 per cent and poor when it was above 4·5 per cent.

To some extent this ranking of countries by performance is arbitrary in that within each group the ranking might vary on a year by year basis. Within group 2, for example, Australia and France may change their ranking positions year by year — and this is the case with some other nations. However the point is that there is a solid group of 'good' performance nations (group 1); there is also another solid cluster of 'poor' performance nations (group 3); and in between there is a clustering of countries that have performed moderately well in the 1970s.

We have discussed the connection between this economic performance and the political arrangements pursued to get social and economic consensus. In Table 4.7 the last column shows the degree to which corporatist arrangements were practised, and the connections between this column and economic outcomes are most striking. In the case of both unemployment and inflation it is clear that strong corporatism is associated with better economic performance. In all countries where strong corporatist arrangements were in force the unemployment rate was low during the 1970s. Furthermore this low unemployment rate was accompanied by relatively low inflation rates. On the other hand, where corporatism was not practised and we classified nations as being weakly corporatist, it is clear that unemployment was severe and that inflation was a relatively more serious concern. In between the strongly corporatist nations and the weakly corporatist nations the grouping of medium corporatist nations generally performed only in our medium rating on unemployment and inflation. Thus the connection between political arrangements and unemployment and inflation outcomes is clear in the developed countries.

However, as we have also seen, the connections between economic growth and political arrangements are less obvious. In group 1 in Table 4.7 the growth record has been good, except in Switzerland, and all these nations are usually classified as corporatist. But Italy and Ireland also achieved good growth in the context of the 1970s and their political arrangements are not corporatist. Furthermore in Sweden, where corporatism is strongly practised, economic growth has been poor. One reason for this lack of connection between political arrangements and growth may lie in investment behaviour. Where investment has declined growth has fallen and on the basis of our evidence here there is no obvious and simple connection between investment activity and political arrangements. One possible reason for the decline in investment may be the increase in public expenditure which has crowded out private investment; but private investment, where it has declined, may also have been affected by other factors. The investment decision is largely controlled by private entrepreneurs in developed countries, and all we can say at this juncture is that investment and growth outcomes do not appear to be as obviously related to corporatism as unemployment and inflation outcomes. The link between investment and political matters will be examined further in Chapter 10.

What is thus suggested in this chapter is that the different economic experiences of the developed countries in the 1970s are partly connected with political matters. I do not mean to suggest that political arrangements are the only explanation for the economic differences discussed—but I do think that political arrangements are so important that they cannot be ignored entirely. Furthermore the prevailing political arrangements and their economic consequences are connected with the distribution of power examined in Chapter 3. It is notable that in those nations where working-class power is relatively strong that corporatist interest intermediation has arisen (Sweden, Austria, Norway, Denmark, Germany). It is also clear that the pursuit of expansionary policies in the UK, Italy, France, Canada, Australia and Ireland has not been successful because wages and prices have not been restrained. And this lack of restraint is partly for political reasons. In these nations the workforce has not been strong enough either to want, or to enforce, consensual corporatist policies. However the workforce has been sufficiently powerful in all countries to cause price and wage movement stickiness and to increase their claim over public goods and services. This suggests that the distribution of power in society and how conflict is mediated is an important issue for economists to consider when analyzing economic policy. It is also an issue that has been virtually ignored by economists of every hue.

This lack of attention paid to the power distributions prevailing in society has led economists to apply neoclassical analysis in quite inappropriate situations. Where there are strong and powerful interest groups in society, as there now are in all the developed countries, the application of neoclassical policies is simply irresponsible and is bound to be ineffective as we have argued already.

The appropriateness of neo-Keynesian analysis is more difficult to assess. It does appear that its application may be suitable in societies where there is a high degree of consensus and corporatism is practised. In this circumstance inflation will not be a big problem. However even in this instance the success of a Keynesian expansion depends on investment being forthcoming, and this is more problematic. The animal spirits of Keynes's entrepreneurs can be upset and if this occurs the only alternative must be an increase in public investment aimed at maintaining and restoring growth. However, *if* a Keynesian expansion is accompanied by private investment increases in corporatist societies it should be successful, and neo-Keynesian analysis and policy is appropriate.

On the other hand, in countries where there is no explicit consensus over policy, the pursuit of Keynesian remedies and the application of Keynesian analysis is not appropriate. Before it can become appropriate the country in question must develop centralized and encompassing interest groups that can mediate their conflicts. This institutional policy prescription may seem difficult to implement and imagine but social and political development is now at a point that makes this institutional innovation imperative. The expansionary policies pursued in the 1970s have clearly been most effective in those countries that have taken this step. In the future if Keynesian analysis and policy is to be appropriate and effective it must combine economics with whatever domestic diplomacy is needed to effect these institutional changes. However even where there is explicit consensus and cooperation around policy, as there is under corporatism, the question of investment and subsequent growth still remains problematic.

This argument suggests that the solution to our present and

persistent economic problems may be extremely difficult. As a first step we clearly need consensus about economic policy, and this implies that the power distribution in society must be accommodated so that economic conflict is avoided. The establishment and maintenance of economic order has historically always been one of the major concerns of the state and ultimately we will turn to address this matter. The pursuit of economic policy must in practice be concerned initially with this question of order.

Concerns about economic order have been remarkably missing from economic theories of policy and the state. In addressing public sector behaviour, economists have sought to give advice to the state about what it *ought* to be doing, and they have also sought to understand what it is that the state *actually* is doing. But in these theories of the state the question of power and order has been generally ignored. This has meant that theories of the state have not been particularly useful in attempts to understand our present economic dilemmas. These existing theories will be considered next, and after that an attempt is made to consider state behaviour when the maintenance of economic order is a principal objective of state action. In the light of that discussion we then return to the economic performance and problems of the developed countries that we have discussed in this chapter. The first theory of the state that is examined is implicit in the economic policy models used to give advice to the state, and I begin with it because it is the most used and usual theory in the economic analysis of policy.

5   The State in Economic Policy Analysis

> If I were the Head of the Church or the State
> I'd powder my nose and tell them to wait.
>
> Auden, *Calypso*

Economists generally regard public sector behaviour and economic policy in particular as something they should pontificate about and give advice on. From countless academic groves and research institutions governments are regaled with often gratuitous advice about what economic policies they ought to be pursuing, why they ought to be pursuing them, and what the quantitative effect of doing so will be. Economists principally see themselves as little more than well-trained technical advisors. This counselling role over economic policy is important, but the notion of the state that is deployed in most economic policy analyses is embarrassingly simplistic and naive. The nature of the state in basic economic policy models pays no heed to the changes in the power distribution in society that we have discussed or to the political arrangements that have evolved to influence economic policy formation. I have argued that these relatively recent historic developments in the polity of Western nations are not without impact on the economy, but in most economic policy analysis such issues are avoided by some quite extraordinary theoretical assumptions. In the act of simplifying to arrive at a theory of economic policy, economists have completely ignored the relationship between the polity and the economy, and the theory of the state that underlies economic analysis is quite astounding when you stop to think about it.

The Basic Economic Policy Model

Peacock (1979) has already drawn attention to the absurd naivety of the assumed nature of the state in economic policy analysis. However his argument has had little impact on either the theory or practice of economic policy. For this reason his work is worth repeating and embellishing; perhaps if enough dissent to usual economic policy treatments is voiced we might eventually get some changes in the theory and practice of economic policy.

The state is treated in basic economic policy models simply as an omnipotent and benevolent actor that pursues and controls economic policy. The role of the state is very straightforward and can be represented as a control system shown in Figure 5.1.

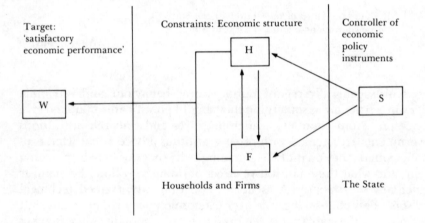

Figure 5.1: The Basic Policy Model

At the right-hand side of the diagram sits the state, a controller, whose goal is to reach some economic target. This target is defined to be a most satisfactory economic outcome in some sense, and may be a social welfare maximum, an aggregate utility maximum or an economic result that is as close as possible to a specified set of objectives. These objectives typically include full employment, price stability, some level of economic growth and a balance of payments target. In Diagram 5.1 the policy objectives are all summarized by the target variable W, on the left of the picture. This is the goal which the state aims to hit.

In attempting to do so the state is faced with various economic constraints represented by the structure of the economy in the centre of the diagram. The economy is composed of firms and households who trade with each other and the outside world, and who are motivated in various assumed ways. It is frequently assumed that firms maximize their profits and households maximize their utility. Then, on the basis of these assumptions, or some similar alternatives, a model is constructed of the economic behaviour of firms and households. This model describes the structural constraints which the state faces in seeking to achieve its economic targets. The entire diagram represents a control system. Given the structure of the economy, the state uses economic policy instruments to achieve its objectives.

In this conceptually simple system all that economic advisors need to do is to specify the state's objectives, along with the structural constraints faced, and the recommended policies can be formally derived. The conception of the state is clearly simplistic. Technically the intellectual exercise involved in advising the state is interesting, but the basic model underneath it all is no more than outlined. This can be demonstrated by looking at those policy models which aim to achieve so-called economic stabilization. This particular policy area is at the moment fraught with debate between monetarists, Keynesians, and 'new' classical macroeconomists. In previous chapters we simply labelled monetarists as neoclassical and ignored the 'new' classical group. Here we will keep the two groups apart as there are differences in their policy analyses. However, the principal concern is that the monetarists, the 'new' classicals and the Keynesians all work within the same simple framework that we have outlined. The state is omnipotent and benevolent and faces structural constraints in society that are only economic. In this sense the state is not political at all as we will now see in some detail.

Keynesians, Monetarists, and 'New' Classical Macroeconomists

Monetarists like Friedman (1948, 1959) advocate a policy where the state follows rules in setting fiscal and monetary policy. A non-Keynesian like Friedman would have three major pieces of advice to the state. First, the level of government expenditure should be set on the basis of benefit – cost considerations, and no attempt should be made to alter public expenditure when business activity fluctuates. Second, given this chosen level of government expenditure, tax rates should be constant and kept fixed at some set level so that the rate of growth in public sector debt averages out over the business cycle at some desired level. Third, the money supply growth should be fixed at a constant rate of x per cent per year, whatever the business conditions. The x will determine the average inflation rate and should be chosen with some desired inflation rate in mind. If this advice is followed, both households and firms know what state economic policy will be; and since this policy is fixed and steady the policy itself will not cause fluctuations in the business sector.

Government- or state-induced instability in the business sector is of particular concern to monetarists who argue that the private sector is relatively stable. If the state does not keep changing its policies, any fluctuations in economic activity that occur will be short-term and effectively mild. In this scenario the major causes of observed fluctuations in economic activity are shifts and changes in government economic policy. This view amounts to using a control system with no feedback from the private sector to the state. If there are hiccups in private economic activity the state ignores these and sticks to its rules. Furthermore, it is argued, the outcome of this rules policy is a satisfactory economic performance. For some monetarists, like Friedman, this objective is achieved *only* via a rules policy. Any other policy approach involving frequent changes in economic policy instruments will achieve an outcome which is worse. There will be larger fluctuations in economic activity if rules are not followed, and these ups and downs involve larger departures from state objectives, such as full employment and price stability.

A more recent wave of theorists, the 'new' classical macroeconomists, argue that if the rules policy is followed by the state it achieves a satisfactory economic performance for different reasons. If the state follows policy rules, the economy, which is viewed as a system of competitive markets, will reach a dynamic equilibrium where resource allocation is optimal. This follows because the Invisible Hand works in the macroeconomic world as well as in the microeconomic resource allocation models. Shifts in economic policy confuse households and firms and cause allocational distortions. If policy rules are followed the competitive markets will guarantee that the state objective of a maximum social welfare is fulfilled. This approach equates the state's objectives with competitive market outcomes but it nevertheless still fits within the control system framework. The state simply pursues policy rules to achieve its target.

Keynesians take a different line on how policy should be managed but they too operate within a control system. Keynesians advise the state to pursue activist policies and not to adhere to steady rules. Policy instruments should be set in the light of what is happening in the private economy and policies ought to 'lean against the wind'. In a boom the economy should be dampened by restraining fiscal expenditure and increasing tax rates. The money supply growth should be cut. In a recession the economy should be stimulated and fiscal expenditure and money supply growth should be increased. Tax rates should be cut to encourage demand and expenditure. This is a general policy of control with feedbacks from the economic system. Whatever is happening to private economic activity affects state economic policy. There are no set policy rules and policy shifts from time to time in response to the condition of the economy.

This alternative Keynesian policy arises because Keynesians consider that the economy is not inherently stable. If the state does not intervene to smooth out fluctuations, the ensuing boom or recession could be long-lasting and severe in its effect. The markets do not operate efficiently and nor do they generate paths of optimal equilibria. State intervention can be stabilizing and set to achieve the state's target objectives.

Whatever the merits of these alternative approaches to policy management, it is clear that Keynesians, monetarists and the 'new' classical economists operate within the framework of a control system. The Keynesians advise a government policy determined by feedback effects which 'lean against the wind'; the monetarists and 'new' classical macroeconomists advise policy rules whatever the state of the economy. All schools accept that the goal of policy should be a 'satisfactory economic performance' in some sense and all assume that the state is little more than a controller. The debate is conducted within the confines of this basic policy model and the simple concept of the state that it implies.

There is not one sign in this approach of any influence of political concerns on economic policy choices or on the responsiveness of the economy to the policy pursued. The economy is viewed as little more than a machine where policy responses can be forecasted and understood by concentrating on entirely economic issues. The polity, in so far as it exists, could be imagined as being extremely pluralist. No actor in the economy has the power to disrupt or encourage policy action or outcomes and there are no powerful interest groups at work. Even if this is not the case the omnipotent and benign state simply presses on in the public interest. This model may be a powerful ideological tool to stop us questioning state actions; but what it certainly is not is a relevant theory about how the state behaves. As we have seen power and political arrangements do appear to influence state economic actions, and in the basic policy model concerned with stabilization this is completely ignored.

The State in Microeconomics and Welfare Economics

Trying to achieve economic stabilization is not the only assumed function of economic policy. Microeconomic and welfare economic analysis concentrates on the distributive, allocative and regulatory roles of the state in the economy. These theories of economic policy, however, also work within the confines of a similar policy model. The state continues to be regarded as a simple controller. Such theories begin by justifying the role of the state in providing certain public goods, overseeing laws and regulations, and generally interfering in the market allocation of economic resources.

The starting point in these studies is the firm and household sector, and this is initially set up and considered as a system of markets with no state intervention. The model at this juncture is strictly hypothetical. It considers only firms and households and there is no state. In this imaginary scenario there is a voluntary exchange of goods and services, and if this economy is perfectly competitive, and there is a full set of markets, the entire outcome is Pareto-efficient. This means that no one person can be made better off without making someone else worse off.

Now this Pareto-efficient outcome serves as an important point of reference, and some economists simply treat it as the objective of state policy. What the state ought to do in this case is to try and get the economy to this Pareto-efficient reference point. To achieve this end the state is told to pursue certain policies which ensure that markets operate effectively. These policies include laws to legitimize property rights, laws of contract and exchange, and regulations that outlaw monopoly and restrictive practices.

Even if this Pareto-efficiency point is reached it is frequently suggested that it may not be all that desirable if judged on an equity basis. It is not difficult to imagine a Pareto-efficient world that is perfectly dreadful: differences in income and wealth between the rich and the poor might be extremely large. But redistributing from the rich to the poor violates Pareto-efficiency criteria because while it would make the poor better off, it would also make the rich worse off, and this is not Pareto-efficient. Nevertheless, on equity grounds redistribution policies from one group to another are frequently recommended. The unemployed are assisted; the severely handicapped are cared for. These policies are redistributive and not Pareto-optimal. One side effect of this type of redistribution may be a decline in economic efficiency and, in economic policy analyses of this type, the policy trade-offs between equity and efficiency are duly examined. In distribution policy the assumed objective of the state is no longer Pareto-efficiency but a more just and equitable society. In terms of the basic policy model the state continues as a controller but its objectives are now defined to include concepts of economic justice. However, these concepts of economic justice are defined by recourse to some system of morality. Distribution is not in practice determined by power arrangements. In this theory the working class improves its position because we all agree that society should be more equitable for moral reasons. It is not a move towards equity that is based on an improved power position by the working class.

The objectives of the state change to include equity simply because society agrees that this is moral and desirable in some sense.

It is not only changes in the assumed objectives of the state that can lead the hypothetical economy away from its Pareto-efficient reference point. Even with vigorously enforced economic regulations, aimed at creating Pareto-efficiency, the economy may not be perfectly competitive. There may be imperfect information resulting in the under-utilization of resources or monopoly power, which can be exploited by those who have more knowledge than others. The outcome of the markets may also be inefficient because of externalities. Producers and consumers are assumed to make decisions only on the basis of the direct effects of these decisions on themselves. They do not consider the effects, whether desirable or not, on other people. As a result the decisions made by firms and households may not be socially efficient. Pollution is a usual example where the cost of polluting is not borne by the polluter, and hence the pollution continues because there is no direct economic motive to stop it. State policies aimed at handling externalities, like pollution, may take the form of regulations, or taxes or subsidies. There is some controversy over the appropriate policy for dealing with externalities but in any case the policy objective assumed is that of attempting to reach some socially desirable and economically efficient position. There are differences in exactly how this objective is defined in the literature but the point remains that the state is recommended to pursue these policies and its role is little more than that of a socially enlightened interventionist.

The same point applies to the economic analysis of the provision of public goods. In a perfect market these goods are not supplied in a socially optimal way. They are particular categories of goods, like parks, basic research and defence, where consumption by one person does not preclude or detract from consumption by others. If there was no state intervention, public goods would not be supplied by the market system at all, or their supply would be extremely limited. To overcome this form of market failure it is advised that the state should intervene in some form to increase the provision of public goods and so achieve greater economic efficiency. There are no political reasons for this intervention.

Now all these recommended economic policies concerned with distribution, allocation and regulation, are analyzed in a similar framework and style, and this corresponds to the basic policy model. As with stabilization policy, the objectives of the state are assumed, the private sector of firms and households is analyzed, and then on the basis of this analysis, the recommended policy for the state is formally derived.

The actual analysis of stabilization policy discussed earlier typically features an income – expenditure model of the private sector, while other economic policies are usually analyzed using a general equilibrium model of markets. But the underlying methodological framework is the same. The economic analyses subsequently advise what the state ought to do on the basis of its assumed objectives. Because the different types of policies are examined using different models of the private sector the total and complete policy advice package is rather difficult to coordinate. The derived stabilization policy may be in conflict with the derived policies for distribution, allocation and regulation.

This particular policy co-ordination problem does not receive a lot of attention in economics partly because of the division of intellectual labour. Macroeconomists focus on stabilization and microeconomists focus on distribution, allocation and regulation functions using general equilibrium models. Co-ordination between the two different economic approaches is usually done in an *ad hoc* way which is not particularly satisfactory. However Dixit (1976) has shown the two analyses might be put together by working within an agreed and common model of the private sector. For telling the state what it ought to do this represents something of an advance, since all policies could be assessed and co-ordinated in a rigorous way. Nevertheless this more recent contribution towards policy co-ordination still rests firmly in the basic policy model framework. State objectives are assumed, the private sector is modelled and analyzed, and the state is told what it ought to do.

The basic policy model, in both macroeconomics and microeconomics, thus implies a view of the state which is rather peculiar. The state is no more than a single-minded and enlightened institution which presumably will accept and follow the wise counsel of economists and act so as to reach various desirable targets somehow defined for the good of the people of the nation. If one were to suppose, quite reasonably, that the state might not behave like this, either because it cannot, or because it does not, then the foundation for this usual analysis of economic policy crumbles.

The Limitations of State Theory in Economic Policy Models

One obvious limitation of this treatment of the state is the mundane recognition that the state is not omnipotent. It has certain limitations to its powers, and in the conduct of economic policy these constraints are broadly social and political as well as economic. It is a perfect waste of time recommending policies which cannot be pursued because of limited capabilities, and as we are arguing one of the limitations that faces the state is the distribution of power in the society in which it operates. In a world where the working class is sufficiently strong to oppose money wage reductions and public expenditure decreases of any large magnitude, it is not pragmatic to recommend policies that are going to be so unacceptable that they cause a breakdown in the economic order. The maintenance of order is usually one objective of any state, and if a breakdown in order is a likely consequence of some economic policy action this policy would never be pursued by a rational government that wished to continue the status quo. On the basis of the evidence in the previous chapters it appears to be worth examining what constraints the modern state faces and how these constraints, whether economic or political, affect economic policy.

To be fair, the basic policy model was never intended to be an analytical tool for understanding actual state actions, but rather a device for developing policy recommendations. But even in this context the nature of the state that is implicitly assumed is not without problems. One limitation imposed by the conception of the state used in these basic policy analyses involves behavioural assumptions which appear to be inconsistent. This is a damaging accusation, since one of the minimal tests that any theory should pass is that its basic assumptions should be logical and consistent with each other. In the firm and household sector in these policy models it is assumed that individuals are motivated in the self-interested fashion depicted two hundred years ago by Mandeville, Ferguson and Adam Smith. The state on the other hand is assumed to act in the interests of the general community. The reason why it pursues the objectives of full employment, price stability, a 'just' distribution of income and so on is because these goals are in the public interest.

Now this is rather odd. The state itself is composed of groups of people and individuals who, when in state employment, are presumed to be motivated by the public interest. But once they are outside the state, in their households, they become motivated by self-interest. In the basic policy model the public servant crosses the steps to the office and behaves in the public interest; upon leaving the office the public servant enters a self-interested world. Each working day involves behavioural schizophrenia for the public servant: sometimes he or she is self-interested and at other times public-interested.

This curious inconsistency needs to be clarified. One rather unconvincing alternative would be to uphold the position in the basic policy model, and to argue that in fact this is the way that individuals in state employment behave. There are real differences in their behaviour when they are in the public sector and the private sector. Philosophers, for example, have argued that there are differences between public and private morality which affect behaviour. Soldiers get medals for killing people when they are acting under orders but should they do so as private individuals they are punished. Behaviour is accordingly modified. This example is somewhat extreme, but public servants in many countries are exposed to an ethos which encourages them to act in the public interest when they are at work. How effective this ideology is in curbing self-interested behaviour while at work is debatable. But for the behavioural assumptions used in the policy model some such argument is required.

Another, surely more plausible, alternative would be to assume that the motivated behaviour of individuals was much the same whatever sector of the economy they frequented. This is the line adopted in what I later refer to as mainstream economic theories of the state, where it is most often assumed that all individuals, whether public servants or not, are motivated by self-interest. This immediately removes the behavioural inconsistency we have noted, but it also implies that the state is most unlikely to act in the public interest. Politicians will pursue their own self-interest and public bureaucrats will pursue theirs. The outcome of such behaviour is not necessarily going to be in the public interest.

This change in behavioural assumptions is important in the context of the policy model because it changes the aims of state economic policy. Policy choices, made by the state, are immediately based on self-interested criteria and are not aimed at a maximum social welfare or any general set of economic goals broadly defined in the public interest. In order to achieve a policy outcome that is anywhere near a public-interested outcome, the self-interested behaviour of individuals must be somehow curbed and controlled within the public sector. Rules of behaviour must be formulated and adhered to in order to have the public interest served.

Another approach to individual behaviour is to abandon the assumption of self-interested behaviour altogether. Whether people are in the public sector or the firm–household sectors it could be assumed that they are not simply egotistical. This raises the possibility of incorporating more forms of human behaviour than the simply selfish. Both simple altruism and commitment to more general ideals might be considered as part of human behaviour, and though this poses problems for analysis it may be a path worth exploring. It has the advantage of avoiding the simplistic self-interested axiom of behaviour; and it also gets around the currently assumed inconsistency of human behaviour in the basic policy model. What this proposed alternative assumption does not do, in common with the self-interested axiom just discussed, is to guarantee that the state will act in the public interest. Once the state is considered as a multitude of individuals motivated by other than public interest, its behavioural outcome as a sector is not necessarily enlightened. This conclusion was obvious to the classical economists before the late nine-teenth century who devoted some attention to the necessary institutions and rules that would be required to achieve good rather than bad or even corrupt government. Even without thoroughly egotistical behavi-our it is naive to assume that any state will automatically act in the public interest.

This point is also obvious if we consider the structure of the state. The state is not the unified actor assumed in the basic policy model; typically it is composed of a central or federal government and local or state governments. Within these echelons there are elected politicians of opposing party affiliations, appointed bureaucrats or administrators at various levels and many other different types of public sector workers. There is clearly no reason why this conglomeration of structures should produce consistent and unified economic policy behaviour aimed at furthering the public interest. Each group may have blatantly conflict-ing aims or milder disagreements. But the way in which these potential conflicts are mediated within the broad state structure is likely to influ-ence both the conduct and the objectives of economic policy. This amounts to suggesting that the behavioural assumptions in the usual normative economic policy models are of doubtful validity and that in practice this matters for both the conduct and the outcome of economic policy. This means that a normative approach to economic policy may only be relevant and useful if it expands its analysis of the state. There is little to be gained from advising a state what it ought to do about econo-mic policy if the state in question is not equipped, either institutionally or in motive, to follow such advice. Thus we should ask what the forces and motives are that lie behind actual state economic behaviour. And, in particular, what are the influences upon the formation and conduct of economic policy?

A further limitation in the basic policy model concerns the definition of the objectives of economic policy. Just exactly what these policy targets ought to be is debatable, and even then achieving them is problematic. To begin with, the policy model we have considered is almost always rooted in nationalism. What the state is concerned with is its own nation; policies are justified on the basis of their benefit to the citizens of a single nation. State benevolence is not universal, and we quite naturally talk in terms of national income and the economic wel-fare of the nation's people.

This nationalistic viewpoint is difficult to justify on moral grounds, and an alternative universal outlook is very rare as Robinson (1962, p.118) has noted. 'The nearest we get to it, usually, is to argue that in a generally prosperous world *we* are likely to do better than in a miserable one. The prosperity of others is not desirable for *their* sake, but as a contribution to *our* comfort; when their prosperity seems likely to threaten ours, it is not desirable at all. This seems such a natural way of thinking, so right and proper, that we do not even notice that it *is* a particular way of thinking; we have breathed this air from birth and it never occurs to us to wonder what it smells of.'

In the real world in which we operate there is good cause for worrying about national economic performance at the expense of more universal considerations. Each nation does compete in international trade, and if markets are not to be lost, with subsequent effects on national employment and consumption, then national economic priorities need to be set and attended to. But in a normative model of economic policy, concerned with what economic policy ought to be, the national orientation of the analysis surely needs more justification than the pragmatic reason we have just outlined. Why should we just recommend policies within a national framework?

The policy recommendations are also narrow in another respect, as we have already emphasized: they are entirely economistic. The only thing the state is concerned with is economic objectives. It has no independent social policy, foreign policy or indeed any broader political or social outlook which may influence its economic objectives. This is very constraining since it is not difficult to imagine social and political policies which are at odds with economic goals. It is also feasible that economic policies which are deemed desirable according to strictly economic criteria are politically impossible to implement. Income distribution policies, for example, which redistribute from one group in society to another, may cause such social unrest that they are never implemented. The state may not be sufficiently powerful to enforce certain policies. Whatever the source of state power it is somehow circumscribed and limited, as we have already suggested in previous chapters.

Foreign policy can also conflict with economic objectives in various ways. Most countries have trade embargos and trade restrictions on certain goods from and to other nations; and economically misguided hostilities between nations are not unknown. All these types of factors limit economic choices in one way or another and constrain economic policy. The objectives of the state are not entirely economic and this does matter for the formulation of economic objectives and whether these will be achieved.

Even if the objectives of the state were simply economic, their appropriate definition is debatable. As the policy model stands, the economic objectives are specified as desirable end-states, such as full employment, a level of public good provision and so on. It may also be worth attaching a value to *how* these end-states are to be reached: in this sense it is not just the end-state that matters but the means of getting there. Hence some writers like Nozick (1974) value individual rights, which they argue are not violated within the market system. Thus any policy which, in its implementation, entails an encroachment on these rights is to be avoided. On a similar tack it can be argued that democracy is to be valued, and any policy which involves a diminution in democratic rights is to be avoided, whatever economic benefits it may involve. These are all philosophical questions which are difficult and probably not capable of resolution. What they suggest however is that great care needs to be taken in specifying desirable outcomes and ways of achieving them. The specialization-induced intellectual poverty from which most of us suffer does not lend itself easily to such matters.

Similar sorts of problems arise when we consider all the economic objectives together as a package. Some of the objectives in fact conflict with each other, and they cannot all be attained simultaneously. This means that some judgement must be formed about what trade-offs to pursue. How much economic efficiency should be sacrificed for equity? How much employment should be sacrificed for price stability if we cannot have both zero inflation and full employment? Economists usually skirt these value-laden issues by claiming simply to be technicians. If politicians tell them what value judgements they have, then these are the trade-offs that economists will use in defining final objectives. But this only passes the buck down the line, and there is not necessarily a guarantee that politicians will choose economic objectives in any broadly desirable sense.

Even if we did have economic objectives specified in some way that was unquestionably acceptable, the problem of whether we could reach them remains. We have already mentioned that the economic targets may conflict with each other and with broader social and political goals; but even within the confines of the narrow economic policy model there are further recognized difficulties. Another constraining influence concerns the international economic environment in which most nations operate. It is well known, for instance, that a small country in an open economy is likely to face difficulties with macroeconomic policy. Imagine an ultra-open economy where all goods, labour and financial assets are tradables and where foreign and domestic commodities are perfect substitutes. If the exchange rate is fixed and all commodities move freely, then the domestic price of goods, labour and financial assets will be determined by demand and supply in the world market. Furthermore if the country is very small in relation to the rest of the world, the world market prices for all commodities will be independent of the economic actions of the country itself.

It follows logically from these assumptions that the room for national stabilization policies is extremely limited. Domestic unemployment is determined by the world market and the national government cannot influence it within this scenario. Aggregate demand management is pointless. The only scope for policy is via the exchange rate, tarriffs and indirect taxes and subsidies on foreign trade. Changes in these policy instruments will affect the commodity price level. But this is all that can be done. This imaginary scenario is an extreme caricature and in practice small countries usually do have more leeway in policy. Nevertheless the open economy can be a severe constraint on policy manoeuvre for a particular country.

These limitations covering both the definition and the attainment of desirable economic objectives suggest that defining and achieving such objectives is not an easy task. Economic targets may conflict with broader state goals, and with each other, and how we then judge what ought to be done is not clear. Even without such conflicts the specification of what is 'good' or 'desirable' raises issues concerned with what we mean by desirable, and for whom such a policy would be beneficial. In the basic policy model the formulation of objectives is frequently taken as given, but we have tried to argue that this short cut may not be without important consequences. As well as looking at what objectives the modern state seems to pursue we must also consider more fully what it ought to do and how it should be instituted so that it would do as 'desired'.

The overall limitations of the basic policy model are thus acute when it comes to thinking about state behaviour. This policy model was of course never intended to be an analytical tool for understanding the state but rather a device for developing policy recommendations. What this approach tends to do, though, is to divert the attentions of economists away from the state, and it is important that this is recognized. We must stop thinking about the state as an enlightened economic despot.

The classical economists, such as Smith, Ricardo, J.S. Mill, and of course Marx, were more concerned with integrating the social and political aspects of society with their economic analysis, and it is on their shoulders that contemporary theories of the state are built. Before going on to discuss these contemporary theories of the state it is interesting to investigate the historical antecedents of the basic policy model. This latter approach which has dominated so much policy analysis in economics has a more recent historical legacy of its own.

The Historical Legacy

Connections between political and economic concerns were largely severed by economists in the late nineteenth century, and this break was of considerable consequence for the development of economic theories of the state. Until the 1860s or 1870s, classical political economy had been dominant in economic thought and economists of this school had devoted considerable efforts to the economic analysis of the state. The classical economists had been particularly concerned about two matters of relevance to the state sector. First James Mill, Ricardo, J.S. Mill and Macaulay, amongst others, were much exercised by the economic and social consequences of the extension of the voting franchise. It was widely feared that franchise extension would lead to the rich, in Macaulay's words, being 'pillaged as unmercifully as under the Turkish Pasha' (quoted by Robbins, 1978, p.199).

The less well off would use their vote to exert pressure for an income and wealth distribution that was more in their interests. Though the extreme scenario feared by Macaulay never happened it does seem clear that the major franchise reforms of 1832, 1867 and 1884 were not without major economic consequences. The Poor Law reform of 1834, the 1844 monetary framework, the 1875 Trades Union Acts, widening union power and permitting picketing, and the 1894 progression in estate duties are generally attributed to the increased franchise and the influence this exerted. For classical economists, like J.S. Mill, who supported the extension of franchise, these developments were welcome though not at all unexpected.

The other major classical political economy theme concerned how government might be organized to work efficiently and for the good of the nation as a whole. The general tendency, from Adam Smith on, was to distrust politicians. For Smith the political arena is populated by 'that insidious and crafty animal, vulgarly called a statesman or politician, whose councils are directed by the momentary fluctuations of affairs'. Decisions are bound to be dominated by 'the clamorous importunity of partial interests' rather than by 'an extensive view of the general good' (quoted in Hutchinson, 1966, pp.7, 8). As a result of this view of the political process, public institutions needed to be organized to avoid, so far as possible, the partial whims of politicians. On this tack Bentham's *Constitutional Code*, and J.S. Mill's *Principles* Book V, are classic examples of attempts to explain how government ought to be set up and run.

These types of political economy concerns were virtually lost from economics when connections between political and economic matters were severed. This shift in the focus of attention of economists seems to have been curiously abrupt, and in Britain it was Jevons who led the change. The thrust of his initial work was taken further by Marshall, Edgeworth and Pigou, and in Europe by Menger, Friedrich von Weiser and Walras. The main concern of Jevons, and those who shared his outlook, was to develop an economic science. For Jevons this discipline was analogous to the science of 'statical machanics', and in his *Theory of*

Political Economy (1871) he viewed his work as a 'positive service to break the monotonous repetition of current questionable doctrines'. The success of scientific economics was to be judged by recourse to logic and facts and not by wishy-washy ethical or moral concerns. Economics was science, not art or ethics, and political concerns, including actual state behaviour, tended to be equated with normative and ethical affairs. He deemed political considerations and most state behaviour to be outside the *modus operandi* of any serious scientific economist.

There were also other reasons why economists shifted their attention away from the state, and several concurrent influences contributed to this course of events and can be identified. First, Jevons's emphasis on economic science opened up new avenues to explore. The introduction of marginalism and the application of mathematics, and particularly calculus, led to exciting new ideas, though these were typically applied to a relatively narrow range of concerns. Economics certainly became sharper and more rigorous but in the process the types of problems it confronted were far more particular than the wide range of concerns of the classical political economy.

Second, the particular narrowing of the focus of economic attention that occurred led to a concentration on the sphere of exchange rather than on the point of production, as Dobb (1973) has argued. This occurred with the introduction of the notion of diminishing marginal utility into consumer theory. Demand became to be viewed as the predominant factor in exchange value. This was in rather sharp contrast with the practice of earlier classical political economy which emphasized the role of costs of production in the notion of value and which thus necessarily focussed on production and supply in some detail.

This new concentration on demand, rather than on supply and production, may not seem particularly relevant to the arguments of this book, but because of this shift in attention, emphasis was placed on the relation between people in the market and on the things they exchanged, rather than on the relation between people, and groups of people, at the point of production. Jevons's theory did not involve latent or open conflict between people, since they were meeting in markets only to exchange things for mutual benefit. On the other hand, in classical political economy the emphasis on relations in production meant that conflict between people was far more overt. At the very least it concerned conflict over the distribution of goods that were produced and it was this relation which Marx developed, though the conflict is also discussed in both Smith and Ricardo.

For Jevons and his followers, property institutions and social relations are taken as given at the start of the analysis, and though these institutional arrangements lurk in the background they are only rarely a matter of comment. What Jevons *et al.* were most concerned with was market behaviour and exchange, and they paid little attention either to conflicts at the point of production or to non-market institutions. This in turn meant that little attention was paid to the state.

Finally, this development in economic thought might not have been so clear-cut if society itself had been in political and economic upheaval, but ongoing practices and institutions seemed stable and secure. Social Darwinism was an important influence at this time, and the economic arrangements that prevailed were regarded as standard and more or less outside the major debates of the time. Marshall for instance, whom one might easily classify as a reformer, thought that competitive markets, a balanced government budget whose size was less than 10 per cent of the GNP, and automatic monetary policy were 'normal'. The late nineteenth century was not a time when existing economic practices were influentially challenged. Heavy critiques had occurred, notably by Marx, but the late nineteenth century was by most historical standards a rather calm period. There was little pressure for questioning the status quo of the economy, and certainly little attention was paid to the role of the state or any other non-market institutions in the economy.

Summary

In this chapter I have argued that the treatment of the state in familiar economic policy models is unsatisfactory. These models, in both their macroeconomic and microeconomic versions, assume that the state is an omnipotent and benevolent controller of the economy. The state is assumed to pursue certain policies, usually after wise counsel from economists, which are aimed at getting to certain objectives that are in the public interest.

The problem with this view of state behaviour is that it is both naive and illogical. There is no guarantee that a state, or its economists for that matter, wish to behave in the public interest. Even if the state wishes to do so it may not have the capacity to act. Political, social and economic constraints can all bind action so effectively that achieving desirable targets is impossible.

Furthermore it is very difficult to specify what these desired objectives of policy ought to be even if it was possible to reach them. Different people in the state have different preferences and these frequently conflict. Also different groups have different power, as we have seen, and this is surely liable to affect what is perceived as a desirable set of outcomes. The state not only operates in a complex world; it is a complex organization itself. It is far from being single-minded and omnipotent.

A more adequate economic theory of the state must address at least two basic issues. What is the state trying to do when it pursues economic actions and what are the constraints the state faces in pursuing these actions? One of the main concerns of the state appears to be maintaining order, and this objective is pursued with due attention to the prevailing power distribution in society. These ideas underlie the political arrangements and the related economic outcomes in developed countries that we have already discussed, but they are completely missing in the basic economic policy model of this chapter. As a result the economic policy recommendations that flow from the basic policy model, whether monetarist, 'new' classical or Keynesian are of limited usefulness. They may not be in line with the objectives of the state, and even if they are they may be ineffective or even inoperative because of the economic and political constraints that the state faces. Some economists however have developed theories about what the state is actually doing and we now explain and discuss these economic theories of the state. None of them really get to grips with the changes in the power distribution in modern society that we have explained in Chapter 2 and which, we have argued, are important.

6 Marxist Economic Theories of the State

So obsessive a ritualist
a pleasant surprise
makes him cross.

Auden, 'Profile'

One major theoretical attempt to analyze what the state actually does is that of the Marxists. Their approach, in contrast to that of the mainstream economists which is discussed in the next chapter, is not concerned with individual behaviour and choice, but with the behaviour of various groups or classes in society. This means that some attention is paid to how the state gets consensus in society and how it preserves social order. It is assumed that power and influence are *not* equally distributed among these social groups. In particular the capitalist class or the bourgeosie has more power and influence than the working class. This situation affects the behaviour of the state, which tends to form and operate in ways which benefit the capitalist class. This analysis of the economic role of the state is obviously a far cry from the view of the state as an enlightened economic despot acting in the common interest of us all, which we have just discussed. It is also an approach in stark contrast to those state actions determined by the self-interested individuals acting in various sectors of the economy that I will discuss in the next chapter.

After examining various Marxist economic theories of the state here, I will argue that their treatment of the power distribution in society is too rigid. Generally their analyses do not allow for any real increase in the strength of the working class; the capitalists always dominate and this domination is always absolute. This rigid treatment of the power distribution in society is not particularly useful in understanding the economic behaviour of the state. To begin with, it implies that these Marxist theorists are rather embarrassed by the very real gains achieved by the working class during this century, which we have documented.

Also the rigid conception of the power distribution that is pursued gives these theorists little understanding of why the economic actions and outcomes of the developed nation-states in the 1970s have been so different.

Capitalists play such a dominant role in Marxist theories of the state because of their control of the material base of the economy. They control production and own the wealth which makes this production possible; and without production, workers could not exist and neither could the state as an organization. Everyone depends, either directly or indirectly, on capitalist production, in a capitalist world.

It is worth noting at the outset that the Marxist analysis has concentrated on the nation-state, and the discussion following will do so too. Supranational state forms, like the EEC, have had little attention, and international bodies such as the IMF, the World Bank, the Bank of International Settlements and other less formal international groups have also been outside the general Marxist theories of state behaviour.

In order to get to grips with the Marxist analyses of the state, some categorization of recent Marxist studies is needed, and here I initially put them into four types. This choice of four groupings is simply one of convenience and both Jessop (1977) and Holloway and Picciotto (1978, Ch.1), in two separate review articles, follow different methods in grouping the Marxist material. The main concern here is to focus on the issues raised, and the typology followed below seems at least useful for that task.

The instrumental approach is the easiest to grasp, and it has the state acting simply in the interests of the capitalist class. The state monopoly theorists concentrate on changes in capitalism and, as capitalism shifts through different forms over time, the functions and nature of the state change to continue serving the dominant class in society. The functionalist view examines the actions of the state and attempts to explain how they aid the continuance of capitalism. The final and most abstract approach is that of the capital logic school which attempts to derive the form and the functions of the state from the social and economic relations in capitalist production. This capital logic analysis has been largely imported from West Germany in response to Marxist criticism of both the functionalists and the instrumentalists.

One obvious point of common concern to all these approaches is an analysis of capitalist production, since whatever is happening there is either affecting the state or being influenced by the state or both. So before getting on to the theories of the state some remarks are in order about the Marxist analysis of capitalism. These remarks are confined to Marxist economic analysis and they are only inserted for readers not familiar with Marxist economics.

78

Marxist Economic Analysis: An Introduction

Marxists base their analysis of capitalism on Marx's own classic analysis which is conducted in terms of the labour theory of value. This theory is fraught with logical difficulties and questions concerning empirical validity, and indeed there is some doubt as to whether the theory can be examined empirically at all. A theory which cannot be examined empirically is not necessarily useless, but lack of empirical examination does open up the danger of permitting a gap to develop between the conclusions derived from the theoretical abstractions and the apparent reality. The theory can become irrelevant to the world it is seeking to explain and understand. These particular difficulties are not trite, but all too frequently they are brushed aside by some theorists in the classical Marxist tradition, using the simple and nonsensical charge that they are ideologically unsound. The particular issues involved are discussed by Morishima (1973; 1974), Catephores (1979a; 1979b), Morishima and Catephores (1978), Steedman (1977), Rowthorn (1980), and Fine and Harris (1976), whose work represents a significant, though not united contribution.

In Marx's work the value of the commodities produced and realized in exchange in the market can be divided into three parts: constant capital, variable capital, and surplus value. Thus the total value of commodities produced, w, is familiarly written:

$$c + v + s = w$$

where   c is constant capital,
             v is variable capital,
             s is surplus value,
and   w is total value of commodities.

This production process takes place over some period of time, say one week. The constant capital represents the dead labour time or hours previously spent that are embodied in the machinery and raw materials that are used in one week's production. This constant capital does not deteriorate during the week and conceptually at the end of the week it is passed on intact without any wear and tear. If production is to expand, so too must constant capital.

Variable capital, v, is the value of labour power. This value is socially determined and represents the number of hours labour must work to reproduce itself in a broadly defined sense. For Marx this value was usually taken to be close to a subsistence level of existence, but it is now understood to be that socially necessary number of hours needed to maintain labour in some given society. In developed nations this value is above the subsistence level, as workers socially define their needs to include such things as paid holidays, gifts to children and a standard of living in general well above that of subsistence. The value of labour power, v, is realized in the labour market where workers sell their labour power to the capitalist.

Now labourers in fact work more hours per week than those determined by the need to reproduce labour. These additional labour hours are surplus value which the capitalist expropriates from the labourers. A position where labour is expropriated in this sense is one where surplus value is greater than zero. The rate of exploitation can be written as s/v and this is also called the rate of surplus value.

Exploitation in this sytem is veiled. Labour is free to sell its labour power at the going market exchange rate, but once this contract is agreed the workers' labour power is in the hands of the capitalist. Labour power is itself a commodity and exchanges as such; and once this exchange is completed, surplus value can be extracted.

There are several situations in this system that can give rise to crises in capitalist production. For an individual firm a realization crisis can result; the entrepreneur purchases labour power and constant capital by exchanging M money units for the purchases. This enables production of the commodity C, say, which is exchanged in the market for M' money units. As long as M' > M the producer can carry on his production but clearly if M' < M the capitalist is in trouble. He is failing to realize fully the value of his production. The money he pays out initially is less than what he realizes in exchange for the produced commodity. It has been suggested by Sweezy (1942) that this situation, on a wider scale, was the position in the 1930s depression. The total value of commodities was not realized in exchange and a crisis of capitalist production ensued.

Another potential crisis for capitalist production comes from the alleged Marxist tendency of the rate of profit to fall. This profit rate is defined as $\frac{s}{c+v}$ and can be more usefully, but equivalently written as,

$$\Pi \quad \frac{s}{c+v} \quad s/v\left(1 - \frac{c}{c+v}\right),$$

where Π is the Marxian rate of profit,
         s/v is the rate of exploitation,
         $c/c + v$ is the organic composition of capital.

It is clear from this expression that if the rate of exploitation, s/v, stays fixed and the organic composition of capital, $c/c + v$, rises, then the profit rate must fall.

Now Marx argued that the organic composition of capital would rise as capitalists were driven to increase their capital accumulation.

This drive came both from the necessity to survive in the competitive whirl of capitalist production and from the desire to get more surplus value anway. The latter not only enhanced survival chances but also increased power and the chance of luxury consumption. But this rising organic composition of capital did not mean that a falling profit rate was a certainty at all stages in time. There were countervailing tendencies that could be mobilized and drawn upon. For example, the rate of exploitation could rise as high levels of unemployment kept the value of variable capital in check. Also new and more productive techniques of production could be introduced. Nevertheless, despite these counter-tendencies it was argued that in the long haul the Marxian rate of profit would decline. This ultimately meant disproportionately less surplus value available to each capitalist, relatively less capital accumulation and a crisis in capitalist production as growth halted.

In brief this is a classical Marxist argument, and I now turn to examining the criticism it has raised. These criticisms are principally concerned with the value schema used. First recall that the total value of commodities produced over some time period, say, one week, is composed of constant capital, variable capital and surplus value. These values are all denoted in labour value units. Now say at the end of the production week a joint product results. This is quite realistically the production of some commodity at the end of the week as well as some machinery which is now one week older. Thus production has resulted in both a commodity and an older piece of capital equipment. In this case Morishima (1973) has shown that a positive rate of profit is not necessarily associated with a positive rate of exploitation. No exploitation might accompany positive profit rates.

Introducing capital goods of different ages also raises the question of a choice in production techniques. So far the technique of production has been implicitly fixed, known and given. But if we allow the capitalist to choose between a whole blueprint of possible techniques in his production process it again transpires that positive profit rates are possible without positive exploitation rates. A similar result also emerges if we assume that labour is non-homogeneous. Some workers are more skilled than others and some are more efficient.

It therefore follows that if either joint production, non-homogenous labour, or a choice of techniques is permitted, then a positive Marxian profit rate can logically occur without a positive exploitation rate. In the assessment of many theorists this amounts to an analytical disaster for Marxist economic theory. In classical Marxian analysis the exploitation of labour that occurs under capitalism is a vital element of the theory. The free contract struck between labour and capitalists by mutual consent results in exploitation and a positive exploitation rate.

81

If however positive profit rates can result from zero or negative exploitation rates, as has been argued under the circumstances outlined, then the whole notion of exploitation can be called into question.

As a consequence some analysts choose to work entirely with so-called surface categories like wages, prices and observed profits. The value schema of Marx is abandoned. The emphasis in the labour process shifts from a free and consenting contract, as in classic Marx, to the struggle between workers and capitalists over their share of wages and profits. As far as fundamental Marxists are concerned, the idea that exploitation is veiled, and that the free contract struck between labourers and capitalists does not abolish exploitation, is replaced by a cruder notion of a more overt distributional struggle. For these theorists the richness in Marx's discussion of such things as social relations, alienation and ideology effectively gets ditched along with the Marxian value schema. These 'pure' Marxists do accept the logical validity of the criticisms, but because they find that the Marxian value system nevertheless provides insights, they tenaciously cling to Marx's classic approach. The value schema of Marx has a powerful pedagogic appeal and a particular usefulness in what might loosely be termed 'non-economic areas of study'; but there is no escaping the fact that Marx's economics and its value system in particular has logical difficulties.

As if this were not enough to contend with, there is also a further problem concerning empirical validation. The value concepts of Marx are simply non-observable. It would be interesting to know if the Marxist rate of profit has fallen, if the organic composition of capital has risen and what has happened to the rate of exploitation over time? But to address these empirical questions some system is needed to shift from non-observable values to concepts we can measure, like wages and profits, and then shift back to the value schema. This is the essence of the 'transformation problem', and several solutions that map from value concepts to surface categories have been suggested. None of these solutions are entirely satisfactory, and in view of the earlier comments about Marx's value system, it is not clear what is achieved by transforming surface categories back into a value system that is fraught with problems. The real world and production are so clearly composed of capital goods of different ages, different techniques, joint production and non-homogenous labour; and for any progress to be made these facts of life must somehow be accommodated.

It is also debatable whether a value schema based on the labour theory of value is relevant as a means of quantifying the present-day capitalist economy, even if all the difficulties already cited did not exist. Taking labour-determined value as the important measure of value seems at least intuitively plausible when actual labour is the main human productive force; but with increased mechanization and capital intensity the labour component is less directly important and using it as a value measure for quantifying the modern economy may yield ideas that are less interesting and of dubious relevance. This matter was indeed recognized by Marx in *Grundrisse* (1973; pp.704−6), who noted the decreasing relevance of the labour theory of value as a means of quantifying the capitalist economy as a result of the development of capitalism itself.

What these comments and criticisms do not make clear is what the correct value system should be, and at present this issue is unresolved. The alternative value schemas proposed to replace the labour theory of value are not without their own particular difficulties. What is pertinent in the context of this study is simply to note that some theorists analyze the state using abstract labour value notions while others choose to use the surface categories of wages, prices and profits. Frequently when commenting on each other's work these two schools of thought are both dismissive and hostile. This venom stems from fundamental disagreements about value theory.

It does not always reflect disagreements about the analysis of the state, though different underlying value systems do logically lead to different ways of thinking about the state. Keeping these matters in mind, I now turn attention to the Marxist theories of the state that have been influential in Marxist thought.

The Instrumental Approach

As Marxists, in the last decade, turned their attention to capitalism's continuing economic problems, one of the earliest theoretical responses was instrumentalism. Within this approach, one of the more influential studies was that of Glyn and Sutcliffe (1972) who provided an historical analysis of the British economy and tacked onto it a discussion of the state's role in choosing and implementing economic policy. A most quoted feature of their work was their historical data on the British rate of profit, which they argued had been falling. This seemed particularly evident in the case of pre-tax profits, but evidence of a falling profit rate also held for post-tax profits after 1965.

Their empirical work necessarily demanded the use of the available statistics, and this in turn meant that the analysis was conducted in terms of observable variables like the measured rate of profit, wages and so on. The upshot of this was criticism from more fundamental Marxists who correctly pointed out that the Glyn and Sutcliffe work was not based on Marx's theory of value. The analysis was carried out in terms of surface categories, like wages and profits, and ignored the more abstract concepts of variable capital, surplus value and other variables of this ilk. These issues have just been addressed, and it is simply sufficient here to note that Glyn and Sutcliffe (1972) took their results to support the hypothesis that the share of resources devoted to profits had been falling. In the particular case of Britain in the 1970s, they argued that capitalists were incapable of halting this trend by their own direct action. The working class resisted wage cuts, and if prices were increased this simply led to both further wage demands and a decline in international competitiveness. Redundancies only led to industrial unrest and days lost in production as strikes resulted. As a consequence, the state was assumed to intervene and act as an instrument of capital; it served the interests of the capitalist class.

Government economic policy, particularly under Edward Heath's Conservative government of 1972−4, was then discussed, and it was suggested that each specific action was directed to aiding the purposes of capital. This crude model of government behaviour is in retrospect the worst chapter in an otherwise interesting book and really demands little serious attention. Their analysis of economic policy is largely ahistorical despite the historical emphasis in the rest of the study. By simply concentrating on Heath's economic record they ignore more interesting questions. The intellectual gymnastics needed to depict Heath's policy as beneficial to business are minimal; but had they attempted to do the same for, say, the first year of the next Labour government, the simple instrumental analysis would have appeared extremely strained. This Labour government in 1974−5, for example, established the Advisory Conciliation and Arbitration Service, relaxed the laws on picketing, made commitments to introduce a wealth tax and price controls, and admitted the Trades Union Council as an integral and powerful input into a 'social contract'. This contract, amongst other things, covered an agreed provision of public services. These Labour Party policies were undeniably an improvement for the working class in 1975, whatever their effect on capitalists at that time.

This gets to the root of the problem of simple instrumentalism. Gains made by the working class through government intervention are either implicitly or explicitly excluded from consideration. The state acts simply in the interests of capital and this overlooks two intriguing questions. First, is it conceivable in a capitalist economy that the state will pursue some policy that is in the interests of both workers and capitalists? The answer to this rather weak question must of course be affirmative. Examples of joint benefits across classes, resulting from state policy, are not difficult to find, and public health provision is an obvious contender. Capitalists gain more healthy and fit workers, and workers gain access to a health service which previously had been either difficult or completely denied because of low incomes.

A second and related question is far more contentious. Is it conceivable that the state might pursue some policy that is in the interests of workers but not in the interests of capital? A positive response to this query is denied by all the recent Marxist approaches, though Ian Gough (1975), whose work is examined later, comes closest to admitting the possibility of working-class gains from state policy with no benefits to capital.

Instrumentalism in its over-simplistic way also fails to deal adequately with other matters. The implementation and formation of economic policy frequently faces a conflict of interest between different groups of capitalists, and it is not clear from instrumentalism how the effects of these conflicts are handled. Glyn and Sutcliffe note the conflicting interests between industrialists and financiers as well as those between small firms and large firms but they do not explain how any state policy is affected or perhaps constrained by these conflicts.

It is worth noting the economic nature of some of these conflicts, although this should not be taken to deny the existence of other social and political conflicts as well. Small firms generally operate in relatively small markets and have less access to sources of funds than do large companies. Consequently, small businesses tend to be more protectionist in outlook than large firms who usually argue for a more free-market-oriented policy. In addition, the effect of a credit squeeze which restricts bank lending is usually more restricting for small companies whose only line of credit may be through a domestic bank. Large companies have more internally generated funds, more access to overseas finance, and easier access to domestic funding sources.

The conflict between financiers and industry is obvious, since industry likes to have cheap loans at low interest rates and financiers may not be able to make profits at these low rates. The basic mechanics behind the functions of banks or financial institutions are quite simple. First they must attract deposits which they can then loan out, and this is the essential source of their business. To attract depositors the interest rate paid on deposits must look more attractive than alternative offers. In an international money market this means the expected return on deposits in London say, must be competitive with returns elsewhere in the world. Both relatively low interest rates in London or an expected devaluation of sterling will cause potential overseas depositors to take their money elsewhere.

But having attracted depositors at some going market rate of interest, the banks must then make a profit if they are to survive; and this they do by lending out these deposits at a higher interest rate than the rate paid out in order to attract the depositors. The interest rate margin between the borrowing rate and the lending rate is the source of

financial profit, provided that the financial institutions can find customers to lend to at the higher rate. Some of these customers are industrialists who, as mentioned earlier, always prefer lower rates on their loans
than higher ones. But lower rates will not attract depositors and thus there
is an obvious conflict between financiers and their industrial customers.

Movements in the value of domestic currency vis-à-vis other cur-
rencies highlight the issue. Devaluation of sterling, say, causes British
export prices to fall and exporting companies would be expected to
increase their profits as sales go up. At the same time the devaluation
automatically raises import prices, hitting both consumers and producers who import raw materials. Consumer demand falls quickly and
companies selling only in the British market find that their sales and
profits go down. They may also face high rates of interest on their loans.
In any case, they will take little comfort in the fact that some of their fel-
low capitalists are exporting more and making more profits. The point
of all this is that the state may somehow mediate or at the very least
recognize these conflicts between different groups in the capitalist
community.

More fundamentally the instrumentalists never make it clear
why the state must act in the interests of capital. This behaviour is
simply assumed, which, in the presence of universal suffrage, for one
thing, is a giant fudge. In the days when voting was restricted to property owners and men of financial means, the election of governments
was in the hands of a group in society whose interests were more compatible with those of the capitalist class. In a nation-state where age is the
only qualification for voting and each person gets one secret vote, the
interests of the majority of voters and those of the capitalist class may
well be divergent. The mechanisms through which this divergence is
either moderated or cancelled out altogether are entirely neglected,
though it is only fair to point out that many other Marxist approaches
also give the existence of popular democracy short shrift, almost as if the
past suffrage struggles by working-class men and women were misguided and ultimately the vote counted for nothing but an illusion of
power and participation. Power and control in capitalist society is obviously not divided equally amongst citizens but the actual location of this
power and how it is maintained and upheld demands explanation.

Universal suffrage and the desire of governments to win elections also affect the conflicts between different groups of capitalists. In
particular, small businesses are a sometimes vocal and in any case
numerous group of voters whose interests cannot be politically ignored in
the quest for votes. This suggests that the unhampered pursuit of economic policy goals that favour big business and/or financial capital is likely
to be constrained by the attempt to maintain democratic popularity. The

conflicts that result from this interplay between democracy and the different interests of different capitalists is often evident in the management of monetary policy. For example in Britain in November 1980 the Conservative government was forced to lower interest rates, as many small business were going bankrupt and popularity for the government amongst this group of small capitalists was at a low ebb. The lower interest rates are less restrictive on the growth of money supply and, at least from the Conservative government monetarists' viewpoint, its attempt to restore price stability is constrained.

Thus the instrumental approach is far from complete in its analysis. It is also not a satisfactory method from which a more complex understanding of state behaviour can be derived. In fact the behaviour of the state in this model is simply assumed and not explained at all. Theory, whether Marxist or otherwise, cannot provide insight when it begins with assertions which are really conclusions. The one achievement of instrumentalism has perhaps been to draw Marxist attention to the state and to highlight the need for a more thorough analysis.

The Theory of State Monopoly Capital

Instrumentalist notions are carried over into this particular analysis of the state in a society of monopoly capital; the state here appears as an instrument of the dominant monopolies. What is of interest, and different from simple instrumentalism, is the attempt to relate the different historical forms of the state to different stages in capitalist development. There are several variants within this approach but all share an underlying stage analysis of capitalist development. In its crudest form it is argued that each society historically passes in an almost fatalistic way through primitive communism, slavery, feudalism, merchant capitalism, competitive industrial capitalism, monopoly capitalism, state monopoly capitalism and finally socialism. At each stage of development a different form of the state is apparent.

Before getting down to the actual analysis of the state, some remarks on this background theory about the stage process of capitalist development are pertinent. Historical evidence suggests that there is nothing mechanical and automatic about the transition of societies through these development stages, and indeed societies have frequently omitted different stages in this development. The USA, for example, never went through a feudal period, and socialism has arisen in societies whose development stage was well back from advanced capitalism. Industrially backward countries who missed out on the industrial revolution of the nineteenth century have followed a path of planned development, and in this way have either short-circuited several stages of the

Marxist schema or stepped right outside it. The USSR is a good example; its material achievements this century rapidly shifted it from a relatively feudal past to its current centrally planned and relatively economically developed position.

As a model of development, the giant step from industrial backwardness to socialism has much appeal. Indeed, the transition to socialism from this early historical position has to date met less resistance than the transition to socialism from the advanced capitalist stage. One explanation for this given by Robinson (1965) is economic in emphasis and thus far from complete. Material development necessarily comes from investment and to get this accumulation in a poor society, any surplus above subsistence needs must be devoted to capital formation. To achieve rapid development, as the surplus grows, it should be diverted into capital formation and very little of it should be released to raise living standards.

Obviously this process is a burden on the people who are bearing a cost, in terms of low living standards, in order to get more development. But this burden is easier to accept when past feudal property rights have been smashed and unearned income is nowhere evident. The hypocrisy of asking or forcing workers to make sacrifices when some people enjoy large property income is avoided; and in time the material advances can be shared. The mass of people were so badly off to begin with that this process of development is most unlikely to meet mass resistance.

The transition to socialism from advanced capitalism is at present less clear-cut in its advantages. There are more people who believe, rightly or wrongly, that such a transition would not be to their material benefit. The obvious inequities under capitalism cannot be denied, but it has also brought better material conditions to more people than classic Marxist thought may have envisaged. The middle class in particular have become prosperous and numerous, and working-class gains have also been substantial.

Many Marxist studies do not deny the drift of this argument. Transition through all these development stages is not a hard and fast rule of life, and this in turn implies that the conditions necessary for a transition both from competitive industrial capital to monopoly capital and from monopoly capital to socialism need careful explanation. Such explanation is provided by building on Marx's early analysis of capitalism. At present this analysis seems more convincing in explaining the transition to monopoly capital than in explaining any subsequent transition to socialism; but in both cases the explanation rests on the logical difficulties and questions concerning empirical validation which have already been discussed.

Monopoly capital develops as the organic composition of capital rises with increased accumulation in the competitive industrial capital stage. This rise in the organic composition of capital is also accompanied by the increased concentration of capital within each industry and also an increased concentration in fewer hands. The myriad of smaller capital owners is replaced by fewer but larger owners of monopoly capital.

This increase in the organic composition of capital is accompanied both by the tendency for the Marxian profit rate to decline and by an increase in the power of the monopolies who come to dominate the capitalist form of production. The state in competitive industrial capital served the interests of many capitalists by overseeing the self-regulating competitive markets. The state judiciary backed up laws of contract and trade; sound money was guaranteed; the defence of the realm was maintained; and certain public goods provided. But the role of the state was essentially a non-interfering role; markets were left to work on their own and the state functioned in an economic way that was limited and which has been explored most thoroughly by classical political economists.

But with monopoly capital and allegedly falling profit rates, the state intervenes to arrest capitalist decline. Basic industries are nationalized; essential services are provided; money and credit is centrally controlled; assistance is given by the state to aid private investment; a large state market is provided for capitalist-produced commodities; wages are state-controlled; research and development is state-sponsored; the economy is programmed to decrease uncertainty, and international agencies of control are established. Monopoly capital becomes state monopoly capital as the role of the state expands. In this final stage of capitalism the state and monopolies fuse together in a single mechanism. This fusion is apparent through such things as the class affiliations of civil servants and the dominance of monopolies in education and the mass media.

This far-fetched story is in need of more evidence than it has received, and the instrumental nature of it is apparent. The political strategies that are derived from it reflect the unsatisfactory basis of the explanation. Because small businesses are excluded from the state monopoly system, it is suggested that they now share an interest with the proletariat in an anti-monopoly alliance. This alliance, it is argued, can capture the state for its own use, but, as Jessop (1977) has pointed out, this argument is quite inconsistent. If the state and monopolies have fused together, how is it possible to transform society to socialism by seizing the state? The state is little more than a system of interventions on behalf of monopolies, and how can popular groups use these forces to get to socialism? The strategy suggested does not follow from the argument.

89

The confusion in part results from the simplified view of the state. Why should the state act in the interests of monopoly to the exclusion of all others' interests? What institutions within the state and civil society bring such behaviour about? What contradictions, if any, are present in decisions? The form of the state is clearly more complex than the one of fusion between state and monopolies which is assumed.

The material basis of the argument also does not necessarily lead to an inevitable socialist transformation, and its foundations are questionable. There is no conclusive evidence that the organic composition of capital has been rising or that the Marxist rate of profit has been falling. And if the rate of profit has been falling, is it because the exploitation rate has been falling, or because the organic composition of capital has been rising? The answer is not objectively clear. If a declining profit rate is assumed, where does the state get the resources to provide services to monopoly capital? Are resources pre-empting surplus value away from capitalist production to provide basic services, or is the state seizing some part of variable capital? Whatever resources the state is using, it must be surely meeting resistance. Capitalists will be resistant to attacks on their surplus, especially if their profit rates are low; and workers will attempt to maintain their variable capital values. The limits on state action imposed through the fact that available resources come largely from the capitalist sector of production mean ultimately in this analysis that the demands on the state exceed its ability to supply. The crisis of capitalism deepens, but again this in no way means that socialism is inevitably going to appear. It is the almost religiously held belief that socialism will come that causes this approach to be far from persuasive. Historically the form and functions of the state have altered; but the relations between these forms and functions and changes in civil society are only examined superficially, and the assumptions made require a great deal more back-up evidence.

The Functionalist Approach

This approach begins with a study of the functions of the state and then explains how each of these actions serves the interests of capital. Monopoly capital and a large state presence are assumed, though different groups within the capitalist class are taken to have different interests. A most typical study in Gough's (1975) analysis, and it exposes several interesting positions. It is concerned largely with an analysis of the British public economic sector, and the form of the state is assumed to approximate that described in Poulantzas's *Political Power and Social Classes* (1975).

This particular state form has several critical implications which

Gough used, and this is the first Marxist analysis discussed which really takes the form of the state in any way seriously. At last the state is not just an instrument of the dominant class but a form of institutions and actors whose interplay is both complex and interesting. The state form is not neutral but the interests of capital are not assumed to be met in any direct instrumentalist sort of way.

The form of the state and the form of capitalist production are assumed to be relatively autonomous, and this is taken to be a specific feature of capitalism. Because of this autonomy, Poulantzas considered that a theory of the capitalist state, as a sort of regional theory standing beside Marx's analysis of capitalism, was possible. The economic features of capitalism are still dominant in the last instance but on this basis a structural theory of the state is constructed. Gough seems to interpret this approach as implicitly meaning that an analysis of the economic functions of the state can be handled fairly distinctly from the more political structures of the state with which Poulantzas was concerned. This interpretation of Poulantzas does not in fact seem correct, but it does facilitate an easy functionalist discussion. Thus economic functions are analyzed, and the more political functions are left to Poulantzas or some other political theorist to cope with.

The state in its relatively autonomous form is given two functions. The first is to organize the disunited and different fractions of the capitalist class. The state can do this because of its apparent relative autonomy within capitalism; and indeed the state must organize these fractions of capital to enable the dominated class to be kept in their place. The second function is to disable the dominated class, and this is largely done by having the state appear as if it acts in the national interest. This appearance of national interest, it is argued, is legitimized by universal suffrage and 'bourgeois freedoms', and this leads individuals to think mistakenly that the state is class neutral. To achieve these functions of uniting the dominant class and disabling the dominated, the state must appear to be separate from class conflicts. In this guise it is to be expected that the state will on occasions appear to act in the interests of the working class. But this is merely to legitimize the state in the popular eye, and in the long term the actions of the state always lie with the interests of the dominant class.

Hence in this approach the state certainly does at times act in the interests of the working class as well as in the interests of the capitalist class. The social welfare functions of the state, for example, are explained as a legitimation device which balance concessions to workers in return for the maintenance of popular consent for the political structures of capitalism. There is class struggle at work but not really any fundamental change in capitalism. Capitalism preserves its structures and support through various legitimation procedures run by the state.

It is difficult to escape the thought at this point that some theoretical rabbit has been pulled from the proverbial hat. The earlier instrumental approaches simply had the state acting in the interests of capital, and in the light of the real world this was never going to be acceptable theory. It was too far from reality. The state often acted to aid the working class. So having got into this theoretical corner, we now see the suggestion that the state does act in the interests of workers, but only as a legitimizing device — that is, the state really acts to serve the overall interests of capital in the given situation. Class struggle and working-class strength certainly help to get these concessions from the state; but concessions is all they are. Implicit is the assumption that these working-class gains also help capital by legitimizing its form. Each concession to the working class somehow strengthens the capitalist class. Class struggle is no longer a zero sum game where one side loses and the other gains; it now apparently results in both sides gaining. While a few class struggles may well have this result, it seems difficult to believe that the outcome of all class conflict can be so categorized. And this categorization implies a theoretical fudge. If working-class gains are written off as simply legitimizing, we are in danger of finding ourselves left with no more than a bit of theoretical semantics.

Gough does seem aware of this issue and at times goes very close to admitting that workers may have had gains that were not in the capitalists' interests in any sense whatsoever. However, to admit this is to accept the possibility that the capitalist class is not always dominant. Social democratic theory and pluralism could enter the scenario, and these theories are, of course, positively alien to Marxist theory. The accepted Marxist alternative is the rather pessimistic one which downgrades working-class successes and triumphs. It will be argued later that this is not the most insightful way to proceed in understanding the state, but with this issue raised, we return again to Gough's functionalism.

Gough concentrates on two laws of capitalist development. These are the increasing concentration of capital and the law of combined and uneven development. The increasing concentration of capital has brought with it a continuous increase in employees, a decline in the number of self-employed, increased urbanization, increased industrial disease, and a higher demand for technically skilled labour. Combined and uneven development on a global scale has resulted in lessened opportunities for capitalist expansion, as liberation movements in the third world do not welcome foreign capitalist exploitation. In addition, the Eastern European bloc limits areas for global capitalist activity. The existence of these socialist nations also provides the model of a system where, whatever its other failings, work is guaranteed for all citizens. Thus capitalism must provide an alternative society which appears at least as favourable as these alternatives; and this provides a constraint on capitalist behaviour. All these developments lead to an increased role for the state.

Now state expenditure in Britain certainly has increased as a share of gross domestic product and these expenditures, following O'Connor's (1973) analysis of the USA, are broadly classified into three types. Social investment covers such government expenditures as aid to industry and infrastructure investment on roads and telephones; its function is to increase the productivity of labour and raise profit rates. Social consumption covers items like government health and welfare expenditures, and these decrease the reproduction costs of labour. The state now covers some of these reproduction costs in the form of a social wage, and this presumably permits the capitalist class to extract more surplus value and raise profit levels by lowering its contribution to variable capital. Social expenses are directed to maintaining the social harmony and social relations needed for capitalist production. These expenditures are a drain on surplus value and cover such items as defence, police, prisons and the judiciary. The national debt is also assumed to be a drain on surplus value and it too is classified as a social expense.

The economic analysis here is far from rigorous and has overlooked the crowding-out debate which is currently flourishing in mainstream economics and which in fact is relevant here. It can also be dealt with in Marxian value terms as the productive versus unproductive labour debate suggests, but whether one uses surface categories or value concepts the issues need more rigorous attention in this context.

In terms of the crowding-out debate, Keynesians argue that whether or not government expenditure aids private sector activity depends on two matters. First, if aggregate demand is less than aggregate supply, the multiplier effects of government expenditure are typically expansionary and stabilizing. But if aggregate demand exceeds aggregate supply, government expenditure may do nothing but crowd out private sector expenditure on investment and consumption and in addition add to inflationary pressures. The size of the crowding-out effect in this latter case depends on how the public expenditure is financed. It can be covered by either bond issues, taxation or a money supply increase and the particular financing mix chosen has different implications both for crowding out and for economic stability.

Thus it is simply not on to categorise expenditure in the O'Connor–Gough manner. In the case where aggregate supply exceeds demand, social expenses will expand the private sector and not be a drain on the surplus. In the reverse case, when aggregate demand exceeds supply, which may have been the case throughout most of the post-1965 period, government expenditure increases in whatever category can crowd out private sector activity, and, in fact, exacerbate the capitalist crisis. But the size of this effect depends on the form of financing used. Gough's attempt to distinguish between the effects of taxation and national debt financing is incorrect in its economic analysis. He argues that deficits are not inflationary if there is unemployment, but unfortunately this is not correct. It is only correct if aggregate demand is less than supply, and this has not been the case. Aggregate supply may be less than demand despite the presence of unemployed workers. The crisis of the 1980s is not analogous to the last 1930s depression, where there was deficient demand, and the current crisis will only be solved if aggregate supply is somehow increased. Stimulating demand will add to inflation. The reverse of Say's Law does not hold: demand does not create its own supply.

More generally the functionalist approach is ahistorical and static and fails to deal with changes in the form of the state. The relatively autonomous state form that is assumed seems more relevant to a society of competitive industrial capital as in the last century. The state did appear then as separate from civil society, but this separate appearance is not at all obvious in the post-World-War-II capitalist state. The more recent state form has properties of corporate bias as we have already seen, and few people are under the illusion that economic and political issues are two separate and unrelated matters. Belief in the state as an actor in the national interest is a more acceptable illusion, but in general this early Poulantzian state form seems to be stuck in a time warp somewhere in the nineteenth century. This issue will be returned to, but at this juncture it is sufficient to note the static nature of the analysis.

Finally, it has been pointed out by Holloway and Picciotto (1978) that class struggle in this model is seen in severely limited terms, as being over the distribution of resources. In part this comes from the static nature of the analysis because no change in either capitalist production relations or the form of the state enters the picture. Hence there is no discussion of how class conflict might affect changes in the form and institutions of either the state or civil society.

Despite these criticisms the functional analysis has moved the theory on from simple instrumentalism. Gough, to his credit, studied expenditure patterns in the public sector and sought to accommodate them into a theory. In doing so it became clear that more attention was needed to explain state form, and that Poulantzas's earlier model is not entirely satisfactory. It is also obvious that the economic analysis needs corrections and that more emphasis on the historical development of both forms and functions within the state and civil society might be a fruitful avenue to explore. It is on this latter issue that the capital logic school has focussed.

The Capital Logic School

The high level of abstraction which characterizes this approach makes it very difficult reading, and its contact with reality often seems fleeting. In this respect, Holloway and Picciotto (1978) have performed a creditable service by introducing the approach to English-language readers and by placing it within the context of both Marxist debate and West German political developments in the 1960s. During this period German economic policy shifted from laissez-faire to intervention and planning as a recession hit in 1966–7. Social reforms were introduced, and the active student movement declined in importance and only rarely received support from the working class. All these developments raised questions about the limits and possibilities of state actions and it was these issues that the capital logic school began to address. The underlying method is 'capital theoretic': this means that the form and functions of the state are derived entirely from the abstract form of the capitalist mode of production.

The capitalist mode of production requires various material conditions to be met for its survival, as well as the continuance of particular social relationships. The previous approaches we have discussed have stressed the material conditions for reproduction, like continued capital accumulation; but in this approach the stress tends to be on the whole totality of capitalist production. This means, for instance, that the consenting social relationship between labour and capitalists must be preserved, as too must be all the legal and property relationships that go with capitalism as a form of production. This brings in much of the richness and depth of analysis in Marx's early work but, as mentioned earlier, necessarily entails working within his value schema and its associated difficulties. There is also another way in which this method meets difficulties, and, as Jessop (1977) has made clear, it tends to ignore all influences on class struggle excepting the social forces of capital and wage-labour. To remedy this failing, he suggests the addition of a neo-Gramscian class theoretic approach which would enable a deeper and more thorough investigation of various other social groups and of the way in which one alliance comes to be dominant and exerts this dominance. A more explicit treatment of ideology and power would be available.

This is an interesting idea and something on these lines might be useful. Nevertheless, the capital theoretic starting point does represent some advance on the simple instrumental and functionalist approaches so far discussed. Specifically, the capital logic school attempts to explain such issues as the structural limitations of state intervention in the capital accumulation process; the structural limitations of political actions to reform and transform the economic system; the continued acceptance of reforms by the working class and its associated latency in class confrontation; and the development of the state as a form of power, apparently separate from capital domination and perceived to exist for the common good.

Explanations of these issues vary within this approach but all begin with an analysis of capitalist production and its requirements to survive. After this analysis of capitalism, two alternative methods of state derivation are pursued. In the first approach, the necessary functions of the state are derived from capitalist reproduction requirements and then the form of the state follows from its functions. The alternative method derives the form of the state from the requirements of the process of capital accumulation and this state form then implies certain state functions. The choice between these two methods of derivation is a matter of dispute within the capital logic approach; the necessary functions of the state in capitalist society to guarantee capitalist survival may well impose limitations on the form of the structure of the state. Likewise, the necessary structure of the state for capitalist reproduction may impose limitations on the functions that the state can perform. Which of these limitation effects is dominant is not clear and it seems quite probable that both effects simultaneously apply. The necessary state structure imposes functional limitations, but the necessary state functions also impose structural limitations on the state.

To maintain discussion within reasonable bounds, attention is centred here on the contributions of Altvater (1978) and Hirsch (1978). Altvater argues, often similarly to Poulantzas, that the separation between the state and civil society necessarily exists because capital cannot continually reproduce itself without 'at its base a special institution which is not subject to its limitations as capital, one whose transactions are not determined by the necessity of producing surplus value, one which is in this sense a special institution alongside and outside bourgeois society'. (Altvater, 1978, pp.40−1).

This point is fundamental to the argument, but its validity is not intuitively clear. If capital is inherently incapable of reproducing itself, it is just as theoretically plausible to argue that capitalism would disappear as it is plausible to argue that these unmet needs necessarily give rise to the state. Exactly in what way and how do these unmet needs of capital give rise to the state? It is incumbent on the capital logic school to explain both why *and how* they consider that capitalism determines the state form and to provide historical and objective evidence for their position. Such an explanation would also require some attention paid to the development of particular institutions within the state form and how institutions such as parliament, the bureaucracy, and local government relate both to each other and to various social classes.

What Altvater suggests is that the conflicting self-interest of individual capitalists precludes their overt co-operation in the general interest of capital as a whole. And thus this co-operative function is provided by the state. As has already been discussed above, different fractions of capital certainly do have different interests and these fractions of the dominant class will at times find co-operation impossible. But it does not necessarily follow that the state will perform some uniting role for the capitalist class. At least tacit co-operation from capital is required for the state to perform this function, and in a sense this co-operation was assumed absent to begin with. Quite how the state meets this corporate need and what limitations there are on the state's form and function in this process demands more examination. On this tack, a recent historical study by David Abraham (1982), using Poulantzian methods, has analyzed the Weimar Republic and shown quite convincingly that at this historical juncture no adequate co-operation between different fractions of capital was possible. The Weimar state collapsed and fascism replaced it. But what is of interest here is that co-operation between capitalists cannot simply be asserted and assumed; and whatever co-operation results undoubtedly has limits which affect subsequent state structures and actions.

Accepting the premise that the state form is like an 'ideal collective capitalist', Altvater derives four functions which the system of competing capitalists requires the state to perform. The state must provide infrastructure, binding legal relations, a regulation of class conflict, and protection for national capital on the international scene. These functions are no surprise and in fact are similar to those attributed by Lord Robbins (1978) to the classical political economists. The Robbins terminology is different, but Altvater really provides no new insight into state functions as such. There is nothing said about how these four functions are constrained or modified with changes in capitalist development. Furthermore, because of the lack of dynamics and the limited attention paid to class struggle, the treatment given to the limits of reform and state intervention is simply mechanical. Because state form is determined by the needs of capital, any attempt to achieve socialism through democratic political efforts is futile. This inference flows directly from the premise that the state is a form of ideal collective capital, and thus the analysis is not particularly illuminating beyond the stated premise. And, as has been argued, this crucial premise requires more back-up support than it is given.

On the issue of the continuing latency of the working class and its consent to capitalism, Altvater has no adequate explanation. He argues that the state is a surrogate for capitalists in their oppression of the working class but there is little discussion of why, therefore, the state is perceived as neutral, and why the working class remains committed to reform and not revolt. The actions of the state that give concessions and reforms to the working class are basically ignored, and only those functions classified as necessary for capitalist reproduction are dealt with.

Hence little progress is made on the development of the state form or the structural limits of intervention and reform. The approach sits so critically on the premise of the state as an ideal collective capitalist that those who are sceptical of this assumption will remain unconvinced; and even those who accept the premise are faced with inferences drawn from it that are only a few steps removed from the premise and thus scarcely enlightening. The approach is too static and insufficiently developed.

Hirsch, on the other hand, has built on this work and contributes a dynamic model of the state with an historical foundation. His analysis is an impressive move forward in Marxist theories of the state and all the more so because of his frank admissions of what the capital logic approach can and cannot achieve at this point in its theoretical development. Hirsch (1978) begins with a critique of pluralist methods which assume that in the face of various conflicting interest groups, the state attempts to serve community goals. He argues instead that the state is an historical product and its specific social form is an organization of domination for the dominant class in society. This dominant class is capitalist and the roots of this dominance lie in the material conditions of life or, in this case, the capitalist mode of production. No statements can be made about the functions of the state, and political management generally, until the basic laws of social reproduction are defined — and these laws have an historical-materialist basis. Thus the state is not to be defined by its functions, though these do enter the analysis at a later point.

This abstract departure is pure Marxist method and the discussion of the capitalist mode of production is right out of *Capital*, Volume 1. The first main point concerns the social relations within capitalism. Workers are free to sell their labour and their subsequent exploitation in production is not based on overt force but on consent. This social relation is necessary for capitalist survival and must be reproduced within the capitalist system. Any conscious organization of social relations which impeded this freedom of the workers would accompany the abolition of the capital relation. The product of labour power is converted into commodities and capital; the labourer produces material wealth but in objects which are alienated from the labourer. The exploitation process is thus effective as a relationship between two 'independent' and 'equal' commodity owners, capital and labour. Hence, political authority and dominance must not be associated with individual enterprise and production. Historically, a central state emerges with a monopoly and centralization of force necessary for the reproduction of capitalist social relations. In this way the state does not institute a general will but separates political and material power from individual and collective interests. And this separation is vital for capitalist reproduction.

Hirsch makes no attempt to detail the history of the emergence of either capitalism or its associated state form, but notes the need for such study in specific countries. Instead he assumes that capital relations are established and that a 'bourgeois society has been constituted'. This approach then shows the objective need of the state by capitalists as outlined; but, he argues, the approach does not define the actual concrete form of the state or its concrete functions. The analysis is too abstract and ony a general glimpse of the social functions of the state can be seen. In this sense the abstract function of the state is simply to create the conditions for the social reproduction process. From the form of the state the possibility and general necessity of functions can be derived. The possibility of functions comes because the state appears as a force separate from bourgeois society; the necessity of state functions, like intervention and reform, results from the need for social conditions so that capitalist reproduction occurs; but those social conditions cannot be provided by capitalists alone. The state's own reproduction as a social form depends on securing its material base which implies a firm interest in maintaining capitalism. The state does not blatantly act as a capitalist-dominated state but its interests are with the maintenance of capitalist production. This is the state's own material base.

The next stage of the analysis concerns capitalist crises, and again, following the classic Marxist model, it is argued that the Marxian profit rate has a tendency to fall. Counter-effects can raise profit rates. For instance, the productivity of labour goes up as new technology plays a part; the value of labour power can be forced down; and the length of effective hours worked raised. But eventually, Hirsch suggests, the profit rate falls and the concurrent crisis redefines the limits of capital accumulation. It becomes necessary to fundamentally reorganize the conditions of production and exploitation; and this reorganization is affected by class conflict, both internally and abroad. There is no mechanical and straightforward outcome. The tendency of the rate of profit to fall does not by itself provide an explanation of subsequent events, as class struggles and strategies enter the stage and affect the course of history. However, three capitalist strategies are noted as important. First, changes in the form of capital emerge; monopolies increase, property relations are changed as joint stock companies grow, and the credit system is extended. Second, capital expands on the world market; and finally, technological progress is accelerated.

In order to make more than abstract comments about the state in this crisis phase, a more thorough analysis of capitalism, class struggle and conflicts is required and this, Hirsch argues, must be the starting point for any investigation of the political. From the abstract it is necessary to move to the concrete, and this analysis will vary across countries and history. Such analysis is not attempted but from the abstract laws of social reproduction several objectively necessary state functions are derived. This final discussion of Hirsch's is interesting but it does not always follow clearly from his preceding work.

First he addresses the growth of the welfare state which is founded on the increasing strength of the working class as well as on the needs of capital to have labour reproduced. These welfare state concessions depend on undisturbed growth and capital accumulation and in a crisis the material basis of welfare benefits is threatened. This can result in open class struggle and violence and threaten the formally legal, peaceful and democratic form of the state.

This threat encourages changes within the state, and intervention and regulatory functions become more closely identified with monopoly and its interests in world markets. Revenue which is centralized is redistributed to individual groups of capital or capital in general. Incomes policy is established to control wages and attempts are made at imposing counter-cyclical economic policies. But contradictions emerge as revenue redistribution to favoured capital groups and to welfare recipients to maintain working-class peace generates opposition. The capitalist class generally opposes welfare expansion in times of crisis and those capitalists not gaining from redistribution will be in conflict with the groups of capitalists who are gaining. Limits to the possibility of state functions are exposed, and these are determined by the state form and the state's attempts to aid capitalist reproduction.

At the same time some capitalists will be going out of business and the state is forced to nationalize or simply fund areas of production in order to safeguard the whole reproduction process. State 'growth policy' becomes primarily 'infrastructural policy', but material barriers are being met by the state. The whole question of the state's capacity to manage the economy and social reproduction is raised. In this climate, Hirsch expects the state to exhibit more overt force and repression but the concrete outcomes cannot be envisaged without more investigation at the specific real-world level.

This abstract theory is clearly more satisfactory than any so far discussed. The complexities of society are more evident and the previous tendency to use assumptions as theoretical conclusions is, thankfully, avoided. However, various problems can be pointed out. As Hirsch himself notes, the abstract analysis must now move down onto the concrete plane of nitty-gritty real world history and happenings if the theory is to be useful for understanding any specific capitalist society. It is also necessary to do this to get any specific feel for the actual limitations of state intervention and reform. In this abstract analysis, limitations are imposed by the social reproduction process, but while this tells us something, it does not impart a great deal. Nor has this level of abstraction had much to say about working-class latency in open class struggle. As structural limitations to state action become acute, the state's legitimation functions supposedly falter and workers become more actively opposed to the system. But recent international experience in the 1980s crisis shows surprising tolerance from the working class. Real wage cuts are accepted; social wage cuts are accepted; and rising and high unemployment is accepted. A more concrete analysis must deal with these issues.

There is also the matter of Marxist crisis theory and the falling profit rate. If the Marxian profit rate has been recently falling, which is likely, has it really been the rising organic composition of capital that caused it? It may well be that the exploitation rate has been falling in the face of strong working-class demands. And if this is one cause of the current crisis, state action will presumably be concerned with more than the type of capital restructuring which Hirsch discusses.

Jessop's (1977) point is also worth reiterating. The capital theoretical basis of this analysis emphasizes the class struggle between labour and capital at the expense of other conflicts, and some class theoretical analysis à la Gramsci might also be introduced. This could better accommodate such influences as religious ideology, racial unrest, sexual divisions, and popular regional pressures for more local autonomy. These issues cannot be dealt with in this current framework.

Further historical study is also required. The derivation of a necessary state form for capital reproduction is one thing, but examining whether and how this form emerged historically is another. In Britain, for instance, the centralized state and politically centralized force predated capitalism, and the state's older aristocratic base lingered throughout capitalist development. The historical shifts in both capitalist and state form, and the relationship between them, require more study before confident conclusions can be derived about current changes in forms and functions.

Nevertheless, Hirsch's study is very interesting and its attempts to handle class conflicts in our society is important. Most economic analysis outside Marxism tends to ignore class conflicts altogether, despite its obvious effects on both the private economy and the state. If the state is not the public-interested and enlightened actor so often assumed in basic economic policy models, and if individuals are not the appropriate unit for analyzing state economic behaviour, then Marxist analysis may clearly have insights to offer.

A Comment on these Marxist Approaches

The particular Marxist analyses of the state that I have discussed in this chapter were chosen because of their influence in Marxist economic theory. What these analyses have in common is their view of the distribution of power in capitalist society. Power is usually taken to be highly uneven and rigid in its distribution and this is particularly true in Leninist inspired theories. Power rests with capitalists and little or any power is left to the wage earners. Within this approach, the ongoing Marxist discussion is also frequently very structuralist. This means that the emphasis is on relationships between rather rigid and static groups of unvarying strength, though in Hirsch's work, and in Gough's, there is some room for the varying strength of classes and groups to exert some sway.

One way in which these anlyses might usefully be extended is to place more emphasis on the nature of the struggle between groups and classes that lies behind the analyses. When the working class is relatively stronger than it is at other moments, do the form and functions of the state alter? Similarly, when the dominant class is relatively stronger at times does this influence the state? What role, if any, does the changing strength of class power have, and within this role what are the limitations on state actions?

These sorts of questions are virtually ruled out of court by those Marxist analyses of the state that are strictly structural. Power rests with capital almost absolutely and there is no room for its diminution except through the tendency of profits to fall and possibly realization crises which weaken capitalism. Power, in these models, is not particularly challenged by class struggle except in so far as it causes profits to fall; and the way that the state is fitted in to these structural analyses is rather limited. Since capitalist power is virtually absolute in these analyses the state must reflect it and the state must always act in capital's interest.

It seems to me on the basis of the discussion in Chapter 3 earlier that a less structurally rigid and more fluid analysis of power might be a more useful way to proceed. Analysis on these less rigid lines suggests in

Chapters 3 and 4 that differences in class power in different capitalist countries have had considerable influence on recent state economic behaviour. More importantly this influence of class struggle on state behaviour has not been principally mediated via falling profit rates. The influence on state behaviour has been more directly through the exercise of political power which reflects changes in the material and economic power of certain groups. Barrington Moore's (1967) historical study of the introduction of democracy in several countries also follows this more fluid analytical approach, as does Abraham's (1982) study of Weimar Germany.

Here I simply wish to make the point that the rigid structures of power in the Marxist economic theories of the state discussed in this chapter do not seem capable of increasing our understanding of state economic behaviour. Their explanation of why states in different capitalist countries pursue different economic policies would basically be that capital in each country has different interests and is in different specific situations. They do not really grapple with why these situations are different or why state economic responses are different in sometimes rather similar-looking circumstances. Thus we are left to conclude, I think rather unsatisfactorily, that the economic size of the state in Sweden, say, is greater than in the USA because this is what suits capitalists in each country. Similarly Britain has a National Health Service and a relatively large public housing sector because this somehow suits capital's interests; and these public activities are now being constrained in Britain because capital's interests have altered. There is, I think, more to state economic behaviour than this, and to understand the economic behaviour of the state we must abandon analyses that do not allow the power resources of groups in society, especially capital and labour, to change. Capital may always be the dominant group but its relative power position in relation to the working class has, nevertheless, shifted over time, as the evidence in Chapter 3 suggested. This matters for economic policy analysis, and we will not be able to understand what is happening if we fail to recognize the implications of changes in working-class strength. But before proceeding to face this issue further it is worth exploring the mainstream economic analyses of state economic behaviour. It is to these that we now turn.

7 Mainstream Economic Theories of the State: The Economic Behaviour of Voters, Politicians and Bureaucrats.

Policy ought to conform to Liberty, Law and Compassion,
but as a rule It obeys Selfishness, Vanity, Funk.

Auden, 'Shorts'

Mainstream economists of non-Marxist persuasions have also attempted to provide an economic theory of the state. They do not work with the rigid class divisions so apparent in the last chapter. Instead they choose the individual as their underlying behavioural agent, and they assume that all individuals, whether in the public or private sector, are motivated by self-interest. The state is usually narrowly conceived to be the government, which includes the elected governing party and the bureaucracy which serves it. These theories concentrate specifically on three not unconnected areas of individual behaviour; these are the behaviour of the voter, the politician and the bureaucrat in public service. Because self-interest is assumed to motivate behaviour these approaches at least avoid the behavioural inconsistency implied in the basic policy model treatment of the state. All people in these theories, whether they are in firms, households or the public sector, are motivated by simple egotistical self-interest. Rational economic man is assumed across all sectors of the economy.

In this chapter I will discuss this approach and finally comment on its apparent strengths and weaknesses as a theory of the state. It is natural to begin with the behaviour of voters and then to proceed to that of politicians and bureaucrats. Some of the policy recommendations and suggested reforms that have been derived from this form of analysis are anti-democratic, and under the guise of individual liberty actually become authoritarian. This interesting, and in my view most worrying, development is also discussed. Bringing the theories about the behaviour of voters, politicians and bureaucrats together yields a cohesive theory about what government actually does, and it is this economic theory of government that I mainly wish to evaluate here.

The Behaviour of Voters

The analysis of voting behaviour begins with Downs's (1957) remarkable book. Written at a time when few economists had recognized the need for a theory of government, this economic study of democracy was truly seminal. Here I will simply concentrate on the economic theory behind voting, since it is the behaviour of voters that is subsequently thought to influence the behaviour of self-interested politicians. The properties of various different voting rules in different situations has been explored in the public choice literature, but because much of this is not strictly relevant it will be left out. (See Mueller, 1979, Chs.3, 4.) According to Downs, the individual voter in a representative democracy acts rationally to maximize his or her individual utility. The value to him or her of the alternative policy packages expected to be pursued by different parties, if elected to government, is initially assessed. On the basis of this assessment the vote is then cast for that party which is going to yield the most net benefit to that individual voter. If the voter assesses the net benefit of all available party choices to be the same then he or she is indifferent between the choices on offer and there is no reason to vote. In this case our rational voter will abstain.

This is all straightforward enough, but when examined more closely it turns out that the individual decision to vote is actually irrational. There is a cost in voting because it takes time and thus if you are going to vote at all you must consider that the value of your vote will outweigh the cost to you of bothering to vote in the first place. Now, the possibility that your particular vote will influence the outcome of the election is infinitesimally small and as a result the expected value of your vote must be very small. It is not rationally in your interests to vote at all. If you do not vote you avoid the cost of voting. If you do vote, whatever the gain of having one party elected over another, this expected gain must be minute since your vote is most unlikely to influence and decide the elected outcome. The simple fact of the matter is that voting is irrational in the economic sense.

Nevertheless, we do observe that many people vote; in national elections this number usually ranges between 75 per cent or over in Sweden and the UK to around 55 per cent in the USA. Why is it that all these people go to vote when they will all admit that their individual vote is unlikely to be decisive? In attempts to answer this question analysts have had to turn to non-economic factors. Our vote upholds democratic values which we wish to see continue; or we identify with a particular class or party and this consciousness causes us to go and support our class or party in the election; or voting is seen to be a duty in some sense. There may be something in these types of sociological explanations, but they are not particularly satisfactory to a mainstream economist. But then economics cannot explain everything.

This paradox of why individual voters bother to vote at all has received considerable attention, and as Mueller (1979, Chapter 6) points out, the economic rationale behind voting is not entirely without interest. It appears that when the race between parties is perceived to be close the voting turnout rises. Even though the probability of an individual vote being decisive is still low this probability clearly rises in a close race and this apparently does affect the turnout. It is also clear that the cost of voting, in terms of time, money and information-gathering, is of some importance to voting behaviour. Tollinson, Crain and Paulter (1975) have argued that the increasing availability of free information about parties increases turnout and Ashenfelter and Kelley (1975) have shown that the poll tax on voting in the Southern USA has a strong negative effect on turnout. Nevertheless it does still remain the case that since an individual vote is always very unlikely to be the decisive vote the only rational reason for voting must be the increase in utility that is gained by upholding democracy or supporting some group with which the voter identifies. Hence quite why rational economic men and women do vote must remain a moot point, but if we simply accept that they do vote we can proceed.

The Economics of Politicians' Behaviour

Once we have accepted that people vote, for some reason, what is next of interest is the economic policies that politicians may follow. Since we are assuming that individuals are rational and motivated by self-interest, we can assume that politicians will also necessarily act to further their own individual self-interest. In particular, in a democracy they will support policies that will lead to their election. To this end they respond to the perceived demands of their electorate and it is simply these perceptions that determine their policies, including their economic policy actions.

In this theory, the general political flavour of any government is determined by the distribution of political opinion in the electorate. Thus if the political opinion of all voters is spatially distributed from left-wing radical to right-wing conservative, as in the diagram below, we can examine how a particular political party responds.

In the Hotelling (1929) model, later developed by Downs (1957),

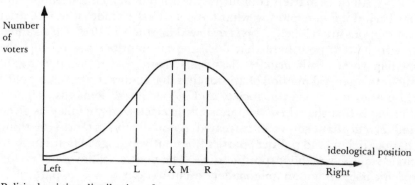

Political opinion distribution of voters

0

each voter is assumed to have a preferred ideological position. The further an electable politician stands from this voter's position the less desirable that politician is to the voter. Preferences are thus single-peaked. If there are two candidates L and R, and if every voter votes, the political candidate at L in the diagram above receives all the votes that lie to the left of X, the midpoint of the segment LR. On the other hand, candidate R receives all the votes to the right of X. In our specific diagram it is clear that R has more votes and would win.

However, our candidate of the left, L, can improve his or her voting position by moving to the right. But our candidate of the right, R, can also improve his or her position by moving to the left. Both candidates are driven towards the centre and ultimately to the position favoured by the median voter M. In this model the ideological flavour of policies that are offered is determined by the median voter. The political candidate who offers this centrist policy package wins and both candidates would be driven towards this policy position. The economic policies that would result would be rather centrist and neither radical nor conservative.

Now, there is a great deal that is unrealistic about this model. Depicting issues in spatial terms such as this has been attacked by Stokes (1963). Some political issues, like abortion legalization or bank nationalization, cannot be depicted spatially. You are really either for it or against it and you cannot make a gradual move from one position to the other. Furthermore, there is not just a single issue that provides the ideological dimension; some candidates and voters may be left-wing on one issue and right-wing on another. Thus many deeply religious people may be conservative on social issues but radical on economic issues. Also, preferences about ideology may not be unimodel or symmetric, not all individuals may vote, and there may be more than two candidates.

107

All these matters complicate the analysis and considerable work has been done in exploring what happens to the model when its strict assumptions are relaxed. This is reviewed in Mueller (1979, Ch.6) and it is sufficient to note here that once the assumptions are relaxed the median voter result usually disappears. Nevertheless, what is useful about this general method of approach is that it does suggest that political parties do respond to society and its perceived demands. What is limiting is first that these demands of the electorate are taken as given and second that each voter is treated as equally important. One thing that politicians and political parties frequently indulge in is attempts to change our views about specific issues. The position that voters take on specific issues is not an independent event but one that is in part influenced by political leaders. This means that the methodology behind this analysis is somewhat questionable.

Furthermore in attempting to win elections it is obvious that some potential voters are more important to a particular political party than others. We might observe policies being directed to favour certain key groups who are perceived as being particularly important to the electoral outcome. The importance of any particular group of voters depends on their power to influence the election result, and this power is not equally distributed among individuals.

Other issues in these analyses of policy decisions are explored more fully in the public choice literature (Mueller, 1979; van den Doel, 1974), and I will not repeat these excellent literature surveys here. The main point that I am trying to make is that these economic-political models are built on assumptions that restrict their relevance. It is I think perfectly correct that politicians seek to win elections and it may also be roughly true that people are motivated by self-interest. What is not correct however is to assume that society is one where individual preferences are fixed and immutable or one where their preferences are of equal importance amongst potential voters. Both these assumptions make this approach of dubious merit in attempting to explain the general stance of economic policy.

This point perhaps becomes more telling when we examine theories that purport to explain specific economic policies. It has been suggested by Tufte (1978), Nordhaus (1975), MacRae (1977), Frey (1978) and other writers, that if politicians are seeking to win elections this will cause a politico-economic cycle in economic activity. This cycle is directly caused, they argue, by shifts in macroeconomic policy which basically stimulate the economy just before elections and dampen economic activity immediately after the election. In order to gain votes, unemployment is cut and growth is stimulated; this also fuels inflation, although this effect is not apparent until after the election when inflation

108

can be tackled by cutting aggregate demand. Through this self-interested behaviour politicians actually cause an economic cycle that goes up before elections and down shortly afterwards. We observe an electoral economic cycle.

Again it is the assumptions behind this model that are particularly worrying and these are worth spelling out in some detail. Most of these studies begin by positing the existence of fixed economic preferences of voters over macroeconomic objectives such as unemployment, growth, inflation and the balance of payments position. In the diagram the iso-vote curves drawn are supposed to be a preference mapping over unemployment and inflation.

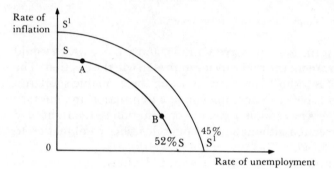

Iso-vote curves

Voters prefer both less inflation and less unemployment and at the combinations of unemployment and inflation shown on curve S, say, 52 per cent of the electorate would support the economic policy that would yield this combination. At point A on S the unemployment rate is low and inflation is relatively high compared to point B on S. However, voters in our diagram are indifferent between A and B. On curve S^1 inflation and unemployment is everywhere higher than on curve S and this combination is less preferred. For argument's sake we can say that on S^1 only 45 per cent of voters would support the economic policies that yield the inflation — unemployment trade-offs depicted on S^1.

Now faced with this situation the government clearly needs to produce policies that will shift the economy onto a desirable iso-vote curve so that it will be re-elected. The government is assumed to face economic constraints that can be depicted by a series of short-run Phillips curves and an accompanying long-run Phillips curve. In the short term the government is assumed able to get onto a short-run Phillips curve that can win it the election but, because of economic constraints, this position is not stable and it will be abandoned after the election. This little drama is shown in the next diagram.

109

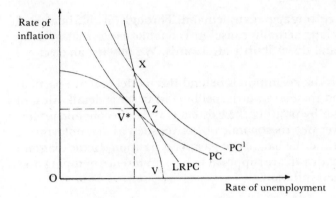

Short and Long Run Philips Curves and an Iso-Vote Curve

Let us assume that the iso-vote curve V drawn above is one which would just give the government the majority it requires to win the election. The Phillips curve PC is a short-run curve showing the available short-run economic trade-offs between unemployment and inflation and it is tangential to V at V*. Any economic policy combination to the right of V will not win the election although any economic policy combination to the left of V will do so.

The government begins its election bid after several years in office and we might assume to begin with that the economy is on the stable long-run Phillips curve at some point, say Z. Since Z is to the right of V this position is not an election winner and the government must engineer some changes to get it to V*, say, where it would be elected. To do so it would increase aggregate demand. Unemployment would fall and in the short-run there would be no change in the inflation rate. The economy would move to V*, and the election would be held and won.

However, V* is off the long-run Phillips curve and is not stable. If the same level of unemployment is maintained, inflation must increase (see Friedman, 1977) and the economy would drift to X. Alternatively, if the inflation level at V* is maintained in the long term, unemployment must rise and the economy would drift back to Z. The point is that V* is a position that cannot be maintained for very long and eventually the economy will move onto the long-run trade-off curve, LRPC. With each election a similar sort of scenario occurs and the upshot is an observable electoral cycle in unemployment and inflation. Unemployment falls immediately before an election and rises after it as demand is cut to bring down the inflation rise that follows the election.

Some economists would take issue with this argument because it is based on Friedman's (1977) theory about unemployment and inflation trade-offs in the short and long run and criticisms of Friedman's

110

underlying labour market behaviour do seem to me to be in order. However, in this context what are perhaps more pertinent are the assumptions about the preferences of the electorate. Not only are they assumed to be fixed, they are also assumed to be myopic. The fact that politicians blatantly engineer cycles to win elections is assumed to be of no concern to the electorate who by the time the next election comes around are supposed to have forgotten the consequences of the last orchestrated pre-election boom. Such assumed behaviour is hardly rational but it is fundamental to this theory.

The electorate is also assumed only to have preferences about economic objectives, and though these are undoubtedly of concern it is not the case that they are always the prime issue with voters. Gallup Poll responses from 1950 to 1975 in the USA and the UK to the question 'What is the most important problem facing the country today?' show a mixed weighting for economic issues. In the USA, the economy dominated other issues only after 1972, and from 1950 to 1972 the major concerns of US voters were domestic, political and social matters, with foreign policy issues rating secondary importance after 1964. In the UK, economic issues have only been clearly dominant since 1965 and before that they shared their primary position with foreign policy matters. The obvious fact is that voting preferences are not only expressed about economic matters.

There have been several attempts to examine the empirical evidence behind these theories of political business cycles, and Frey and Schneider (1978a, b, c) and Tufte (1978) all claim empirical support. However, Nordhaus (1975) found little evidence of such electoral cycles, and quite detailed work by Alt and Chrystal (1980) also comes down on the negative side. At present, the empirical evidence must be classified as inconclusive, but given the restrictive assumptions about electoral preferences it will not be surprising to find that these theories eventually fall from favour.

Furthermore, in common with the basic policy models of Chapter 2, these theories assume that politicians can do what they want within the bounds of the economic structural constraints they face. The anecdotal evidence of some political leaders, such as is evident in Crossman's diaries, casts some doubt on this omnipotence. Politicians and their policies are affected by a bureaucracy which is not without its own influence and which need not necessarily always support the desires of the elected representatives.

The Economic Behaviour of Bureaucrats

While politicians are pursuing their self-interest it is similarly assumed

111

that bureaucrats in the public service are pursuing their particular self-interest. The bureaucrats maximize their own utility which is defined over a varying set of arguments. Niskanen (1971) assumes that all the dimensions of bureaucratic utility are a monotonic function of the total budget of the bureau. Thus a bureaucrat's utility goes up with salary, perquisites of office, public reputation, power, patronage, output of the bureau, ease of making changes and ease of managing the bureau. All of these items, except possibly the last two, increase with the size of the bureau's total budget, so we can simply assume that bureaucrats in their attempts to mazimize utility will attempt to maximize their total bureau budget.

In doing so however the bureaucrats face a budget constraint. This constraint is generally assumed to be the expenditure that politicians are willing to allocate in order to provide varying levels of output. The politicians set the budget constraint for the bureaucrat and the budget allocation they decide upon is determined by the policitians' self-interest. This particular political decision, as discussed in the last section, depends on the perceived preferences of the electorate and the perceived intensity of these preferences. To stay in power the politician may satisfy the median voters' preference or indulge in logrolling behaviour (Mueller, 1979, Ch.3). For simplicity we can simply assume that politicians will wish to allocate expenditures so that the marginal cost of the output produced is equal to the marginal benefit that this output provides the politician. In the figure below,

B is the size of the budget,

Q is the output of the bureau,

TC is the total cost of production,

V is the marginal value of the goods produced, to the politicians,

and MC is the marginal costs.

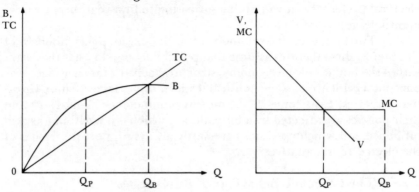

The Bureaucratic and Political Optimum

The political optimum for production, Q_p, is where the marginal cost and political marginal value of production are equal. However bureaucrats who are attempting to maximize the size of their budget, subject to covering production costs, will prefer to produce Q_B. At this point Q_B, total costs are equal to the size of the bureau's total budget, and Q_B is in excess of Q_p. This diagram simply assumes that total production costs increase linearly with output and that the budget output curve is parabolic as shown. This curve B can be interpreted as the maximum that politicians are prepared to spend, if necessary, to get a given output. The analysis is very simple but it suggests that if bureaucrats are self-seeking, as in Niskanen (1971), then the total public output they desire will be in excess of the political optimum desired by the politicians.

This immediately raises the problem of the actual outcome of such behaviour. If politicians are acting in their own self-interest, and want Q_p, and if bureaucrats are acting in their own self-interest, and want Q_B, what actually happens? Niskanen (1971) argues that the outcome will favour the bureaucrats and that Q_B of output will be produced. Politicians are not aware of costs; all they know is what it costs to produce the prevailing level of output and this information is provided by the bureaucrats. For this reason bureaucrats can generally use their monopoly power to gain the position they favour. Furthermore the fact that public bureaucrats and public sector workers can vote, and that they comprise a not insignificant part of the electorate, is also seen by Bush and Denzau (1977) as further reason to believe that bureaucrats are likely to get their own way. In the face of considerable bureaucratic power the politicians are expected to be accommodating.

On the other hand a great deal of the literature in public administration takes the line that politicians are sufficiently powerful to get their own way. If this were the case Q_p would be produced in our simple model. In this body of literature the bureaucrat is not seen either as self-interested or as all-powerful. Instead the bureaucrat is viewed as a responsible and reliable professional who fulfils his or her duty as determined by the elected government. Decisions are made by politicians and bureaucrats simply implement or administer them, as in Woodrow Wilson (1887) and Weber (1922).

This benign view of public bureaucratic behaviour is probably not entirely warranted as no elected politician running a large government department can hope to oversee every facet of its activities. Bureaucrats will generally have some room for manoeuvre, and the outcome in our simple model of public output production simply depends on how relatively powerful one assumes the bureaucrats and politicians are.

In other developments of this model, different arguments have been used in the bureaucrat's utility function. Ames (1965) in his study

113

of the Soviet bureaucracy simply assumed that bureaucrats attempted to maximize physical output. Galbraith (1967) assumed that the technical elite in firms would attempt to maximize production increases. Williamson (1964, 1974) assumed an 'expense preference' on the part of managers. They attempt to appoint new staff who will thus enable the bureaucrat to increase his or her own salary, security, status and power. Williamson's hypothesis, like that of Migue and Belanger (1974), directly evokes labour inefficiency and suggests that the labour input per production unit output will be higher than in a similar profit-maximizing concern.

Whether or not these theories of bureaucracy are pertinent can be examined empirically. If bureaucrats are self-interested and sufficiently powerful to implement their aims we would expect to see inefficient public production, possibly characterized by labour-biased production techniques. It is more difficult to test whether or not output levels are above a political optimum since this latter concept is elusive and difficult, if not impossible to define. Despite this problem the available evidence certainly does suggest that bureaucracies are prone to inefficiency.

Bradford, Malt and Oates (1969) attempted to measure the rate of productivity change in education, police, fire and hospital services in US local government. Their findings, also supported by Spann (1977), suggested that productivity changes tended to be either negative or zero. However these results do not necessarily prove inefficiency since in these services an increase in inputs, and costs, may well indicate an increase in the quality of service offered. Perhaps more convincing are those studies that have compared productivity in private and public agencies that produce similar goods and services. Davies (1971) has shown that the private domestic airline in Australia is more efficient than the comparable public airline which operates similar routes. Similarly Ahlbrandt (1973), the Ralph Stone and Company Survey (1973), and Orzechowski (1977) have found lower productivity in public agencies than in private companies supplying fire services, garbage collections and university education respectively. In all these studies the public bureaucracy employed more labour than the private concern.

In some quarters these findings are taken as evidence that public agencies are necessarily less efficient than private companies, but this conclusion may not be always warranted. What the economic models of bureaucracy suggest is that all bureaucracies, whether they are public or private, are likely to be inefficient. The arguments apply to all bureaucrats, not just to public servants. This is why studies of health care provision are also important to note. A recent study at York University (1982) found that public health care provision tended to be more cost-effective than private provision and Spann's (1977) study in

114

the USA also confirms that non-profit hospitals tended to have lower unit costs than for-profit hospitals. In some ways these findings about health care are no surprise since private health provision shares many properties of a bureaucracy and it is usually less controlled in its bureaucratic power than is public health provision. Because of the nature and structure of health service there can be more inefficiency in private provision than in public care. Whether or not this is generally the case depends on the controls that are placed on the particular bureaucracy, and in this case particularly on how much the monopoly position of doctors is constrained.

We might sensibly conclude that any bureaucracy is likely to be inefficient, and from a policy point of view what is important is to consider how to go about making bureaucracies more efficient. Whether bureaucracies should be made private or public is in this sense a separate matter. In both cases if bureaucracies face competition and hence are forced to be more cost-conscious their efficiency is likely to improve. However in cases where competition is not possible or desirable for some reason, some form of regulation is required to provide the necessary constraints for efficiency. And this is as true in private bureaucracies as it is in public bureaucracies.

Exactly how bureaucracies can be made more efficient has been examined by van den Doel (1979). He begins by arguing that bureaucracies are inefficient because of the self-interested aims of their leaders and the possibility of achieving these aims through the monopoly position of the bureaucracy. If these two causes of inefficiency are removed, he suggests that the outcome will be closer to a social optimum. To remove the first cause van den Doel suggests that the hierarchical bureaucratic structure should be replaced by a self-management system run by all civil servants in the bureau. These people elect representatives to run their bureau and decide the bureau's policy. This institutional change is not likely to lead to behaviour that maximizes the bureau's budget or increases its staffing levels unduly because the additional power that would follow does not accrue to lower-ranking civil servants when the bureau expands. Indeed chances of promotion from lower ranks may well decrease with increased staff. Furthermore he suggests that no single government department should have the exclusive right to provide specific public goods. This introduces the threat of competition and removes the monopoly power of the bureau that is one of the causes of its inefficient behaviour.

This concern for achieving better bureaucratic economic outcomes is not shared by all economists, and Breton and Wintrobe (1975) have argued that in the present system of government, politicians already have sufficient power simply to enforce the decision they want or something close to it. This just takes us back to the point that the economic behaviour of public bureaucracies depends on the relative power distribution between politicians and bureaucrats. However whether the outcome is determined by bureaucrats or politicians, or even a negotiated settlement between them, there is no reason to believe that this outcome will necessarily be in the public interest.

We have thus arrived at what has been the main thrust of mainstream economic theories of the state. If politicians and bureaucrats and voters are all motivated by self-interest the economic behaviour of the public sector is not going to be aimed at the public interest. Partly because of the assumed myopia of self-interested voters, the politicians will tend to run economic policies that generate political business cycles. And because of the monopoly position of public bureaucracies the output of bureaus will be excessive and possibly produced inefficiently with a bias towards high labour inputs.

This general view of the actual behaviour of government has led to recommendations for change that are aimed at securing action that is more in line with the public interest. But the particular reforms suggested depend on the particular definition of public interest that is adopted. In the work of van den Doel (1979), reform is concerned with decreasing the monopoly power of bureaus and thus making them more efficient. This general concern about bureaucracies is not new and can be found in the earlier writings of Bentham and J.S. Mill.

Writers in this tradition overtly or implicitly assume that democracy is to be valued and not altered in any fundamental way. For all its faults, and inefficient bureaucracies may be one, it is the best system going. Care should be taken to root out corruption and to see that bureaucracies do not run without due control, but basically the system is acceptable. This too was Downs's view on the position. In a democracy, he argued, the outcome of government action would favour the better informed higher-income groups as well as producer interests, because their influence on decisions would be relatively more powerful. However, despite this inequality Downs accepted the current system because he apparently could not envisage any practical changes that would improve matters. Any democracy that operated alongside the current economic system was bound to be somewhat unequal in its government actions, but democracy was valued highly and ought not be changed in any basic way. This high valuation given to democratic ideals, often implicitly, is not present in more recent recommendations of reform that flow from this economic theory of government. This work has led to suggestions for fundamental constitutional changes and argues that the public interest is served when individual liberty is not violated. This alters the definition of the public interest because what becomes the dominant concern is the need to avoid encroaching on individual liberties.

The Constitutional Contract

The most dramatic suggestions for reform of this type have emanated from economists at the Center for the Study of Public Choice in Blacksburg, Virginia. Their general concern is how the public sector can be instituted so that it serves the public interest as they define it. They perceive a public domain that is inhabited by self-interested politicians and bureaucrats whose behaviour leads to outcomes that are well removed from any public-interest criteria. For Buchanan (1975) the public interest is served when individual liberty and freedom are enforced. All individuals should be treated equally in this enforcement and the state must not violate individual rights.

This stress on individual rights, as in Nozick (1974), tends to place democratic values in a secondary position. As Niskanen (1975, p.531) explains, 'Democracy is an instrument, not an ideal...A government that serves only the interests of the majority is neither achievable, desirable, nor stable.' In the view of these writers what is most desirable, and in the public interest, is individual liberty. Any individual should have a right not to do as the majority may wish. Thus if you are ordered by the state to pay taxes against your will this is a violation of rights and is to be avoided.

Given this notion of public interest as individual liberty they proceed to examine what can be done to achieve it. Buchanan and Wagner (1977) analyze a democratic state's economic activity and proceed to suggestions for reform. These mooted reforms depend on both their conception of the public interest and the assumption that individuals are motivated by self-interest.

Now because both politicians and bureaucrats are motivated by self-interest they suggest that the fiscal conservatism of balanced national budgets has been replaced by Keynesian policies. In a democracy with self-interested rulers and bureaucrats Keynesian fiscal policies in effect become budget deficits. There are two reasons for this. First bureaucrats, as we have discussed, prefer large bureau budgets. Second, politicians seeking election compete for patronage and this involves offering economic policies and programmes that enhance their goals. This encourages politicians to spend money to woo certain groups to their support base.

If there was a law that forced budgets to be balanced so that taxes completely covered public expenditures, the politicians and bureaucrats would be constrained in their behaviour. Voters would directly perceive the cost of the public goods and services they get and would weigh up the costs and benefits when deciding on their economic policy preferences. However once the possibility of funding public goods and services by either borrowing or printing money is used, the direct link between costs and benefits is broken. Voters in this sort of world tend to underestimate the costs of public good provision since they no longer directly perceive the link between costs and benefits. They do perceive the direct taxes they pay, but the immediate cost of public borrowing, increases in the money supply and increases in indirect taxes, are not well perceived by voters. They underestimate the price of public goods and hence demand more of them. This of course suits self-interested bureaucrats and politicians very well since they can now offer more public goods. The politicians can more effectively compete for patronage and the bureaucrats can increase the budget.

This behaviour then leads to budget deficits which continue to exist. Keynesian policy that envisaged fluctuations in the budget position, between deficits in slumps and surpluses in booms, is replaced by a world of continuing deficits. Keynes, they argue, was an elitist who believed in the economic policy model (as described in Chapter 5). Bureaucrats and politicians simply did as wise economists, like Keynes, told them. However, if self-interest prevails this is a delusion, and the outcome is a run of continuing budget deficits. These deficits they argue, despite contrary evidence (discussed in Chapter 4), cause inflation. They also cause slow growth and are seen principally as the cause of current economic problems.

To get out of this perceived nightmare, what is required is a constitutional contract. This contract will lay down laws that constrain politicians and bureaucrats; in particular it will say 'thou shalt balance the government budget'. It would also concomitantly limit money supply growth, public borrowing and indirect taxation. In this way, and only in this way, they argue, will the public interest be served.

Furthermore the constitutional contract may be decided by individual consensus. No individuals' rights may be violated by the constitution. This is an extremely heavy condition, of course, since any individual has the power of absolute veto. The richest voter, with little demand for public goods, could veto provision even though all other voters may demand provision. This problem is recognized, and to get some flexibility in practise it is more usually suggested that the laws embodied in the contract should simply be carried by two-thirds of the voters. This gives the contract a large populist backing though it violates the wishes of those individuals that do not support it.

Should this type of reform ever be instituted, its effect they suggest would be to decrease the expenditure on public goods and services.

This might well be true, though it depends on the extent to which voters are self-interested. If over two-thirds of voters are altruistic they may well prefer to pay for public goods even when the benefits do not accrue directly to them. People without children are frequently happy to pay for schools and people who are not unemployed or handicapped are usually happy to support those voters who are. Furthermore, why we should have a contract that is supported by two-thirds of the voters is not clear. If one-third of the electorate is against the constitution there are a lot of individual rights being violated, and if rights are so sacrosanct by what moral or ethical judgement do we decide whose rights to ignore?

These philosophical issues are outside both the scope of this book and my expertise. I personally would not value individual rights above democratic values, but the main point here is not what the state ought to do or how it should be doing it. The issue is whether these mainstream theories of state economic behaviour explain what is happening and whether the theories appear to be logically coherent.

An Assessment

In this chapter we examined how the state would behave if politicians, bureaucrats and voters were self-interested. The evidence that politicians' behaviour produces electoral cycles in economic activity was inconclusive, though there is some evidence that bureaucracies tend to be inefficient and perhaps therefore serving only the interests of their bureaucrats. The increased relative size of the public sector in the economy may in part be due to this behaviour, but it is not altogether clear that a large public sector is necessarily in the interests of politicians. If voters do not wish to have a public sector that is so large, they can, at least to an extent in these models, force through policies that decrease its size. Fiscal illusion, where the costs of public goods are unperceived, is myopic behaviour and not rational for a self-interested voter; and in any case the size of the effect of fiscal illusion, if it exists, may not be large.

An interesting study by Borcheding (1977) into the sources of US public expenditure growth shows that population growth, the demand for public goods and services, the relatively low productivity of the public sector, and urbanization increases account for only 50 per cent of the increase in US public expenditures. Since politicians in the models of this chapter respond to voters' demands and since relatively low public sector productivity suits the self-interested bureaucrat, these effects on public expenditure growth are at least partly included in Borcheding's measured sources of growth. But we are still left with 50 per cent of public sector growth in the US unexplained. This unexplained public sector growth may partly be due to fiscal illusion but it would seem nonsensical to claim that this is the sole source of explanation for this large unexplained component. Perhaps more damaging for these theories are the cross-country differences in public spending behaviour. If voters in all democratic countries suffer from fiscal illusion and face self-interested politicians and bureaucrats, what is the cause of such wide variation in government spending and indeed public deficit behaviour? This issue is not addressed. And I have argued that it cannot be explained without recourse to changes in the power distribution in society and the differences in this power distribution between countries.

We have also noted that these mainstream economic models cannot explain why a rational person votes, and their explanation of other types of political action are also limited. Since the expression of preferences through voting is a fundamental basis in these approaches, the fact that voting behaviour cannot be explained in a rational economic model is rather damaging. Also the preferences of voters in these models are meant to cover preferences about each macroeconomic objective and the provision of each public good and service. Since in a representative democracy we usually only get to vote for a politician, there is no way that all this assumed information can be transmitted. And in any case in practice the revelation of preferences via voting is fraught with difficulties, as discussed in Arrow (1951) and Mueller (1979).

Thus I am inclined to conclude that application of these theories has yielded some insights but that this application does have severe limits. Fiscal illusion and the monopoly position of bureaucrats are the only reasons cited for the difference in power between the citizenry and the state. While these factors are probably not insignificant, it is I think far-fetched to say that they are the major factors in determining where economic power lies in society. And they are surely not sufficient to explain the increase in government expenditures this century or the cross-country variation in this item.

In these models a self-interested voter would not bother to vote. If irrationally he or she does vote, politicians compete for this vote by offering policies that are perceived to be demanded. Fiscal illusion suggests that more public goods will be demanded than is socially optimal but this too is irrational in a long-term sense. If voters are self-interested, a lapse of myopic behaviour will not last forever. Political business cycles that are stage-managed by self-interested politicians to win elections also depend on voter myopia, and this too is irrational if voters are self-interested. Meanwhile bureaucrats are posited as having so much monopoly power that they can override both the wishes of politicians and the preferences of voters. But if everyone is self-interested, any politician who competes for votes could win on a policy platform that undertook to constrain this bureaucratic behaviour. Hence in a world where everyone is self-interested and rational it is difficult to argue that these models are always logical. They involve odd mixtures of rational and irrational behaviour and they are limited in only looking at a very narrow power distribution.

The mainstream economic theories of the state, along with the Marxist theories discussed in Chapter 6, do not pay heed to the import-ance of interest groups and their changing power resources over time and across countries. The Marxists assume power is rigidly set and unvarying so that the workers are completely dominated and any increase in their power position vis à vis capitalists is almost irrelevant. In the mainstream theories of government the use of individual agents and an assumed pluralism ignore the power of all social groups except that of bureaucrats and elected politicians. The different power posi-tion of elected politicians and bureaucrats probably does have some effect on actual government actions, but to ignore the power distribu-tion in the society outside the state appears to be a massive oversight. This is apparent if we consider the role of the state in maintaining civil order and it is to this that we turn.

8 Economic Order and the State

> If we, dear, know we know no more
> Than they about the law,
> If I no more than you
> Know what we should and should not do
> Except that all agree
> Gladly or miserably
> That the law is . . .
>
> Auden, 'Law Like Love'

The general idea that the state is concerned with maintaining order has not been absent from the economics literature. In this chapter I begin by discussing the approaches to economic order that have been followed. I then go on to assess these and point out that they generally ignore the presence of established interest groups, both fragmented and encompassing, which do exist in modern democracies.

The Rationale of State Formation

In addressing social order economists have mainly been concerned with explaining why this order prevails. Their approach, at least outside Marxist economics, does not begin with the assumption that power is unevenly distributed between different groups; instead these mainstream analyses concentrate on individuals and ask why individuals consented to the establishment of a state or a form of government. Why is it that we do not simply have a society of crude anarchy?

The starting point in economic analysis really goes back to the old Hobbesian problem: how is social order possible? Why does order exist at all and how is it maintained? In answer to these questions, Hobbes (1651) concluded that centralized coercion, and hence some sort of law-and-order state, was a necessary but not sufficient condition for social peace. People are also motivated by moral codes to maintain

122

social order, but as far as Hobbes was concerned, if the society was composed of a large number of people, moral constraints were not enough to maintain order. Thus, for Hobbes, if social order was to be maintained, some centralized and coercive force was required and this implied a strong state presence.

Many other scholars have pondered this Hobbesian problem, but the work of Parsons (1937) is of particular interest. Parsons found the idea of a coercive state repugnant and instead he took the line, in some ways similar to the anarchists, that social order would not disintegrate if the coercive state withered away. Social order, as far as Parsons is concerned, is maintained by internalized value restraints that are based on common values. People are socialized, especially in childhood, and this forms their basic attitudes, which along with society's institutions contribute sufficiently for social stability. There is thus no functional need for a coercive state though the state can of course play a role in the socialization process. Obviously, if even this socializing role for the state is not necessary for social order, then the anarchists, like William Godwin, are correct and we do not need a state for social order. On the other hand, one could argue, and this is more accepted than the anarchist position, that the state and its institutions are vital in the socialization process that establishes order.

These basic positions about the existence of the state have now been examined by economists, and the rigour and simplicity of economic argument tend to make the opposing position of Hobbes and Parsons quite clear and indicate the different assumptions they have used, even though these assumptions are often only implicit, especially in Parsons. The economic analysis begins from an imagined state of anarchy and each individual is assumed to be motivated by self-interest. People try to maximize their own utility which is simply defined to depend on the material possessions they individually own.

In this crude anarchy it is assumed that people can negotiate rules of behaviour and they can choose freely whether or not to abide by them. More formally, individuals have choice of exit and non-commitment. The idea is easily explained in the simple case of two individuals, X and Y, who grow wheat and graze sheep, and who can negotiate a rule that simply says 'thou shalt not steal'. A set of hypothetical choices facing persons X and Y is set out in the matrix below.

In cell 1 of this matrix both X and Y choose to abide by their negotiated rule. In cell 2, Y is law-abiding but X is not; and in cell 3 neither X nor Y obey the rule. In cell 4, X obeys the rule but Y does not. The cells of this matrix represents a case of the familiar Prisoner's Dilemma game. Both X and Y are better off if they both do not steal but each is even more well-off if only they steal and the other individual does not (as in cells 2 and 4).

X\Y	Do Not Steal	Steal
Do Not Steal	1. X (14 sheep, 8 wheat) Y (7 sheep, 5 wheat)	4. X (5 sheep, 4 wheat) Y (9 sheep, 8 wheat)
Steal	2. X (16 sheep, 9 wheat) Y (4 sheep, 2 wheat)	3. X (6 sheep, 4 wheat) Y (6 sheep, 4 wheat)

In this example when X and Y do not steal they devote all their time to the production of their wheat and sheep. Thieving is a time-consuming business, and as cell 1 demonstrates when compared to cell 3, there is more produced when stealing does not occur. When one person devotes all their time to production and only one person thieves, the total output produced is more than when both thieve. This is clear in the example if the total production in cells 2 and 4 are compared with production in cell 3. However in cells 2 and 4 the individual who steals from the producing law-abider is better off.

What this set-up implies is that there is good cause for these individuals to negotiate the no-stealing rule so that their utility can increase by moving to either cells 1, 2 or 4 from cell 3. It does not imply that the rule will be obeyed, since cells 2 and 4 are possible options once the no-stealing rule is negotiated. A movement from cell 3 to cell 1 is Pareto-optimal since it makes both X and Y better-off, as Bush (1972), Bush and Mayer (1974) and Buchanan (1975) have also pointed out. But the departure from cell 3 may not necessarily be to cell 1, as it is in the interest of Y to move to cell 4 and it is in the interest of X to move to cell 2. These two latter moves would follow the establishment of a nego-tiated rule which is then broken, but by only one of the individuals. Thus we can argue that negotiation which establishes property rights, over sheep and wheat in this case, and individual behaviour constraints, in this case of no stealing, is likely if individuals are utility-maximizing. This agreement is a simple form of social contract between the members of the society. However, there is no guarantee that the contract leading to this simple social order will be upheld. This is the crux of the dilemma.

Say the contract is negotiated and X obeys it and Y does not. What happens next depends on X and Y's next moves. The most likely outcome, assuming that Y is now known to cheat, is to return to cell 3 where neither obeys the contract, because at least here X is better off than in cell 4. Law and order breaks down completely. At this point, for the next move they both may recognize the properties of the dilemma and choose the Pareto-optimal outcome in cell 3, but the stability of this choice as the game continues is not absolutely assured because stealing strategies always dominate at least for a single play of the game.

This analysis is similar in many ways to that of Hobbes and leads to the conclusion that coercion is required to 'force' both the people into the Pareto-optimal position and to maintain it. Hence a state which enforces the social contract, possibly through punishing offenders, is needed and is set up by individual agreement to ensure social order. This either tacitly or overtly coercive state is accepted by the society because the outcome it enforces is preferable to that where all individuals do not obey the contract. As long as the individual cost, in taxes say, of running the state does not exceed the gains the state provides to that individual, through the established social order, then this solution will prevail. But it is in a sense a coercive solution even though it may be one that is agreed between the individuals.

But where does the Parsons position, that suggests that state coercion is not necessary for social order, fit in with this? Parsons's emphasis on socialization and adherence to moral values can be analyzed here by dropping the assumption that individuals are motivated by self-interest. Instead, let us assume that our individuals X and Y are now so well socialized that their behaviour is not based on self-interest but on altruistic morality. Two possibilities on these lines have been discussed by Sen (1974). In the first case, assume that X and Y behave according to the contract as long as each other does the same. They do not however obey the contract if the other person does not. In this assurance game there are two equilibrium points: the Pareto-optimal position is reached if no-one breaks the contract, and if one individual breaks the contract the other equilibrium point is where both steal. This latter equilibrium does not of course satisfy the Pareto criteria. Hence, and almost trivially, in this assurance game we arrive at the Pareto-optimal position only if the socialization of individuals is so successful that none of them ever break the social contract.

The second case, again assuming behaviour that is based on altruistic morality, posits that individuals obey the constitutional contract even when others refuse to do so. In this sense they are so successfully trained in the moral code of accepted common values that they adhere to them even though they know it is possible that another individual may not do so. They consider not obeying the social contract a worse outcome than any other. In this set-up, called an 'other-regarded game', the Pareto-optimal position is always assured since all individuals benefit from it. The social contract is negotiated and by assumption each individual obeys it.

What is of interest in these two games discussed by Sen (1974) is

125

that they clearly show the role that a socialization process, whch instils moral codes and values, can play. The weakness of the analysis, and of the Parsons position too, is the requirement that moral values and codes of conduct are followed at all times. Any emergence of self-interested behaviour can destroy this delicate balance and Hobbes's conclusion becomes more relevant: moral values help maintain order but they are not sufficient; and coercion, in the form of a law-and-order state, is required for Pareto-optimality.

This discussion seems to leave us with several possible conclusions. First, if individuals are motivated by self-interest a state is required, and may be established by individual agreement, to maintain and enforce the social contract as in Hobbes. Second, if individuals are motivated by altruistic morality to the extent that they always abide by the negotiated rules, then no state is required unless it is needed in the socialization process. Anarchists would believe that the state is not needed for this socialization process, but less extreme theorists, like Parsons, would argue that some role for the state, in education and so on, is certainly required. This state need not however be overtly nor even tacitly coercive like the Hobbesian model. The conclusion that one favours ultimately depends on one's view of individual behaviour and on whether or not one believes that this behaviour is mainly motivated by pure self-interest or whether it can be fully socialized to be altruistic. It is clear that even only partially successful socialization, say through the partial instilling of religious and moral codes, will assist social order and the move towards Pareto-optimality in this simple example. But it may well be naive to believe that absolutely no tacit or overt coercion will be required.

Finally, it is worth moving the analysis on to more complex scenarios of the Prisoner's Dilemma game. Experimental studies by Siegel and Fouraker (1960) and Sherman (1971) have found that the emergence of a cooperative solution depends on three factors. These are the number of players, the number of plays of the game, and the size of the gain from adopting the cooperative strategy relative to other possible alternatives. I will discuss each of these in turn.

If the numbers playing the game are large, it is easy for one or a few individuals to adopt a non-cooperative strategy and either not be detected or not be punished, since this is too costly. This has led Coase (1960) and Buchanan (1965) to argue that small communities are more likely to comply with the agreed social contract than larger societies. In small communities what is going on is easier to ascertain and individuals who do not comply can easily be detected and punished with little cost. As a consequence, some people have argued for the decentralization of decision-making because people in small groups feel themselves liable for the influence their behaviour has on the result reached by the community, which clearly includes themselves. This idea is behind Schumacher's book *Small is Beautiful* (1973), and has been examined by Taylor (1976), van den Doel (1977) and Olson (1965).

In large communities on the other hand, self-interested individuals have an incentive not to comply with the social contract since they may not be detected or punished. This is particularly true where the society is highly mobile or heterogeneous and in these instances formal rules need to be made known before individuals can even be aware of what conduct is consistent with the common interest. Also, the expected value of strategy outcomes are more difficult to assess in larger communities.

Thus we might generalize that small homogeneous societies are more able to achieve the common interest position of Pareto-optimality by simple social pressure and mores, and thus have little need for a state presence at all. If there is a state, we might expect it to be relatively small. In larger and more heterogeneous communities the moral code will not be as efficient in getting the group of Pareto-optimality and a larger state presence will be required. This individually agreed state presence would not only publicize the negotiated contract rules and see they were known, but it would also detect and punish non-compliance.

Taylor (1976) and Buchanan (1975) have argued that this may be why the modern state is so large. Increased mobility and urbanization this century are linked, by these writers, to the increases in government expenditures. As the community grows in size the number of individuals who fail to comply with the social contract increases. This increases the need for further law enforcement and state intervention in society increases. This in turn, Taylor argues, makes individuals feel less responsible for the enforcement of social mores themselves, since they come to be viewed as a state responsibility. Asocial behaviour increases further, as does state intervention, and a spiral of government growth is observed.

This theory is not disproved if we look at just the evidence relating to increased public expenditure in one country. However, there are other factors at work, and one of these, as we have argued already, is the increasing power of the workforce, who have pushed for more public goods and services. The fact that state expenditure out of GDP is very high in some relatively small countries with a powerful workforce (Sweden, Norway, Austria), and relatively low in large countries with a less powerful workforce (the United States), does not square with the Taylor and Buchanan theory. Furthermore this theory also presupposes a view of behaviour which some writers find unbelievable. Rawls (1971), for example, has argued that a society can evolve where the compliance of one individual to the code of conduct encourages and reinforces

127

others to behave likewise. The more individuals who comply the stronger the social fabric becomes and a co-operative solution emerges. This idea is not dissimilar to the two games of Sen (1974) that we have already discussed, and it depends on altruistic morality as a behavioural driving force. Thus we are drawn back to the Hobbes – Parsons debate and to the underlyng problem about the appropriate assumption one should make about human behaviour.

The second factor in experiments that influence whether or not a co-operative solution emerges is the number of times a game is played. Typically in laboratory conditions individuals reach a cooperative solution only after about six or eight plays and this solution is maintained until just before the end of the game is announced (Mueller, 1979, p.16). The reason why the total co-operation strategy is not reached immediately is because it takes various trials for individuals to learn what others will do when faced with different strategies. In a stable society, we might expect that sufficient 'trials' are available for co-operation to emerge, though the more people there are the longer co-operation will take to appear as there is more knowledge of strategies to acquire. What perhaps is of more interest is that the agreed solution breaks down at points towards the announced end of the game. This phenomenon might be compared with episodes in history where riots and rebellions are occurring or appear to be imminent. These are certainly an announcement that the society is changing and individuals who up until then have been law-abiding may see little point in continuing with this strategy. Looting and thieving, for instance, may be carried out by people who until that moment have been compliant law-abiders. It is not simply that they now think they will not be detected; it is also a recognition that the established social contract is about to be broken, and if they are self-interested, they should change their strategy of compliance.

The final factor that influences the choice of the co-operative strategy is the relative size of the gain from adopting it over other alternatives. This is so obvious on one level that it deserves little comment, but Olson's (1965) work has made some excellent use of this argument. He has argued that to get more individuals to participate in a constitutional contract, selective incentives can be offered to people. These can be either positive or negative and effectively change the values in the cells of the game matrix we have been discussing. To encourage co-operation, both negative sanctions, say in the form of fines for non-compliance, and positive sanctions, in the form of individual subsidies for compliance, are offered. These make co-operation more attractive and the co-operative strategy more likely. The positive and negative sanctions may even be arranged so that the co-operative strategy is absolutely dominant and there is no dilemma.

Hence if the values in the cells of the matrix we have discussed earlier are not likely to generate a stable and lasting strategy of Pareto-optimality, or full agreement to the constitutional contract, then these cell values can be altered by some agent such as a state. This point rather begs the question of why the state should be motivated to act in such a way as to gain Pareto-optimality and social order, but the idea here is that the state does so because its actions are agreed and then its rules followed by all individuals, because this makes them all better-off. In terms of our simple game, the strategies in cells 2 and 4 may be attractive and utility-maximizing for an individual for one play of the game, but they are unstable strategies that will not last. Over many plays of the game the utility-maximizing strategy is the cell 1 Pareto-optimal strategy, and for this reason agreement for a state presence to maintain this solution is the 'best' outcome.

In this sense the state forms because self-interested individuals agree to its formation and its code of conduct, and the policing of the negotiated contract. If individual behaviour is not self-interested but altruistic, then perhaps there is no state formed because it is not needed for getting the best outcome, and there is anarchy. Alternatively, under the altruism regime, there is an agreed state formed, and its negotiated role is to socialize all individuals in the moral code required for the Pareto-optimal outcome. Perhaps more realistically the solution may be an agreed state formation which both socializes people and acts as a police officer when required. In this sort of state, individual behaviour is a mixture of altruism and self-interest.

An Assessment of this Economic Rationale for State Formation

I have argued that this rather simple economic analysis of state formation gives some new insights into the older Hobbes – Parsons debate about how social order is achieved. In particular, I think it makes very clear the effect of different individual behaviour assumptions and shows that Hobbes and Parsons each chose different views of personal motivations. Also, the one reason why a community of people may agree to the formation of a powerful state is quite apparent. Whether the state serves as an agent of socialization, or as a law-and-order state, or indeed both, is because all individuals agree to this role for the state in order to maximize their defined utility. This conclusion is not dissimilar to Locke's (1939) conception of the state as a trust which is created by citizens for the benefits of themselves.

What this analysis does not do, and to be fair does not try to do, is to take account of the different power that certain individuals and groups may have. It is implicitly assumed that all people are equal excepting that they may have different individual material endowments. Despite these possible differences in endowments each person has an influence in the negotiation which it has been implicitly assumed is at least roughly equal. Everyone gets a say whatever their material stake.

Now the relevance of this analysis for understanding the development and the role of the modern state can be questioned on three fronts. First in at least some societies there are groups and individuals who are excluded from the agreements reached. The laws or rules which the black and coloured people in South Africa are faced with are obviously not agreed and negotiated by them; these codes of conduct are imposed on them. The state form which they face has not emerged as the result of an agreement in which they participated. The same is true of other oppressed groups one can think of throughout the world.

This approach is also entirely concerned with individual behaviour, but, as we have shown, modern developed society is composed of interest groups and some of these appear to be rather powerful. The democratic state formation we are faced with is not necessarily Lincoln's 'rule by the people, and for the people'; not all individuals are equal in the influence they exert on the state and its negotiated laws and settlements.

Lindblom (1977) has argued that in Western democracies it is indeed the case that political influence on the state is not exerted in any equal sense by its citizens. Businessmen as a group take on a privileged role within the state sphere, he suggests, because jobs, prices, production, growth, the standard of living and everyone's economic security rests in their hands. For this reason the state cannot be indifferent to their demands, as ultimately they control the economic base of society. This idea is clearly borrowed from Marxism though Lindblom himself does not use Marxist analytical methods. The state can encourage and induce business to perform but it cannot command this performance since it does not own the basic means of production. Constitutional rules, and particularly laws concerning private property, limit the power which the state or any other agent exerts over business. Furthermore, if a radical state attempts to change these laws, production can be halted by the private sector and the concurrent economic crisis leads to a breakdown in order and a probable overthrow of the state. The experience of the Allende government in Chile is a recent example. Thus, for the state and its officials, businessmen are not simply representatives of an interest group; they are people performing functions that are indispensable for the maintenance of society and the state itself.

This view is sometimes challenged by the assertion that labour organizations also exercise a privileged power position within the state. Labour and trade unions provide essential services and through strike threats can have their special demands met. However, the counter-argument to this is perhaps more convincing. First, workers will, and do, work without special inducements from the state; their livelihoods depend on this work and there is little element of choice about it. On the other hand, businessmen can decide whether or not to undertake entre-preneurial ventures; if conditions do not seem favourable, business can be set up elsewhere or postponed. Second, even the threat of strikes by workers is a limited weapon. Stopping work in one industry, and even a general strike, is impossible for very long because it provokes the state to break the strike. Labour can be, and is, forcibly commanded in a way which is impossible with business leaders. Thus trade unions are only privileged in special circumstances when they are essential workers, and even this position cannot be maintained indefinitely. New workers can be trained to replace them.

The special position of business in relation to other groups and individual citizens is also evident empirically. Many interest groups attempt to influence state actions, and about a decade ago the US House of Representatives made an estimate of the expenses of various interest groups trying to influence legislation. The results are quoted in Lindblom (1977, p.195). A sample of 173 corporations, the principal national farmers' organizations, the AFL-CIO, and the major independent national unions were queried. The reported expenditures for a three-year period of these interest groups were:

173 corporations	:	$32·1 million
Farm organizations	:	$ 0·9 million
Labour unions	:	$ 0.55 million

The disproportionate expenditure by business in this area is obvious. Similar sorts of disproportions in those expenditures aimed at influencing state actions is also obvious in the UK. The election campaign of 1964 for example had its publicity funded from the following major sources:

Conservative Party (financed by itself but largely through corporate contributions)	£950,000
Aims of Industry (an industrial association)	£270,000
Steel Federation (an industrial association)	£621,000
Stewarts and Lloyds (a single corporation)	£306,000
Labour Party (financed largely through trades union contributions)	£267,000

131

Again the business sector appears to be easily the major source of funds, and the expenditure of just one company alone, Stewart and Lloyds, was larger than that of the entire Labour Party.

It is clear that the political contributions from business virtually swamp those from labour unions, and on the basis of this evidence one should surely not unquestioningly accept the 'equal influence of all citizens' assumption that was implicit in the last section. This means that the negotiated game I have been using as an example is not relevant in Western democracies. Even in democracies where there is universal suffrage one must doubt if each citizen really has equal influence before the state.

The third way in which the theory about state formation and its role can be questioned relates to the form of the state that emerges from the implicitly or explicitly negotiated and agreed settlement. The analysis give no clues about why a democratic order has emerged or indeed why in some countries it has not. If analysis is restricted to individual agreements between citizens who all get an equal say in the negotiations, it appears that a rather democratic notion of the state is assumed right at the start.

Historical studies of the emergence of particular systems of government take an entirely different approach. Historians would not accept that the rise of the modern state can be understood as universally negotiated settlement between individuals. They instead focus on social groups and the way the influence of these groups has waxed and waned with their material fortunes and through the alliances and coalitions they have formed. These shifts are reflected in the type of state that emerges. The point is made most forcefully by Barrington Moore (1967), who has analyzed the emergence of democracy in several nations. The starting place for historians interested in the emergence of particular state forms is not an abstract anarchy but the social order that prevailed under feudalism.

In his study, Barrington Moore identifies several groups as being important actors in the maintenance and periodical breakdown of order that occurred after the feudalist period. These groups include the crown, the landed nobility, the town bourgeoisie, the peasants and the urban plebs. Each of these groups had different amounts of power at particular times and formed varying coalitions with each other in pursuit of their own interests. The coalitions were both tacit and overt and some were cemented by coercion. Those groups that were not part of an alliance were either too weak to be of use or sufficiently weak so that they could be repressed without great cost, or alternatively they had interests that were opposed to the alliances formed. In this way, the march of history can be examined rather like a game of 'Diplomacy' using bargaining theory and assessments of the relative power and interests of each group at a particular moment in time.

The initial coalition was typically one between the crown and the landed nobility. In those countries in which democracy eventually emerged, this coalition was one of balance in the sense that the nobility had a degree of independence from the crown which enabled it to form other alliances and at times to be quite hostile to the crown's interests. However, the crown was sufficiently strong to keep the nobility controlled and ordered so that it did not plunder the countryside.

The town bourgeoisie in this early period were not strong or powerful. They were not numerous and their economic strength had not yet developed. The material base of the nation was land and its produce, and it was taxes on this base that largely maintained the crown. In England the landed nobility developed an interest in commercial agriculture and this in turn led to the farming of large tracts of lands which were seized in enclosures from the peasants. The peasants were weak and their only ally was at times the crown to whom they looked as an upholder of conservative values. Both Elizabeth I and the Stuarts did at times ease the burden of the peasants in their clash with the landed nobility, but this alliance was always weak. The crown depended on land taxes from the nobles for its existence, and the peasants certainly never offered a substitute material base for the crown.

At the same time the success of commercial agriculture in England led to a strengthening alliance between the landed nobility and the town bourgeoisie. This particular alliance between nobility and bourgeoisie was a peculiarly English experience in many ways. The commercial interests of the nobility lay in wheat and wool, and the trading of these goods took place in the towns. The nobility needed the towns to extend their commerce and the towns profited from their role in this agricultural trade. It supported the rise of industry and at the same time the declining population in the countryside provided an input of labour into the town's growing industries.

In England this alliance between the town bourgeoisie and the nobility was one of the causes of the English Civil War, which itself ultimately led to an extreme weakening of the crown, if the beheading of Charles I can be represented as such, and the emergence of an embryonic democracy. The power of the parliament at this stage lay with the landed nobility but the bourgeoisie were partly represented through the rotten borough system. As the town bourgeoisie grew in strength, both economically and numerically, their representation in parliament also grew and their influence over legislation grew with their strength. The repressive powers of the English state were never very great internally, since England, largely for commercial reasons, had concentrated on the development of its navy rather than its army. Partly for this reason, the nobility were forced to accommodate and ally with the town bourgeoisie rather than turn on them. They had little internal firepower at their command even if they had wanted to use it.

In France, by comparison, the alliances and behaviour of the crown, the nobility, the bourgeoisie, the peasants and the urban plebs were rather different. The crown and the nobility were close but the nobility never showed very much interest in commercial agriculture. The taxes which it raised were taken from the peasants in the form of produce and cash and this was partly passed on to the crown. The peasants paid rent and were not forced off their land as in England under the enclosures. At the same time, the town bourgeoisie were employed in the production of arms and luxuries for the court. The nobility, the crown and the bourgeoisie clung together and the aristocracy's power was not smashed until the French Revolution. The power behind this revolution was an alliance of peasants and urban plebs. The peasants were exploited by their nobles, and as the demand on the peasants for their surplus rose, so did their misery.

The revolution destroyed the aristocracy, but the alliance between the peasants and the urban plebs did not last. Each group had different interests and the demand by the town for cheap food, and the more radical demands by the urban plebs, were ultimately in conflict with the needs of the peasants and their more conservative demands for property rights and protection. Once this alliance fell apart, the town bourgeoisie were free to grasp the leadership of the state and quell the more radical demands of the urban plebs. However, through the smashing of the landed nobility and the crown, the way was opened for a democratic state, though its beginnings were rather different to those in England.

In Germany, democracy did not emerge because there never was a lasting alliance between the landed nobility and the town bourgeoisie. This latter group were weak, and though the landed Junkers exported their grain, this never passed through the towns and there were few moves to form alliances. The alliance that was eventually formed between the nobility and the bourgeoisie was held together by a powerful crown through the exploitation of an external threat and the internal militarism and unity that was perceived to be needed to deal with it. It was through this form of the state that Germany, and also Japan, modernized. In both these countries, the crown and the nobility were initially too strong and united for the bourgeoisie and society to modernize via the liberal capitalist route.

These simplistic caricatures of the broad sweep of several nations' history are, of course, far from adequate but they are sufficient to suggest that the form of the state that emerges, and the particular sort of social order that was and is established, depend on the particular balances of power and strength among various groups in society. The state that emerges reflects this balance of power and continues to accommodate and react to it. This is as true today as it was in the general sweep of history before us. It is this fact that economists must keep in their minds and their models of state behaviour. It cannot be sufficient to explain the social order or the state behind it in terms of individual motivations and reactions; these individuals must be linked to the group which they come from and identify with.

The major point that this discussion again poses is that to understand the economic actions of the state, including its economic policies, we must pay attention to the power distribution in society. One of the basic aims of state behaviour has always been to maintain social order, and historically this has necessarily meant accommodating the powerful. The modern world is no different in this respect, though evolving changes in the distribution of power have led to historical shifts in state economic behaviour, as already argued. It is impossible to understand this simply by concentrating on individual units of behaviour.

9   Towards a Systemic Theory
of the State

Slowly we are learning
We at least know this much,
That we have to unlearn
    Much that we were taught,
And we are growing chary
Of emphatic dogmas;
Love like Matter is much
    Odder than we thought.

Auden, 'Heavy Date'

Introduction

In the light of the lavish criticisms I have been heaping on current economic theories of the state I now move on to an attempt to develop an approach which may be more appropriate. This approach should be appropriate in the sense that it is applicable to the developed countries we have discussed earlier, and in common with all economic theories of the state it is concerned with explaining *actual* state economic behaviour. We are concerned with what the state *is* doing, rather than with what it *ought* to be doing in some sense.

Now the functions of a state obviously vary from one society to another. A feudal system of governance is clearly different from a democratic capitalist system for example. However, every state, except one on the point of collapse, has one overriding and basic function. It maintains the social and economic order. This function of the state is fundamental and it necessarily dominates all other state activity. Indeed, without order it is nonsense even to talk of a state.

In conventional economic policy analysis, this function of the state is ignored and order is simply taken as given. This is also the case in what I have dubbed mainstream economic theories of the state, where order in civil society implicitly prevails while politicians seek votes and bureaucrats seek bigger budgets. When the question of order is considered, it is used, following Hobbes, as a justification for state existence and not as an underlying and dominant state function which might interfere with the self-interested behaviour of politicians and state bureaucrats.

Marxist theory has to its credit been more concerned with the issue of order, but this aim of state activity is oddly not seen as particularly problematic. Because the capitalists are so rigidly dominant in their control, any recent threat to the existing order has been strangely regarded as being quite manageable. Concessions to the working class may be made in this quest for order, but at a fundamental level the stability of the capitalist system is not called into question by these concessions. The day when revolution occurs and the capitalist bourgeois democratic order is smashed is apparently assumed to be a long way off. The Marxists have been keen to explain why the existing system has been so long-lived and stable, but by the very act of addressing this question they have failed to ask whether the present order is really as stable as they assume. A workers-led revolution certainly does not seem to be just around the corner, but this does not mean that we can count on the continuing existence of order under capitalist democracy. Their theory needs to be less rigid in accommodating the problem posed for a state trying to maintain economic and social order in a system where, as we have seen, the working class has become more powerful over the century.

This increase in the power resources of the working class, and the concentration of capital, also suggest that an appropriate theory of the state should not be built on the individual as a unit of analysis. Civil society is not pluralist. Power is not spread rather evenly around among many individuals or myriads of small groups. It is, in all the developed countries, manifest in a few groups. These might be fragmented or encompassing groups, but in maintaining economic order the state is principally concerned with tacit or overt group mediation. In this way my suggested approach to understanding the state is systemic. We are not just concerned with the institutions and actors within government but with the whole social and economic system of a nation which the state is attempting to maintain.

A Static Bargaining Problem

In maintaining the economic order, the basic conflict in society that must be sorted out is that of the distribution of resources. Conflict between groups over this distribution must be mediated so that governance

137

prevails. As a start let us assume that there are just two powerful groups in society which we will call workers and capitalists. The workers are a unified coalition and the capitalists are another and the resources of the nation are to be divided between them. Each group is attempting to maximise its share of resources, and the total resources available at any time are a finite amount, u. This amount u is to be distributed on the basis of agreements that are co-operatively struck between the workers and the capitalists. Thus we can pose a simple bargaining process over society's resources. Further if no consensus is reached over this distribution of resources, and order breaks down, we can assume that each group will receive some conflict pay-off. This conflict pay-off will be less than what would have been achieved had a co-operative agreement been reached. It is in both groups' self-interest to achieve consensus. This seems sensible enough to assume, because if there is consensus the production levels achieved and the resources available will be higher than those reached where conflict was present.

One possible bargaining game that could be used to formalize this view of affairs is a two person Nash co-operative bargaining process. We will begin with this because it implies some interesting results, but we will then proceed to investigate and develop it further.

Let the total amount of resources available be u; if there is consensus the capitalists get u_1 of these resources and the workers get u_2. On the other hand if no consensus is reached and there is conflict the capitalists get c_1 of the resources and the workers get c_2. As we have already noted the conflict pay-offs, c_i (i = 1,2), are assumed less than the agreed pay-offs, u_i (i = 1,2). The situation is represented in Figure 9.1.

In this diagram, Figure 9.1, C is the conflict point which represents the resources that workers and capitalists get if there is no agreement. At this conflict point the workers get c_2 of resources and the capitalists get c_1 of resources. The line DE is the negotiation line which represents the total resources available when there is agreement. At E the workers get all the resources produced and the capitalists get none; at D on the other hand, the capitalists get all the resources and the workers get none. These two points, D and E, are polar cases where society's resources are intuitively divided in the most inequitable way available. The winner takes all.

Given the conflict point C, it is clear that not all the negotiation line is relevant to the bargaining process. In an out-and-out conflict the capitalists can get c_1 so they will never rationally agree a bargain which is below the pay-off c_1.

Similarly in a conflict the workers can by assumption get c_2 of resources and they will never agree a position that gives them a lower

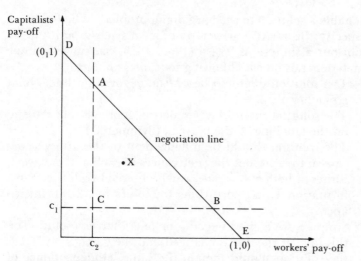

Figure 9.1: The Nash Bargaining Game

pay-off than c_2. This means that the relevant segment of the negotiation line must be AB; any agreed division of resources between A and B on the negotiation line will make both capitalists and workers better off than if there is conflict and they are at C. Thus the bargaining process is basically about determining where on the segment AB the agreement point will be established. If the agreed division of resources is near A then the capitalists will get a relatively high proportion of resources as their pay-off. If the agreed division of the resources is near B then the workers will get a relatively high proportion of resources as their pay-off.

Points within the triangular area ABC we assume can only be reached by some agreement too, but these points are not Pareto-optimal and can be ruled out if our workers and capitalists are rational. Thus some point like X would not be an agreed division of resources, since by moving from X either horizontally or vertically, some new point on the negotiation line can be achieved. At this new point one group will be better off than before, in its achieved pay-off, but the other group will be no worse off. Thus X, and all other points inside the ABC area are not Pareto-optimal and we can ignore them for the present.

This means that the basic bargaining problem is now clear. Given the conflict point C, where on the segment AB will agreement be established? Intuitively the solution will depend on the relative power of the two groups in the bargaining process. The workers will want to achieve some division of resources that gives them a maximum pay-off; they will wish to be as near B as possible. On the other hand the capitalists will wish to maximize their share of resources, and they will wish to be as near A as possible.

To enable a solution to the bargaining problem to be found we must now specify the relative power position of each group and be explicit about our assumptions. Nash (1950; 1953) has suggested one solution which depends on the following four assumptions:

1. The solution ought to be on the negotiation line. (Joint efficiency.)
2. The solution should be symmetric. It should not depend on the labelling of the players. (Symmetry.)
3. The solution should be independent of the utility scales chosen to represent the preferences of each of the players. Either or both of the scales can be altered by a linear transformation withut perturbing the solution. (Linear invariance.)
4. Suppose, for a given negotiation line, there is a solution on this line. If the line is changed and the game is replayed, the solution should remain the same. (Independence of irrelevant alternatives. The result is invariant with respect to irrelevant restrictions of the pay-off space.)

These assumptions behind Nash's solution are discussed in detail in Weintraub (1975, pp.48−50) and Harsanyi (1977, p.144). In terms of our figure the first assumption says that the solution must be on the segment AB, as we have already argued. The solution must be Pareto-optimal. The second assumption is self-evident; the solution must be an intrinsic concept. The third assumption reflects the notion that interpersonal comparisons of utility are meaningless. Changing the scale of measurement ought not to affect the outcome. The fourth assumption states that in a negotiated settlement, if both sides reject one alternative, the result of the negotiation is not affected by this rejection − provided that these rejected, but offered, alternatives do not alter the conflict point.

Now under these assumptions Nash has shown that there is a unique solution to this two-person simple bargaining game. Given the conflict point C, some solution can be found. This unique outcome, (u_1, u_2), is determined by the conflict point and Nash's equilibrium is found by maximizing, the product Π,

$$\Pi = (u_1 - c_1)(u_2 - c_2),$$

where (u_1, u_2) lies on AB somewhere. In our simple bargaining process this solution amounts to sharing out the resources in a proportion $(u_1 : u_2)$ that is the same shareout proportion as at the conflict point $(c_1 : c_2)$. This is easy to see mathematically. For Π to be at a maximum we must have,

$$u_1 - c_1 = u_2 - c_2.$$

If we now let the u_i and c_i represent a share of resources, which in our example is being split only two ways, we can write,

$$u_1 = 1 - u_2 \tag{1}$$

and $$c_1 = 1 - c_2 \tag{2}$$

Then $$u_1 - c_1 = u_2 - c_2$$
$$= (1 - u_1) - c_2 \qquad \text{from equation (1)}$$

and $$u_1 = \frac{1 - c_2 + c_1}{2} \tag{3}$$

Similarly $$u_1 - c_1 = u_2 - c_2$$

so $$(1 - u_2) - c_1 = u_2 - c_2 \qquad \text{from equation (1)}$$

$$u_2 = \frac{1 - c_1 + c_2}{2} \tag{4}$$

Then $$\frac{u_1}{u_2} = \frac{1 - c_2 + c_1}{1 - c_1 + c_2} \qquad \text{from equations (3) and (4)}$$

$$\frac{2c_1}{2c_2} \qquad \text{from equation (2)}$$

Thus $$\frac{u_1}{u_2} = \frac{c_1}{c_2} \tag{5}$$

The Nash solution to our problem is a point (u_1, u_2) on the negotiation line segment AB where the resources are divided in proportion $(u_1 : u_2)$. This proportion is the same proportionate split as that proportionate split which occurs if there is conflict $(c_1 : c_2)$.

Intuitively this solution equates the power of workers and capitalists with the share that each group could get in a conflict situation. Imagine that there was conflict and each group say got 50 per cent of resources. According to the Nash solution the appropriate *agreement* solution would also be one where resources were split equally on a 50 – 50 basis. Imagine again that the conflict situation was one where capitalists got 80 per cent and the workers got 20 per cent. In this scenario the Nash equilibrium under agreement would be one where capitalists got 80 per cent and workers got 20 per cent. Both groups would get more under the agreed solution, because without conflict, production is higher and the level of resources available is higher. But this higher level of resources is split on an 80 : 20 basis. Thus the concept of power here is quite directly related to the share of resources that would be acquired in an out-and-out conflict. This is just one possible way of determining where on the AB segment we end up, but the fact that the Nash agreement solution does depend on this particular conception of power is worth bearing in mind.

If we stay with this Nash solution to the problem we can note several interesting features relating to it. The conception of power that lies behind it will be returned to shortly but for the moment we will just investigate what this solution implies.

The Increasing Power of Workers and Economic Order

If the power of workers in this model increases, vis à vis capitalists, there is a shift in the conflict point C. The change in the power distribution means quite explicitly that when there is conflict, and no agreement is reached, the workforce can gain a higher level of resources than before. The shift in this conflict point is shown in Figure 9.2 below where the conflict point moves from C to F.

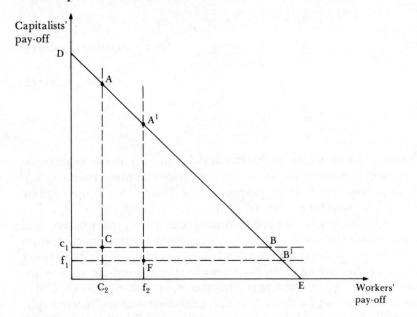

Figure 9·2: A Shift in the Conflict Point

At the new conflict point F, workers get f_2 of resources which is greater than c_2. In conflict they do better. Also as we have drawn it the capitalists now do worse in a conflict. Instead of getting c_1 of resources in a conflict they now get f_1 which is less than before.

If there is an agreement under this new conflict point arrangement it must now be on the negotiation line somewhere between $A^1 B^1$. The part of the negotiation line that is relevant for the solution has changed from AB to $A^1 B^1$. The particular new agreement point, where resources are split, will be one where society's resources are divided so that now,

$$\frac{u_2}{u_1} = \frac{f_2}{f_1} > \frac{c_2}{c_1}$$

This means that the workers' share of resources, u_2, under an agreement has gone up from what it previously had been. The increasing power of workers, as represented by the shown change in the conflict point, means they can command a higher share of resources under agreement.

This seems intuitively reasonable in the sense that if workers' power has increased we would expect that they could command an increasing share of the agreed resource pay-off. This increase in power, in this model, is exemplified by a shift in the conflict point that makes the workers' pay-out under conflict more favourable than hitherto. Hence in this narrow sense, the increase in workers' power, vis à vis that of capitalists, leads to an increase in their pay-off share under consensus and agreement and order.

The Behaviour of the Mediating State

Within this system we can investigate the behaviour of the state by simply assuming that the state's only function is to preserve order. The state is nothing but a mediator and in this role it would facilitate the reaching of an agreement. Since the agreed Nash solution is one that shares out resources in the proportion $(u_1 : u_2)$ as before it is the purpose of the state to see that the Nash agreement is reached. If agreement is not reached in the Nash world the only alternative is conflict and it is this disorder which the state is anxious to avoid.

Let the existing conflict point be C; when there is conflict total resources are divided in the ratio $c_1 : c_2$ with capitalists gaining c_1 and workers gaining c_2. At this point there is disorder and for agreement and order to prevail under the Nash regime the resources should agreeably be divided so that capitalists get u_1, and workers get u_2. As we have already seen (in equation 5) there is a unique agreement point (u_1, u_2) where

$$\frac{u_1}{u_2} = \frac{c_1}{c_i} \qquad (5) \qquad \text{and } u_i > c_i$$

As a mediator in this system the state must attempt to see that resources are divided according to this formula.

Now to facilitate this particular division of resources the state has several options it can exercise via its taxation and expenditure policy. Specifically let total private resources, Y, be composed of wages (W) and profits (Π). Both wages and profits can be taxed at rates t_1 and t_2 respectively. Also the state can give public goods, services and direct monies to either group.

143

We can thus write,

$$u_1 = \Pi(1 - t_1) + (1 - \gamma_1)G \tag{6}$$
$$u_2 = W(1 - t_2) + \gamma_1 G \tag{7}$$
$$Y = W + \Pi \tag{8}$$
$$G = t_2 W + t_1 \Pi + D \tag{9}$$

where

u_1 = total resources available to capitalists,
u_2 = total resources available to workers,
W = total wages,
Π = total profits,
$Y = W + \Pi$ = private income,
G = government expenditure,
D = public sector deficit or surplus (expenditure less taxes),
t_1 = tax rate on profits,
t_2 = tax rate on wages,
γ_1 = proportion of government expenditure benefiting the workers.

It is clear from equations (6) and (7) that the state can manipulate the resources available to workers and capitalists by both setting tax rates and manipulating the distribution and level of government expenditures. In terms of the Nash solution the devised $(u_1:u_2)$ proportion for an agreement solution can be achieved by changes in t_1, t_2, and γ_1. In addition the level of G itself can be shifted by changing the size of the public deficit or surplus and the tax rates. (See equation (9) again.) There are so many possible options facing the state that there is no unique path it must follow. However if a Nash solution is to be achieved, and economic order with it, then changes in t_1, t_2, γ_1, and G can be used to achieve the solution. And in its role as mediator, and seeker of order, the state will change these variables and facilitate agreement.

If the ratio of total wages to profits in society happened to be the same as the Nash solution $(u_1:u_2)$ there would be no need for a mediating state. In this extreme instance we have,

$$\frac{u_1}{u_2} = \frac{\Pi}{W} = \frac{c_1}{c_2} \qquad\qquad u_i > c_i, \ i = 1, 2.$$

and $t_1 = t_2 = G = 0$

This extreme case might approximate the minimal state economic presence earlier in the century in developed countries where order, and specifically a Nash agreement, was forthcoming because wages and profits happened to be close to the desired ratio for consensus. Hence this approach does not necessarily entail a large public sector.

The Nash solution might also cast some light on why different states have differences in the size of their public sectors. Suppose we have two states where the power distribution is the same so that their u_i are distributed in the same proportions. Further assume that tax rates are similar but that in the first state the share of resources going into wages is low vis à vis the other state. In this situation if the first state is to be stable the share of public resources being transferred, in cash or kind, to the workers, must be higher than in the second state.

Similarly if the share of resources allocated to profits in this first state is relatively high, compared to the second state, we would expect to see relatively lower public transfers to the capitalist group. Thus the public sector, as controller of the flow of resources, has an important role to play in maintaining stability. The decision made by the government about tax rates and expenditure transfers must be compatible with the decisions about wage and profit shares in the sense that the final outcome must conform to the Nash equilibrium solution. The entire system must be made to reach an agreed outcome.

Now we have already suggested that if the relative strength of the working class increases so too does its expected proportionate pay-off if stability is to be maintained. We can now add that this increased pay-off can take the form of increased post-tax wages or increased public transfers, in cash or kind, or indeed a bit of both. Similarly if the post-tax share of profits should fall, without decreasing the power of the capitalist class, their public transfers from the public sector will increase. Hence in a state where the working class is increasing its power, we would expect to see increases in their post-tax wage share, increases in public expenditures that benefit this class, or some suitable combination of the two. If the capitalist class is relatively weaker it will be experiencing declines in its post-tax profits and possibly declines in its public sector transfers. However if post-tax profits are falling, but not because of any decrease in power, the public transfers to the capitalists would be increasing to maintain state stability.

During the post-war period it is possible that the working class has improved its relative power position, as we argued in Chapter 3. This suggests that both post-tax wages and public transfers to this group, or some increasing combination of the two economic resources, will have occurred. It is also probable that capitalist power has declined relatively — and this would decrease their relative pay-off, and post-tax profits and public transfers taken together will have declined as a share of resources. However to the extent that the fall in profit share has not been accompanied by a decline in power, and say has been caused by factors exogenous to this model, we would expect to see increased public funding of this sector.

Thus in this scenario the public sector is intimately involved in maintaining the stability of the entire system. If it fails to do so, each group simply gets its conflict pay-off and any other considerations of public sector behaviour are purely peripheral. This concern to achieve order is the overriding and principal objective of state action.

Up to this point we have implicitly assumed that the utility of wages, public goods, services and transfers are all interchangeable to workers; and that the utility of profits and public goods, services and monies are interchangeable to capitalists. It is easy to abandon this simplifying and implicit assumption in this context by interpreting u_1 and u_2 as utilities. The role of the state is then to balance the utilities u_1 and u_2, acquired by capitalists and workers respectively, and this can be managed through changes in taxation and government expenditure levels and allocation as before. The particular ratio of the utilities agreed, u_1 to u_2, is determined by the relative power of each group in conflict situation but the state must now weigh up the contribution to these utilities of wages, profits and government expenditures. If for example, the capitalists have a strong relative preference for post-tax profits over public expenditures that benefit them, the government must take this into account in its attempt to facilitate agreement. However the principal aim is still to maintain order and facilitate the Nash agreement.

The State as a Mediator and a Self-interested Actor

It is possible to extend this approach to allow for self-interested action by the state. In mainstream economic theories of the state both politicians and bureaucrats are assumed to act in a self-interested fashion; politicians seek to win elections and bureaucrats seek to extend their power by increasing the size of their department's budget. In these theories the overriding state objective of maintaining social and economic order is ignored but within the simple Nash bargaining process both the quest for order and a public sector that is motivated by self-interest can be accommodated. We continue to assume that the maintenance of order is the overriding and dominant concern. As before we also assume that private sector workers are formed into a unified coalition, and capitalists are another unified coalition. But now we add a third group, the public sector, composed of politicians, bureaucrats and public sector workers. This third group, the public sector, also seeks to maximize its pay-off, and we assume that all the individuals and groups within it are another unified coalition. There are now three groups and each is attempting to maximize its pay-off.

Further let us assume that the amount of total utility or resources available in society is some finite amount u. This utility is to be distributed amongst our three groups on the basis of agreements that are co-operatively struck between each group. Thus we have an assumed bargaining process which is now represented by a Nash three-person simple bargaining game. Each group, $i(i = 1, 2, 3)$, chooses a pay-off demand u_i and these are chosen simultaneously and independently of each other. If the u_i chosen are compatible then each group receives u_i; if on the other hand the u_i chosen are incompatible then there will be conflict between groups and in this case I assume that each group gets c_i, $i = 1, 2, 3$.

The solution to this particular game is $u = (u_1, u_2, u_3)$ where u is the pay-off vector that maximizes the three-person Nash product,

$\Pi = (u_1 - c_1)(u_2 - c_2)(u_3 - c_3)$ subject to
$u \ \varepsilon \ P$, where P is the agreement space,
$u_i > c_i$ for all $i = 1, 2, 3$
c_i = constant for all $i = 1, 2, 3$.

Now as before u is unique and always exists under these conditions (Harsanyi, 1977, Chs.8, 10).

The interpretation of this co-operative game with a binding threat is what is most interesting in this context. First if an agreement is reached the society can be said to be internally stable and each group receives u_i, in pay-off. The capitalist class gets u_1, the working class gets u_2, and the public sector get u_3. On the other hand if no agreement is struck the system is internally unstable and each group gets c_i. In this conflict situation the capitalist class gets c_1, the working class gets c_2, and the public sector get c_3.

In a capitalist state let us suppose that in a state of conflict each group knows it will get the following pay-offs,

$c = (c, ac, bc)$
where $a < 1$, $b < 1$.

This amounts to saying that in a conflict the capitalist class will get proportionately more of the total utility of the state than either of the other groups. If we define total utility as the total available resources in the state, the relatively favourable position of the capitalist class in a conflict seems a reasonable assumption. This group controls the main means of production and in a state of social disorder and conflict they will be able at least to utilize some of their resources. Their pay-off in conflict is likely to be more than that of the working class who have relatively fewer material resources to draw upon. Similarly the public sector also has access to few productive resources in a capitalist economy and in a conflict situation their pay-off is unlikely to be relatively as great as that of the capitalist group.

Now these assumptions about the conflict pay-offs to each group must be interpreted as before as a statement about the relative power positions of each group. We can say that the capitalist class is relatively most powerful because even in a conflict situation they will do relatively better than the other two groups. And furthermore this underlying distribution of power, as depicted in the conflict pay-off vector, will influence the agreement that is reached. Because both the working class and the public sector do less well in a state of conflict than do the capitalists, they will take this fact into consideration when bargaining for an agreement. But it is in each group's interest to get an agreement since in a stable state their pay-offs are greater than in a state of conflict.

We can thus now suppose that the agreement pay-off vector reached will be u* where the Nash product to be maximized is Π,

$$\Pi = (u_1 - c)(u_2 - ac)(u_3 - bc) \tag{10}$$
$$a < 1, \ b < 1.$$

If we put $u_1 + u_2 + u_3 = 1$ we can solve equation (10) and look at the proportion of resources that each group gets when the state is stable and there is agreement. Thus we solve the following equations, (11) to (13).

$$u_1 - c = u_2 - ac \tag{11}$$
$$u_1 - c = u_3 - bc \tag{12}$$
$$u_1 + u_2 + u_3 = 1 \tag{13}$$

The solution to these linear simultaneous equations is:

$$u_1 = \frac{1 + c(2 - a - b)}{3} \tag{14}$$

$$u_2 = \frac{1 + c(2a - b - 1)}{3} \tag{15}$$

$$u_3 = \frac{1 + c(2b - a - 1)}{3} \tag{16}$$

These equations (14) to (16) show u* the proportionate distribution of total utility between the three groups when agreement is reached. Since $a < 1$, $b < 1$ it is clear that the capitalist class will have a higher proportionate share of total utility or resources than the other two groups. If $a > b$, the power of the working class is stronger than that of the public sector in the sense that in a conflict they will get proportionately more than the public sector, and in this case their agreement pay-off is proportionately more than that going to the public sector group. On the other hand if $a < b$, the public sector group does relatively better out of the agreement than does the poorer working class.

Now if a and b increase it is clear that the share of utility going to the capitalist group will decline. If the working class *ceteris paribus* becomes more powerful so that in a conflict its pay-off rises, and a increases, then the share going to the working class increases and that going to the capitalists declines. Also if a increases the share going to the public sector decision makers declines. Thus an increase in working-class power, in the sense that a goes up, causes the working-class pay-off to rise proportionately at the expense of both the capitalists and the public sector.

If the power of the public sector increases, so that b increases, then their relative share of total utility or resources goes up at the expense of a decline in the share going to capitalists and a decline in the share going to the working class.

Though this is a very simple analysis it does seem to suggest that an agreement, with binding threats, will be reached so long as the expected pay-off of the agreement, u_i, i = 1,2,3 is greater than the conflict pay-off c_i, i = 1,2,3. We have mentioned that the Marxists have had some difficulty in explaining the ongoing stability of capitalist states. They have not erupted into conflict and revolution as some Marxists expected. This can be explained here by arguing that the expected pay-off from agreement and co-operation, and system stability, has exceeded the expected pay-off from conflict. If the expected pay-off from conflict was to exceed the expected pay-off from agreement for any group then stable or co-operative social systems would break down.

Furthermore this explanation of stability in capitalist systems does not depend on any assumptions about the relative power between groups in society. Stability simply depends on the pay-off from agreement to each group being in excess of its conflict pay-off. If conflict should occur in this simple model it is because c_i, the conflict pay-off for any group, is in excess or equal to the agreement pay-off u_i. Thus conflict could be caused by the working class when $c_2 > u_2$ but it could also be caused by the capitalist class if $c_3 > u_3$. In any of these conflict cases each group simply gets their conflict pay-offs c_i.

However, as we have seen, the agreed distribution of total resources or utility reflects the underlying power distribution of the system. This power distribution is interpreted in this model by the relative distribution in the conflict pay-off vector. The group that is most favourably represented in this conflict pay-off vector is also most favourably treated in the agreement pay-off vector. And groups that are relatively less powerful get relatively unfavourable agreement pay-offs. Hence this model suggests that the distribution of resources between groups will be inequitable if power is distributed inequitably. If power is equally distributed so that the conflict pay-off is the same for each group then the agreement pay-offs to each group will also be equal. If the power of the working class goes up so too does its agreement pay-off at the expense of the capitalist group and public sector group shares. Similarly if the power of the public sector group goes up so too does its share of the distribution under agreement. And this increase is at the expense of both the capitalist group and the working-class group.

The structure of this bargaining game implies that it is in the interests of each group to try and increase its expected conflict pay-offs or its power, relative to other groups. It is clear from equations (10) to (16) that the capitalist group can increase its relative conflict pay-off by decreasing that of both the working class and the public sector group. The capitalist class would attempt to decrease the power of both these groups. Similarly the working-class group and the public sector group would attempt to increase their relative power as represented in the conflict pay-off vector. Hence any relative increase in power in one group will be opposed by both other groups in this analysis.

Now the Nash solution with three independent groups in the system implies that if conflict is to be avoided each group must receive u_1, u_2 and u_3 as specified in equations (14), (15) and (16). If we now let the u_i represent some level of economic resources flowing to each group we can write

$$u_1 = \Pi(1 - t_2) + \gamma_2 G \tag{17}$$
$$u_2 = W(1 - t_1) + \gamma_1 G \tag{18}$$
$$u_3 = G(1 - \gamma_1 - \gamma_2) \tag{19}$$
$$Y = W + \Pi \tag{20}$$
$$G = t_1 W + t_2 \Pi + D \tag{21}$$

where

Y is total private income,
W is total private wages,
Π is total profits,
G is government expenditure,
t_1 is tax rate on wages,
t_2 is tax rate on profits,
D is public sector deficit or surplus (public expenditure less taxes).
γ_1 is the proportion of government expenditure benefiting the workers,
γ_2 is the proportion of government expenditure benefiting the capitalists

The capitalists get utility from post-tax profits and government expenditure that benefits them. The workers get utility from post-tax wages and government expenditures that benefit them. The public sector gets utility from government expenditure which it does not distribute to either group and which it keeps for its own benefit.

Now if the system is to be stable we know that the relative proportions $u_1:u_2:u_3$ must be as before. (Equations $(14)-(16)$.) If all decisions are made independently and simultaneously this means that $t_1, t_2, \gamma_1, \gamma_2, W, \Pi$ and G must all be values that conform to this solution. Clearly there are a lot of values of these variables in combination that would conform — but the state, in its arbitrating role, is in a special position to facilitate the solution. By altering tax rates and government expenditure allocations and levels it alone can affect the values of u_1, u_2 and u_3. Hence at the same time as maximizing the public sector pay-off, u_3, the state can also act to facilitate the agreed Nash solution and this would achieve the state objective of maintaining order. Indeed if this agreed solution is not reached, the conflict solution (c_1, c_2, c_3) is assumed to prevail, and it is in the self-interest of each group to avoid this as long as $u_i > c_i$ for all i, i = 1,2,3. Thus taxation and government expenditure transfers will be agreed independently by all groups so long as the outcome is the unique Nash solution. In this sense the state both mediates and acts in its own self-interest. It maximizes its own pay-off but it also facilitates the reaching of an agreement and the maintenance of order. This objective of order maintenance is compatible with a self-interested public sector.

The International Dimension

Up to this point we have simply been talking about an isolated nation state. However this state exists within an international system, and this has immense implications for the behaviour of our simple model. Suppose we have two countries, Britain and Japan, where the power distribution in society is different. The working class in Britain is in a relatively more favourable position than is the working class in Japan.

Now in our initial year let us suppose that the total resources in each country are the same. Their GNP is 30 million dollars and it is distributed so that we have agreed pay-off vectors:

Japan 30 = (14,8,8)   Britain (12,9,9) = 30

In Japan the workforce gets 8 million, while in Britain it gets 9 million. The public sector group get similar pay-offs, say, but the capitalist group in Japan is relatively more powerful and it gets 14 million compared to the 12 million pay-off to capitalists in Britain.

Now let us suppose that the GNP available at the end of this year for distribution depends on the level of investment throughout the year. Furthermore let us suppose that in a capitalist society it is capitalists who invest and that they invest all their available resources. Also let us imagine that Japanese and British capitalists are equally efficient in their choice of investment so that they each have identical investment functions.

151

Thus let $I_t = \alpha (Y_t - Y_{t-1})$

and for simplicity put $\alpha = 1$.

Now in Japan at the end of the year the GNP will be $30 + 14 = 44$ million. In Britain the GNP will be $30 + 12 = 42$ million. These GNP's for each country will be allocated according to our initial power assumptions. Thus at the end of this year the pay-off vectors will be,

$$\text{Japan} \quad 44 = (\frac{14}{30} \times 44, \frac{8}{30} \times 44, \frac{8}{30} \times 44)$$

$$44 = (20 \cdot 5, 11 \cdot 7, 11 \cdot 7)$$

$$\text{Britain} \quad 42 = (\frac{12}{30} \times 42, \frac{9}{30} \times 42, \frac{9)}{30} \times 42)$$

$$= (16 \cdot 8, 12 \cdot 6, 12 \cdot 6)$$

Again the British working class gets a bigger pay-off than its Japanese counterparts. However it is clear that Britain is running into difficulties since its investment rate, and GNP growth rate, are falling behind the Japanese. In this little example, at the end of the next two coming years the pay-off vectors will be,

Japan $(30, 17 \cdot 2, 17 \cdot 2) = 63 \cdot 5$ Britain $(23 \cdot 5, 17 \cdot 6, 17 \cdot 6) = 58 \cdot 8$
and Japan $(44, 25 \cdot 2, 25 \cdot 2) = 94 \cdot 5$ Britain $(32 \cdot 9, 24 \cdot 7, 24 \cdot 7) = 82 \cdot 3$.

Hence by the end of this year the Japanese working class have overtaken their British counterparts even though their share of resources has not increased. Because the Japanese have invested more and increased their growth rate faster they have improved their absolute pay-off though their relative power distribution has not altered.

Now this example highlights two points. In a dynamic situation it appears to be in the interests of groups that do not invest, the workers and the public sector here, to forgo some of their pay-off so that their capitalist group can keep up their investment and growth. However the problem with this argument, as Lancaster (1973) has pointed out, is that workers have no control over the investment decision. The workers could decide to consume less, leaving more resources for investment, only to find that their capitalist group consumed the resources. The workers have no guarantee that their sacrifice will be invested for their benefit and thus lead to more consumption later. Because of this problem it is not rational for workers to forgo their pay-off unless they are certain that it will be invested for their future consumption.

One way in which this dynamic inefficiency of capitalism can be overcome is a corporatist solution. The workers, the capitalists and the public sector group can all agree on some pay-off vector ratio which will be adhered to only if the agreed investment strategy is followed. This investment, it should be pointed out, need not be done by capitalists in a mixed economy. Thus if this group will not invest, the public sector or the workers themselves could do so. However it is only by investing at the same rate as other countries that a state will grow at the same rate and hence *ceteris paribus* maintain its relative world economic position. Failure to maintain this relative position will mean a decreasing share of world trade and subsequent devaluations of the state's currency. As we have seen in Chapters 4 and 5 corporatist solutions have been attempted with varying degrees of success in several countries. Where they have not been attempted, and where the working class has been relatively powerful vis à vis other states, there have been economic difficulties relative to competing states.

The second issue that this simple example highlights is the constraints on a single state acting within an international system. As the investment rate slows down relative to other states so too does growth. Within the international system this shift is going to change the underlying international power distribution. Once powerful states can become relatively insignificant over time as the relative size of their resources fall vis à vis other countries. This will make it increasingly difficult to exercise power over such matters as international trade policies, and the relative decline can then become even more disastrous for the country in question. For these reasons the introduction of corporatism in countries where the working class is relatively more powerful is no surprise. If such agreements are not introduced when the working class is relatively powerful, the relative economic success of the nation in an international context will in all likelihood decline. On the other hand where the working class is weak vis à vis other countries and investment is not constrained, in comparison with other competing nations, there is no need to contemplate the introduction of corporatist arrangements.

An Evaluation of the Static Nash Bargaining Process

The discussion of economic bargaining outcomes in an international context, where investment was admitted to the scenario, shows how vital it is to consider the dynamics of the bargaining process. In the simple static bargaining process explained in this chapter the maintenance of economic order was only considered at one moment in time. But the objective of pursuing and maintaining order is also a dynamic objective. For a state to exist without disorder there must be a consensus and agreement which prevails across time. The function of maintaining economic order also includes the reproduction of that economic order. This dynamic objective was only touched on briefly in this static treatment. It was mentioned that shifts in the power distribution, and specifically a relative increase in working-class power, implied changes over time in the pay-off to various groups. The introduction of investment and growth showed how important a dynamic process would be for the economy and the static bargaining process must be developed further to incorporate this dynamic aspect. In the next chapter the dynamics of a capitalist economy are explored in an attempt to accommodate this oversight.

However the lack of dynamics in the Nash bargaining process just considered is not the only problem with this approach. For this particular bargaining process to be applicable we must accept that power is starkly equated with what resources a unified group could gain in a conflict. The Nash bargaining process is technically a game with a binding threat; it is a co-operative game but the agreement solution depends quite explicitly on the conflict point and the threat of conflict that is entailed.

The equating of power with conflict pay-offs is a giant simplification which it is important to consider. In the discussion of power in Chapter 3 we argued that the working class in developed countries had increased its relative power position, but there we argued that this was achieved through an increase in unionization and greater political control. It is a moot point whether this rise in working-class power resources means that in a state of disorder the working class would do better now in getting resources than, say, in a state of disorder in 1900. If in a state of disorder the workers can now possess more resources than earlier then the simplification used may be an adequate approximation but whether or not this is so may be doubtful. Power is a difficult notion to define but it is surely more complex than is implied in the Nash bargaining procedure.

For one thing, power appears to be multidimensional. Workers have some influence and power over money wages through their union structures. They also have some influence and power within the government through their political influence. This is exercised both by their votes and their influence or control over a political left-of-centre party. However union power and political influence are two rather separate dimensions to power, and the empirical evidence discussed earlier suggests that this multidimensional concept of power matters. In nations where working-class political control has been weak (the United States, Canada, and Australia for example), the size of public expenditure out of GDP has been relatively low. On the other hand where political control by the workforce has been strong, the size of the public sector has been rather high compared to other countries. The level of unionization in a country does not appear to be a dominant influence on public expenditure. In Australia, for instance, the level of unionization is very high but the public sector is relatively small as is the degree of political control by the workforce. Thus the degree of unionization appears to be a critical influence on wage outcomes and bargaining but the degree of political influence is more directly related to public sector expenditures and their allocation. Within the simple Nash model this two-dimensional facet of power is ignored completely. The particular way in which an agreed workers' allocation is split between wages, public goods, services and transfers is omitted. Perhaps the bargaining process should not be all lumped together in one game but be considered as several related bargaining processes.

The Nash bargaining game is also in a different category from that which is often used to explain collective bargaining. The Nash co-operative game is a process with a binding threat, but co-operative games have also been developed for the case where there is no binding threat. Two analyses by Hicks (1932, Ch.7) and Gilpin (1981) fall into this latter category. In Hicks's analysis there are two players, a labour union and an employer. The union will strike, or seriously threaten to strike, only when the strike will cost the trade unionists less than accepting a lower wage would. Similarly the employer will refuse to grant a wage increase only if the strike likely to result from his or her refusal will cost less than allowing the wage increase. Each party tries to maximize their net conflict pay-off. This is the value of the concessions that will be extracted by the conflict strategy less the costs of the conflict.

However if both parties expect to reach an agreement this behaviour seem irrational. They should maximize the pay-offs they will receive under this agreement. Their conflict pay-offs are important only to the extent that they influence the strength of the bargaining positions with respect to the pay-offs that they will agree upon if a conflict is avoided. Hence the conflict strategy must not be judged in terms of its pay-off in a conflict situation if each party expects an agreement. The conflict strategy ought to be judged in terms of its effect on the net pay-off in the agreement position. That is in terms of its effect on the two parties' relative bargaining positions in case they do reach an agreement and avoid a conflict. In this case they will not have to implement their threats.

Similar comments also apply to Gilpin's (1981) interesting study of international political change. He assumes that a state will attempt to change the international system when the expected benefits exceed the costs and that this change will continue until the marginal costs of further change are equal or greater than the marginal benefits. Again the idea is that each party is maximizing their net expected gain, but surely before embarking on a conflict strategy that changes the international system a rational state ought to judge this potential conflict in terms of its effect on the net pay-off in the agreement position. A rational state would try and increase its potential conflict pay-off, and enhance its bargaining position for when agreement is reached. This agreement, if it is reached, will reflect the underlying conflict pay-offs and any new agreement reflecting a change in the international system will embody a change in the conflict pay-off vector. However the new agreement, if there is one, does not need to be accompanied by any more than the binding threat of conflict.

Thus in analyzing agreements and conflict in social systems I would argue that Nash's model of a simple bargaining process with binding threats is an appropriate place to start. If the players are rational, then the game without binding threats used by Hicks and Gilpin is not appropriate. Agreement is expected and the role that conflict plays is as a binding threat and not an actuality. Nevertheless the particular bargaining process that is used in analysis needs careful consideration, and it would not be a waste of time to explore alternatives to the Nash approach. At this stage of research it is difficult to be confident about the choice of bargaining process to apply. Certainly history suggests that the maintenance of economic order involves a pay-out to social groups that reflects their power position within society, and as this power distribution shifts so too do the pay-outs if order is to continue. But from this basic starting position there is considerable room for alternative applications of bargaining models.

One further problem is that the bargaining model used here assumed the existence of unified coalitions. The working class, the capitalists, and in later sections the public sector, were all formed and working coalitions of individuals and groups. Formal treatments of coalition formation suggest that a coalition will form only when the expected pay-off to an individual from joining a particular coalition is equal or in excess of the expected pay-off from joining any other coalition or acting alone in the bargaining game (Luce and Raiffa, 1957, Ch.10). People join coalitions simply because it is rational to do so and it maximizes their expected pay-off. This behaviour also implies that members of a coalition may be prepared to distribute the total coalition pay-off amongst individuals in the coalition in such a way that they tempt individuals to remain in, or join, a coalition if this strengthens the coalition, and hence the subsequent total coalition pay-off in the bargaining game. This type of distributive behaviour within the coalition occurs when it is rational for the individuals involved, in the sense that their expected pay-off is maximized by the behaviour. The expected individual benefit of strengthening the coalition exceeds the expected cost to that individual of strengthening the coalition.

An example may make the idea clearer. Within the working-class coalition in our example we may observe higher-income workers transferring some of their income, and utility, to a lower-income group. This behaviour, achieved say by progressive taxation and transfer payments, causes the lower-income group to get a pay-off in excess of what they would get if they acted alone and outside the coalition, and as a result they are happy to join the coalition. Their membership of the coalition strengthens it, increasing the size of the conflict pay-off, and this means that the total agreement pay-off will be larger than if the low-income group were absent from the coalition. This added pay-off increases the net benefit to the better-off individuals even though they distribute some of their income towards the low-income group. If this were not the case the low-income group would be excluded from the working-class coalition. Hence within our three simple coalitions we would expect to see resources being distributed within the coalitions in order to strengthen the coalition and maximize each person's expected pay-off.

The rational reasons, just cited, for joining coalitions do not however appear to be able to explain the existence of very large coalitions or groups of the type we have postulated (Olson, 1965). There is no reason why some individuals would not wish to free-ride on the collective actions of others. If there is a union and it is engaged in bargaining, the non-union member will frequently get the pay-off that is agreed by the union. There is no incentive to join the union. Similarly, as we have argued already, there is no rational reason why an individual would vote. But in developed countries we do observe mass participation in both voting and unionization, and this has led to other explanations about coalition formation.

Hardin (1982) has proposed that groups form and can continue their existence and increase their size through a contract of convention. Tacit co-operation within a large group is established because over time each individual learns and gains knowledge of a convention to co-operate. The group is small to begin with, and there is less incentive for free-riding. But the existence of this small coalition establishes a convention of commitment amongst its members. This convention then governs the forms of action of the group and underpins the reasons for its existence. In this way the functions of a group are partly formed by the historical circumstances that contributed to the particular convention.

In the case of unions Hardin suggests (Hardin, 1982, Ch.14) that they began as small collective groups in small factories and workplaces. This established a convention which initially occurred in small groups. Federation of these small groups into a centralized organization then took place for strategic reasons and a large union formed. The formation of a large group does not happen statically, at one point in time; it happens over time by gradual conventional amalgamation.

The reasons behind the formation of unified coalitions is another area where more detailed and careful research is in order. Specific case studies of the formation of union and employer organizations in different countries will eventually lead to more knowledge about this phenomenon. But the point here is simply to emphasize that we have assumed unified coalitions, which is another gross simplification. Both workers and employers are organized into groups in most developed countries, but these organizations are not always unified and even when they are there are conflicts of interest within the coalition.

There is one final property of the Nash bargaining process that is worth mentioning. In this process we either arrive at the unique agreed solution or we end up at the conflict point. Since the outcomes at the conflict point are worse for all groups than those at the agreement solution, there is a general and self-interested aim to reach consensus. However in the real world the alternatives faced are not simply two stark outcomes of this type. We can use as an abstraction the polar notions of total disorder and complete agreement but what we tend to observe is economic order punctuated by minor skirmishes of conflict between groups here and there within society. In all developed countries there are occasional lockouts and strikes and disputes about public sector economic behaviour. These relatively minor conflicts could be signs of conflicts within coalitions, such as in union demarcation disputes, or they could be strategic reminders by one coalition to others of the importance of their binding threat. In either of these two cases the analysis of the bargaining process might be extended to accommodate the smaller conflicts for whatever reason they occur.

There are thus several problematic features within the simple static bargaining process we have been using. It is static and it would certainly make more sense to look at the bargaining game in a dynamic context. The state does not just require order in the here and now, but continually. The simplified concept of power, equating the relative pay-offs under conflict with power, is also problematic. Power is not simply unidimensional like this, and even if it was its specific dimension may not be the relative conflict pay-out. In the light of the historical behaviour of social systems it does seem important to emphasize the role of power in the maintenance of order, and what this implies in terms of economic pay-offs to groups and the economic behaviour of the state. However I do not wish to assert that the Nash approach is necessarily the most appropriate. It tentatively appears to be more applicable than co-operative games without binding threats, but the appropriate choice of a bargaining model remains an area to explore further. The fact that unified coalitions were assumed is another simplification that opens up a thicket of further problems; and future case studies about coalition formation will add to our knowledge in this field. Finally the real presence of minor conflicts in stable economic systems also suggested a need to develop the analysis. All these problems imply a big research effort, and in the next chapter I modestly begin by looking at a dynamic model. This does not deal with the other issues raised here, but by mentioning these issues I have tried to assess the contribution of the static bargaining problem in understanding state economic behaviour.

On the positive side, the simple Nash approach does show the vital importance of the power distribution in society on economic distributive outcomes. The simple bargaining model, despite its problems, suggests that as the working class gains in its relative power position it becomes economically better off. Furthermore if the state is seeking to maintain economic order, this simple bargaining process suggests that the state will arbitrate and mediate so that economic pay-offs are the Nash agreement solution. The government, whether or not it is self-interested, is in the unique position of being able to change taxation and expenditure policies so that order and agreement prevails.

When power is explicitly recognized, as it has been in this approach, and when the maintenance of order is sought, the economic behaviour of the state is quite different from that implied in previous theories. The state is not naively benevolent or omnipotent. It seeks order to maintain and continue the sytem. The state may be motivated by self-interest, but in seeking to feather the public sector nest it must be constrained by the power of workers and capitalists and their subsequent claim over resources. In this sense the state cannot be an unconstrained Leviathan, as such behaviour would conflict with its overriding objective of order maintenance.

This simple approach also shows that those Marxist theories of the state that simply assume that the state acts in the interest of capital must be more cautious. If the state was no more than an ideal collective capitalist it would co-operate in the distribution of resources towards capitalists without apparent limits. But as other Marxist writers have stressed, there are limits upon the capitalist state, and in the Nash approach these limitations are quite explicit. Establishing order is in the interest of capital but it is also in the interests of workers and the state itself. Furthermore, the actual distribution of economic resources, over which the state presides, must conform to an agreement solution. This entails a recognition of the power of the working class and its claim over resources. This group in capitalist society is not the most powerful, but if it does not achieve the pay-off that its power position warrants, then disorder and conflict prevail. In this position of conflict all groups are worse off. Thus it is not surprising to see the working class improving its economic position along with its increased power. The quest for order and the attempt to reproduce it suggest that this behaviour will continue until one group in society finds that its agreement pay-off is less than its conflict pay-off. Then, and only then, will economic disorder occur and stability break down.

159

In conclusion then this simple bargaining process does provide a formal analysis that explains why power has an important effect on economic distribution and the behaviour of the state. It is not by any means a completely acceptable analysis, as we have noted, but it does provide several insights that previous theories of the state have neglected. In stressing the maintenance of order, and power, the economic behaviour of the state is neither naive, Leviathan-oriented or simply that of an unconstrained collective capitalist. The state behaves within the constraints of the economic and social power distribution so as to achieve order within the whole social system. In this sense the state behaves systemically, and this approach, while not perhaps sufficiently developed to be a theory, is a move towards a systemic theory of the state.

10 Economic Order in a Dynamic Capitalist System

> Bound to ourselves for life,
> we must learn how to
> put up with each other.

Auden, 'Shorts'

Introduction

In view of the discussion in the last chapter I now attempt to develop a dynamic model. In the static approach just examined, consensus and order were established when resources were allocated to groups in proportion to the prevailing power distribution. But when investment and growth are introduced the scenario becomes more complicated. Intuitively it would appear to be in the interest of all groups to maintain investment, since without it there would be no growth and fewer resources in the future for distribution. If the future returns on investments are shared amongst all groups in society then it is in everyone's interest to maintain investment.

It is thus not difficult to imagine a scenario where a consensus prevails that depends on investment behaviour and the shareout of its returns. As before this consensus would in some way be affected by the relative power of social groups, in particular workers and capitalists, but the agreement in a dynamic model also depends on the expected return from investment to both workers and capitalists. This implies that the interests of capitalists and workers may not always be irreconcilable, and the proclaimed Marxist inherent instability of capitalism may be in error, at least under certain circumstances.

The fact that capitalism has been a rather long-lived arrangement in many countries does seem to suggest that the conflict between workers and capital has not been irreconcilable as yet. The continuance of economic order under capitalism has typically been explained by

161

Marxists by looking beyond the system of production to the relatively autonomous state. If irreconcilable conflict has been muted in capitalist production this must be because of some outside state intervention. In this capacity the state comes to the rescue of capitalism by repressing conflict, organizing ideological dominance for capital, and co-opting the working class.

But this explanation of state behaviour is also generally rather static. How does the position of our economy at any particular point in time affect consensus? Does the behaviour of the state in maintaining order alter at different economic instances? Why do different capitalist countries pursue different political arrangements and why have these varied historically?

These types of questions are also pertinent to the problems facing developed countries today. The persistence of slow growth, unemployment and inflation has been blamed on the unfortunate and unusual bunching of a number of exogenous events. Oil and commodity price rises and changes in the international monetary system are not without economic influence, but any theoretical explanation that simply blames present economic difficulties on exogenous occurrences must be suspect. Indeed when a dynamic model of capitalism is studied along with the economic power distribution in society, further reasons for current economic problems present themselves. The recognition of the importance of power in a dynamic, economic analysis of capitalism does appear to add to our understanding of the present situation as I will now argue. I begin by setting up a simple model of capitalism.

Setting up the Dynamic Analysis

Let us continue with our earlier assumption that society is simply composed of two unified coalitions, workers and capitalists. The role of the state in this society is to maintain order and to reproduce it. Capitalists and workers are self-interested and as before they attempt to maximize their pay-offs, but this maximization now occurs over some foreseeable and finite time horizon. Pay-offs are not just a static concern. Because the society is capitalist we also assume that capitalists control the investment decision and this investment is undertaken from the resources available to the capitalists.

This capitalist control over investment is a crucial part of the dynamic model because it affects the strategy of workers. Workers can forgo consumption, and leave resources aside for investment, but they have no guarantee that the capitalists will actually invest these resources. If capitalists do not invest the worker's forgone consumption there is no future pay-off for the working class. Workers give up some resources in return for nothing in the future. On the other hand, if capitalists do invest all the consumption that workers forgo there is a future pay-off to the workers who can consume more later. Investment now means more consumption later but the investment decision is not controlled by the working class.

Within this model, or perhaps more correctly hovering outside it, is the state, whose aim is to perpetuate order. Conflict between capitalists and workers must be avoided, and if the economy is to continue in existence investment must occur at a rate that is at least sufficient to maintain the economic system. The economic order which the state is now seeking is not simply static but dynamic; order must be reproduced. If it is not, capitalism will be replaced by some other system and the capitalist democratic state will be replaced by another form of governance.

We now assume that the proportion of total resources that workers consume is v_1. This is partly determined by their power position and partly by their decision about how much of their consumption to forgo for investment. The proportion of resources devoted to investment is v_2. This proportion is decided by capitalists at the same time as workers are choosing their consumption. If capitalists do not invest (and $v_2 = 0$) we can assume that they use the resources available to them in a way which will benefit them but not the workers. Capitalists might for instance consume all their resources and not invest at all. The aim of both workers and capitalists is to maximize their resources over time. The only reason for undertaking investment is to add to resources later.

Thus we are positing a simple model of capitalism derived from Lancaster (1973). The capitalists have complete control over investment decisions and workers are sufficiently strong to insist upon some proportionate claim over resources which they then consume. Basically capitalists decide whether or not to invest the resources that they control. On the other hand workers decide whether to consume immediately the resources they control or alternatively whether to leave some of these resources aside for investment. The reason why workers might choose to leave some of the resources they control aside for investment purposes is because this investment causes growth and the possibility of more consumption later. We treat public and private goods as if they were the same and continue with the assumption that capitalists alone make the investment decisions.

The objective of the workers is to maximize their (undiscounted) consumption over some time horizon. This assumption, of no discounting, can be relaxed without any loss of generality though the details of the subsequent solution alter (Lancaster, 1973). There is just one sector in this caricatured economy which produces output using a particular investment technology. Output can either be consumed or invested, and the capital stock is assumed to have zero depreciation.

If v_1 is the proportion of total resources devoted to worker consumption we assume that this has an upper and lower limit. At the upper end, $v_1 = b$, and this variable b is determined by the power of the working class. This is the maximum proportionate claim over resources that the workers can make. If the workers are very powerful we might imagine that $b > \frac{1}{2}$ so that the workers can claim over 50 per cent of total resources. On the other hand if $b < \frac{1}{2}$ the workers are less powerful and they can claim a maximum of resources that is less than 50 per cent. The lowest claim that workers will make over resources is in proportion c and then $v_1 = c$. This lower limit is the minimum consumption level that workers are willing to put up with at any point and they agree to do so because this frees resources for investment. This lower limit is not determined by their power position but by their desire to forgo present consumption in return for investment and future consumption.

The proportion of the remainder of total resources that is devoted to investment is v_2. We assume that when there is maximum investment, $v_2 = 1$. In this case the future return on investment to the capitalists is sufficient for them to choose to invest as much as they can. On the other hand, when there is no investment $v_2 = 0$. Hence the lower limit for v_2 is zero and the upper limit is unity.

Now if,

v_1 is the proportion of resources devoted to
    workers' consumption, $c \leqslant v_1 \leqslant b$.
v_2 is the proportion of the remainder devoted to
    investment, $o \leqslant v_2 \leqslant 1$,

k is capital stock,
q in total output,
a is the fixed output/capital ratio,
we can proceed to write out the model algebraically. The capitalist economy is depicted by the following equations:

Total output q_t $= ak_t$ (1)
Workers' consumption C_w $= ak_t v_{1t}, \ c \leqslant v_{1t} \leqslant b$ (2)
Capitalists' consumption C_c $= ak_t (1 - v_{1t})(1 - v_{2t})$ (3)
Investment   I $= ak_t (1 - v_{1t})v_{2t}, \ o \leqslant v_{2t} \leqslant 1$.   (4)

These equations are quite straightforward. The first relates the level of output to the existing capital stock. The second equation says that workers consume v_{1t} of this output and this proportion of consumption can vary between b and c. The upper limit b is determined by the power of the workforce, and the lower limit, c, by their minimal consumption

164

requirements. The rest of the output is either consumed or invested by capitalists. Equation (3) shows their consumption and equation (4) shows their investment. The proportion of resources invested, v_{2t}, can vary between zero and unity. If v_{2t} is zero there is no investment and the capital stock remains unchanged. If at the other extreme v_{2t} is unity all resources available to the capitalists are invested. They choose to consume nothing and invest everything for the future.

This is the simple structure of the economy and to this we now add the behavioural elements. The objective for the workers is to maximize their consumption over some time horizon. We let this time horizon be from o to T and the workers' aim is then to maximize J_1 where,

$$J_1 = \int_o^T ak_t (1 - v_{1t}) \, dt. \tag{5}$$

To achieve this objective the workers choose v_{1t} which is limited by their power position and the consideration that investment can add to their later consumption. But if they consume less now, thus leaving more resources available for investment, they can consume more later if, and only if, the capitalists undertake this investment.

The objective of the capitalists is also to maximize their consumption over the same time horizon, o to T. From equation (3) we can see that this will amount to maximizing J_2 where,

$$J_2 = \int_o^T ak_t (1 - v_{1t}) (1 - v_{2t}) \tag{6}$$

The capitalists choose v_{2t}, the proportion of resources they invest in each time period, to maximize their consumption. However, like the workers, they also know that if they invest now rather than consume, they will have more to consume later.

We thus have what is intuitively a fairly simple problem. The workers must choose v_{1t}, the proportion of resources they consume at each point in time, so as to maximize their consumption (equation 5). On the other hand the capitalist must choose how much of their available resources to invest, v_{2t}, over time, so as to maximize their consumption (equation 6).

The solution to this joint problem gives the path of v_{1t} and v_{2t} over time. It tells us what proportion of resources go to consumption and investment at each point in time, between o and T. What is of interest about this solution is that it implies that at certain junctures the workers will be willing to forgo consumption and enhance investment. There are periods when agreement is perfectly rational under the terms of this model and workers do not exercise all the power at their command. However there are other periods where workers will exercise their power and demand to consume all the resources they can get. The solution also depends on the power position of the workers, and it suggests when the maintenance of order by the state may be both easy and difficult. In this dynamic context the maintenance of order does not simply depend upon the power distribution in society, as in the static model. It is also influenced by the position of the economy.

Solving the Dynamic Problem

The solution which has been posed of the dynamic model of capitalism demands some mathematical expertise, and those readers who would prefer to take the results on trust should simply skim this section and carry on to the next subheading. There the results are summarized in a way that is not mathematically difficult. For those who are willing to be more mathematically intrepid the rest of this part will work through the solution.

Formally the solution is two separate maximizing problems, one for workers and the other for capitalists. Each problem is in a form that allows Pontryagin's maximum principle to be applied and I begin with the workers. We drop time subscripts for ease of exposition. Their problem is to choose v_1 so as to maximize,

$$J_1 = \int_0^T ak_t v_1 \, dt$$

subject to $\dot{k} = ak(1 - v_1) v_2$

$$c \leqslant v_1 \leqslant b$$

and some anticipated choice of v_2 by the capitalists. The workers' Hamiltonian is,

$$H_1 = akv_1 + y_1 ak(1 - v_1) v_2 \tag{7}$$

where y_1 is the costate variable associated with k, the capital stock. This must satisfy,

$$y_1 = -\partial H1/\partial k = -[v_1 + y_1(1 - v_1) v_2] a \tag{8}$$

Here y_1 represents the value *to workers* of a marginal increase in investment. Since workers do not look beyond some time horizon T the marginal value of investment at this point T is zero, so $y_1(T) = 0$. From the maximum principle, the optimal path for v_1, given some anticipated v_2, is

$$v_1 = c \qquad \text{whenever } y_1 v_2 > 1$$

and $\quad v_1 = b \qquad \text{whenever } y_1 v_2 < 1$

Note that v_1, the workers choice of the proportion of resources to consume, depends on y_1, the value of investment *to workers* and v_2, the anticipated proportion of resources that will be invested.

For the capitalists the problem is the choice v_2, the proportion of resources to invest for some anticipated v_1. Thus they maximize,

$$J_2 = \int_0^T ak_t(1 - v_1)(1 - v_2) \, dt$$

166

subject to $\quad \dot{k} = ak(1 - v_1)\, v_2$

$$0 \leqslant v_2 \leqslant 1$$

and the anticipated choice of v_1. The capitalists' Hamiltonian is,

$$H_2 = ak(1 - v_1)(1 - v_2) + y_2\, ak(1 - v_1)\, v_2 \tag{9}$$

The costate variable y_2 is different from that in the workers' problem because it represents the marginal value of investment *to capitalists* rather than to the workers. Following similar reasoning to before,

$$y_2 = -\partial H_2/\partial k = -\{1 + (y_2 - 1)\, v_2\}(1 - v_1)\, a \tag{10}$$

Since the capitalists also do not look beyond some time horizon T, $y_2(T) = 0$ and the capitalists' Hamiltonian is linear in v_2 with coefficient $ak\,(1 - v_1)\,(y_2 - 1)$. Now $(1 - v_1)$ is always positive so the capitalist solution is,

$$v_2 = o \text{ when } y_2 < 1$$
$$v_2 = 1 \text{ when } y_2 > 1$$

Combining the two solutions we can see that there are four potential combinations of v_1 and v_2 to consider. These are,

I $\quad v_1 = c, v_2 = 0$ when $y_1 v_2 > 1,\ y_2 < 1$

II $\quad v_1 = b, v_2 = 0$ when $y_1 v_2 < 1,\ y_2 < 1$

III $\quad v_1 = c, v_2 = 1$ when $y_1\, v_2 > 1,\ y_2 > 1$

IV $\quad v_1 = b, v_2 = 1$ when $y_1 v_2 < 1,\ y_2 > 1$

Now combination I can never be possible since if $v_2 = 0$, $y_1 v_2 > 1$ is incompatible. This leaves three combinations to consider and in problems of this type it is usual to begin at the end. There is an end boundary condition $y_2(T) = 0$ and y_2, the return on investment to capitalists, must be a continuous function of time. Thus at the end we must have $y_2 < 1$ and also for some period, say t^* to T, before the end. In this final phase of the capitalist dynamic we therefore must have combination II ($v_1 = b$, $v_2 = 0$) because $y_2 < 1$ in this phase. Furthermore we know that this final phase, which begins at t^*, must begin at the point where $y_2 = 1$ and since y_1 and y_2 are both declining linearly during the final phase we can compute t^* as,

$$t^* = T - \frac{1}{a(1 - b)} \tag{11}$$

Hence provided

$$T > \frac{1}{a(1 - b)}$$

the capitalist system enters its final dynamic phase at t^*. After this point in time the return on investment to capitalists is not sufficient to induce them to invest at all and from t* to T all resources are consumed by both the workers and the capitalists. The workers take proportion b of these resources, from t* to T, and the capitalists consume the remainder $(1-b)$. This maximum proportionate amount that the workers can consume is b and in this problem b is entirely determined by workers' strength or their effective claim over resources.

Now the only way in which this final phase is interesting is that in a sense it denotes the death of the capitalist dynamic based on that particular investment technology. After t*, the 'crisis point', there is no additional investment and resources cease to grow. Between t* and the end point T there is no growth and no investment and resources are simply consumed. Hence the final phase of this capitalist dynamic is reached at a crisis point t* where additional accumulation ceases. After t* the system theoretically continues to the end point T but over this final period the economy ceases to grow and resources are simply consumed.

The period prior to t* can now be examined and it is clearly going to be either combination III or combination IV. In both these combinations y_2, the marginal value of investment to capitalists, is greater than unity and there will be investment. However in combination III the workers choose to consume their minimal proportion of resources, c, and in combination IV they choose to consume the maximum proportion of resources they can get, b. Since in both combinations III and IV we have $v_2 = 1$ we must have $y_1 > 1$ in combination III and $y_1 < 1$ in combination IV.

This means that if the return on investment to workers, y_1, is greater than unity, they will choose their minimal consumption plan, c, and leave some resources aside for investment. When $y_1 > 1$ it is worthwhile for workers to put resources aside for investment so they can consume more later (combination III). On the other hand if $y_1 < 1$ the return on investment *to workers* is not sufficient to induce them to forgo any consumption now and they will take b, the maximum of resources they can get. In this case, combination IV, there is no rational reason for them to leave resources aside for investment since they will get insufficient return on their forgone consumption.

Returning to the final phase, between t* and T, note that $y_1(T) = 0$ and that y_1 declines linearly at a rate of ab during this period. At t* the value of y_1 must therefore be

$$y_1(t^*) = ab(T-t^*) = b/(1-b) \tag{12}$$

from equation (11). Hence if $b > \frac{1}{2}$, so that workers are sufficiently strong to claim over 50 per cent of resources, the phase before the final phase must be combination III. Here $y_1 = b/(1-b >1)$ and workers choose c, their minimal plan. The reason they do this is because they can consume proportionately more later when investment ceases. The return to workers on investment is high enough to warrant them setting aside resources for capitalist investment and subsequent growth.

On the other hand if $b < \frac{1}{2}$ so that workers can claim only less than 50 per cent of resources the combination before the final phase is combination IV. In this phase $y_1 = \dfrac{b}{1-b} < 1$ and workers have no inducement to set aside resources for investment. The return on investment to workers is not sufficient for them to restrain their immediate consumption plans and they consume all they can get. When $b < \frac{1}{2}$ there is also a stage before combination IV and this stage is combination III. Thus when the workers are less powerful, so that $b < \frac{1}{2}$, there are three regimes. We begin with combination III, switch to combination IV, and then at t^* switch to combination II. Working through this case, when $b < \frac{1}{2}$, is more complicated though the method is similar and I will ease the tedium by simply spelling out the result.

Summarizing the Results

In solving the problem outlined earlier we were seeking the values of v_1, the proportion of resources that workers chose to consume over time, and v_2, the proportion of resources that capitalists chose to invest over time. Both groups were attempting to maximize their consumption or their claims on resources over some finite time horizon, and workers would vary their consumption between proportion c and b. The upper limit, b, of consumption was set by their power and the lower limit by their minimal consumption requirement. The capitalists on the other hand could choose to invest v_1 of their resources and v_1 could vary between unity and zero.

Now there are in fact two solutions to this problem and both depend on the value of b, the power of workers. When $b > \frac{1}{2}$ so that the workers are powerful enough to claim over 50 per cent of resources, the path of total consumption in the capitalist economy is given in Figure 10·1.

In the first phase of dynamic capitalism in this figure the workers consume the lower limit of their consumption proportion. They agree to forgo consumption in the knowledge that the extra investment will add to their consumption in the future. Over this phase capitalists are investing all their available resources, and consumption is growing as investment occurs and adds to growth. During this stage workers' consumption goes up each time period at a rate of cak_1; the capital stock grows exponentially at a rate of $a(1 - c)$ and output increases at a similar rate. By the time we reach t^* output has grown to

$$q(t^*) = a\bar{q}\ e^{\,a(1-c)t^*}$$

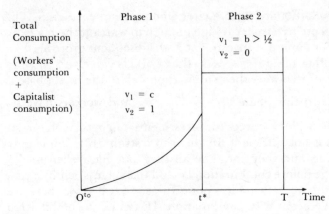

Figure 10·1: The Path of Total Consumption with Powerful Workers, b> ½

where $\bar{q}$ is the output existing at time, t_o, the beginning of the period. This phase is one where the return on investment to workers is sufficient to induce lower current consumption; and the return on investment to capitalists is sufficient to induce a total investment commitment.

In the final phase of the solution, phase 2, there is no investment. Workers consume the maximum of resources they can gain (b>½) and capitalists consume the remainder. Consumption by either group during this phase does not increase and at each point in time they consume the same stationary amount of output. Because the capital stock does not depreciate, by assumption, there will be output to consume but there is no growth. Investment has stagnated completely because the return on it to capitalists is not sufficient to warrant further investment.

Now what is of special interest about this solution is that it implies co-operation from the workers in the first phase. The workers are powerful to the extent that they could claim over half the resources for immediate consumption but they do not do so because they are assured of further consumption gains later. Thus in this model a very powerful working class does not necessarily imply conflict. In their own self-interest, workers are co-operative so long as their investment is forthcoming. While this investment occurs worker consumption goes up each year and the workers become better off.

In the final phase however, when investment halts, workers exercise their power to the extent of claiming over 50 per cent of resources for consumption. There will be conflict at this stage if they do not get their warranted share of resources but if they do so their earlier abstinence will be rewarded and conflict averted.

The second solution reached was one where the working class was less powerful. The maximum of resources that the workers could

170

claim, b, depended on their power but this claim amounted to less than 50 per cent of resources (b < ½). In the case of this less powerful working class the solution was that shown in Figure 10·2.

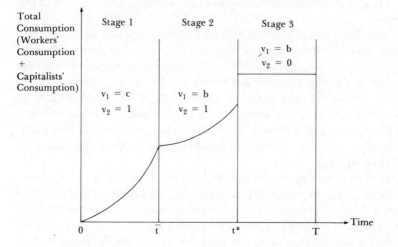

Figure 10·2: The Path of Consumption With Less Powerful Workers, b < ½

This solution where the workers are less powerful has three stages. In stage 1 the weaker working class decide to forgo consumption in the expectation of higher consumption levels in the future. Investment is forthcoming and at some later point in time the workers expect to consume a proportion b of the output. However in stage 2, where investment is still forthcoming, the workers switch to their maximum consumption level. The expected rate of return on investment to workers is not sufficient for them voluntarily to forgo consumption and they take all the resources they can get. However this proportion is less than 50 per cent of total resources (b < ½). The final third stage is similar to the final stage discussed earlier, when workers are powerful. Here new investment ceases and both workers and capitalists consume all the output with workers taking the maximum they can command.

Though the solution to the simple dynamic model we posed is rather technical and a terribly simplified caricature of capitalism, it does appear to lead to several implications that are intuitively reasonable. Furthermore it provides some further insights into the connections between power, consensus and economic performance which we discussed less formally in Chapters 3 and 4. The simple dynamic problem here involves a basic conflict between two groups in society over the distribution of resources. It is clearly in each group's self interest to try and maximize the share of resources over which it has control. The lower the

171

workers' command over resources (b) the higher is the share available to capitalists to either invest or consume. This basic conflict is ever present and as strategies we would always expect to see each group attempting to increase its power and command over resources at the expense of the other group.

But this basic conflict does not imply that workers will not sometimes appear to be quiescent. When the resources that they command are not consumed, but are available and actually are invested the workers will not press for their maximum consumption share. Investment by capitalists ultimately means future consumption for workers, and so long as this future return is adequate and forthcoming the workers will be quiescent in forgoing their maximum consumption claim. It is then, and only then, in their interests to 'co-operate' with the capitalists who control investment.

It is clear in this model that this rational quiescence is not however always going to occur. It depends quite directly on the actual occurrence of new investment and the expected gains to the workers of this investment. Once new investment halts so too does workers' quiescence. There is no longer any point in this group maintaining its low consumption plans, because there is no future gain in doing so. This implies that conflict in society over the distribution of resources is likely to be muted and even non-existent when investment is at high levels. On the other hand once investment stagnates workers will press for their maximum claim over resources and conflict is likely to be more evident.

The point at which workers cease being co-operative in this model, in the sense of forgoing consumption to allow more investment, depends on both the power of the workforce and their expected return on this investment. Perhaps surprisingly, a strong working class, who have command over *more* than 50 per cent of resources ($b > \frac{1}{2}$), are quiescent for a longer period of time than a weaker working class, who have command of *less* than 50 per cent of resources (see Figures 10·1 and 10·2 again). The reason for this initially startling result is that a strong working class can claim a higher percentage of consumption once new investment halts and thus the return to them on investment is higher than is the case for a weaker group. Hence it is no paradox that a strong working class may at times be less militant than a weaker one. With strength, more gains can be claimed in the future, and there is thus a rational reason to forgo current claims for a time in return for substantial future returns. Quiescence is a rational strategy.

If there is any credibility in the conclusion drawn so far we would at least expect to observe relatively high militancy by workers in countries where investment is low. In this instance, whether the working class is strong or weak, there is no rational reason to moderate workers' claims over resources since the future returns on doing so are low. We would also expect that in countries where the working class is strong and investment is high that worker militancy is rather muted. Workers are expecting to gain from this investment and do not press their current claims over resources. These hypotheses can be examined by looking at Table 10·1 below.

The countries are arranged according to the presence or otherwise of corporatist arrangements. As we have suggested in Chapters 3 and 4, corporatism, as presently practised and defined, is consensual, so that several groups in society work together according to voluntary arrangements between peak interest groups, which typically include three groups: workers, employers and the state. Thus the countries at the top of the Table 10·1 are in this sense more consensual and less conflict-ridden than those at the bottom, in terms of their institutional arrangements around economic policy decisions.

If we examine the strike activity data in Table 10.1 and the proportion of resources invested, it is notable that countries where strike activity is high are also countries where the proportion of resources invested is relatively low. The USA, the UK and Italy all invested less than 21 per cent of the GDP and had high strike militancy records. On the other hand Austria, Norway, Japan and Switzerland all devoted over 26 per cent of their GDP to investment and recorded low strike activity. It is remarkable more generally that the strong and medium corporatist countries had lower strike activity than the weak corporatist countries and higher investment levels out of GDP. Also some of the countries recording low strike activity and high investment ratios were nations where the working class is strong. It is both highly mobilized and in stable political control as we discussed in Chapter 3. Austria and Norway clearly fit this category. Only Finland and Australia had relatively good investment figures and relatively high strike activity. Thus while this data is not conclusive evidence in support of the conclusions reached it does imply that the conclusions are at least credible and worth further attention.

Additional support is also provided by noting the ratio between strike activity and the change in money earnings. The correlation between strike activity and the change in average earnings is ·80 and this suggests that militancy has been used to establish claims over resources. Furthermore in Italy, Canada, the United States, Ireland, Australia and the UK, where either investment has been relatively low (USA, UK) or the working class is less powerful (Italy, Canada, USA, Ireland, and Australia), the exercise of militancy is most evident. As can be seen in Figure 10·3 those countries where militancy has been low are by no means countries where the working class is weak. In Sweden, Norway,

173

Table 10.1: *Corporatist Arrangements, Strike Activity and Investment as a percentage of GDP, 1960–80*

	Strike activity[a] (working days lost)	Investment as % of GDP
Strong corporatism		
Austria	5·2	26·5
Norway	15·8	29·6
Sweden	26·1	22·3
Japan	69·1	32·7
Switzerland	0·9	26·4
Medium corporatism		
Germany	11·6	23·9
Denmark	47·2	23·4
Netherlands	15·9	23·8
Belgium	144·5	22·1
Finland	284·1	26·2
Weak corporatism		
France	150·9	22·8
Australia	394·2	24·8
Italy	845·8	20·9
Ireland	465·4	22·4
UK	329·3	18·3
Canada	702·2	22·2
USA	400·4	17·8

[a] Comparative data on strike activity is difficult to interpret precisely because of different national customs in recording strikes. The figures here are from Cameron (1983) and are the working days lost in industrial disputes for 1000 in the total labour force.

Denmark, Germany, Austria and the Netherlands there has been little militancy despite the power of the working class.

The Implications for Consensus and Conflict and State Behaviour

The argument that when new investment is occurring, there is likely to be labour quiescence seems intuitively reasonable. Claims are moderated in return for future gains. More evidence of course needs to be carefully examined before we can feel confident about this hypothesis, but at least on the basis of the data we briefly examined there does seem to be some credibility in the idea. Furthermore this idea also adds to the arguments I presented less formally in Chapters 3 and 4.

In those earlier chapters we noted that wage moderation in the developed countries was associated with consensual arrangements. In particular in nations where corporatist arrangements were practised, the level of wage inflation was moderate and this was accompanied by low price inflation and other economic benefits. This economic

Figure 10.3: The Relation between Strike Activity and Increases in Earnings, 1965–81

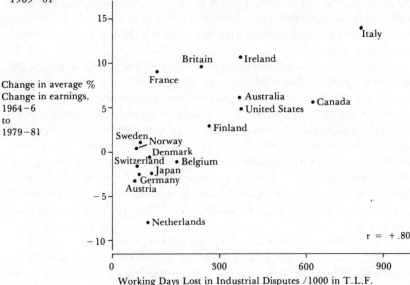

Change in average %
Change in earnings,
1964–6
to
1979–81

Working Days Lost in Industrial Disputes /1000 in T.L.F.

consensus and co-operation was not present in all countries and where it was lacking there was much higher wage and price inflation.

In the sociology and politics literature, as well as in public choice theories, the establishment of corporatism is usually linked to institutional factors. Where the working class has historically developed as an encompassing group that is not fragmented, it is capable of dealing with both business leaders and the state, and the benefits from this interest mediation flow to all the members of the encompassing group. Because the group is encompassing it acts for everyone in the labour force and this encourages outcomes that are in line with a broader social interest. On the other hand, where labour is fragmented in its organizations there is little possibility of high level tri-partite interest mediation, and even if there is each fragment would simply pursue its own self-interest. The outcome would not be in the wider social interest.

These institutional reasons for the success of corporatism in some nations do appear compelling, but in the light of the simple dynamic model here we can now also stress the importance of economic factors. It is obvious in this dynamic economic model that maximum claims over resources by the workers will be pressed when new investment stagnates and when the return on investment does not warrant labour moderation. At this point we would expect corporatist arrangements, and any other type of consensus, to come under stress. For economic reasons there is no sense in the workers maintaining co-operation

175

any longer, and they will in all likelihood become more militant and press their maximum claims. Thus it is no surprise to find that the consensual interest mediation arrangements that prevailed when the economy was performing successfully begin to break down when investment and growth falter.

This amounts to little more than saying that when the size of the cake stops growing the conflict over the size of slices becomes more intense. When there is growth and output is increasing the workers decide to moderate their claims. Because of growth they do get more each year; proportion c remains the same but the size of the cake is going up. But once investment and growth stops the conflict heightens considerably. Workers increase their share of consumption (to b) and moderation on the part of workers ceases. Hence I would suggest that corporatism is not a particularly stable arrangement. It fails once investment and growth stagnate and it does so for quite rational economic reasons.

From the point of view of a state that is attempting to maintain order, and sustain it, this clearly presents a problem. Order should be forthcoming when there is capitalist investment and growth and the state need do no more than oversee a rather stable-looking regime. But once investment and growth cease, the state is going to have more difficulty in maintaining order. Furthermore these difficulties for the state are acute when it tries to sustain this order continually.

In this context it is instructive to consider the dynamic model at the point where new investment ceases. The reason why capitalists cease new investment in this model is because the rate of return on that particular investment technology has fallen to a point where, for the capitalists, it is no longer worthwhile investing. New additions to the capital stock cease, not because of worker's claims over resources, but because the return on investment has fallen over time to a non-viable level. If the economic capitalist order is to be sustained, what would necessarily happen at this stage (stage 3, in Figure 14.1 and stage 3 in Figure 14.2) would be restructuring. Capitalists would search for a new investment technology that would give them a suitable return on their investment. If this does not occur there will be no new investment and eventually the stagnant economy will decay and the prevailing economic order with it.

Hence if the economic order is to be sustained we would expect (at some point after t*) a shift in the capitalist dynamic back to its beginning phase. A new investment technology would imply a different rate of return on investment to both workers and capitalists and with restructuring the new returns on investment would be greater than before. The system would begin its dynamic again with a different technology.

176

It is also clear that restructuring is likely to pose several problems. The resources for the new investment technology are unlikely to be sought until the 'crisis point' is reached; before this time the existing investment technology is yielding adequate returns. However, after the crisis point workers will be expecting to get their maximum claim on resources and this will limit the resources available for new investment. Other things being equal it is obvious that restructuring will be easier the lower the strength of the working class and the lower their claim over resources.

The conflict and possible strategies of both workers and capitalists in the general vicinity of the crisis point, where new investment stops, are of interest. Just before this crisis point the return on investment to capitalists has almost fallen to the point where accumulation in the existing investment technology ceases. The economy is approaching stagnation. At the crisis point and beyond there is total stagnation: no new investment and no growth. As a rough approximation for argument's sake, we might consider that the developed countries have been somewhere close to this crisis point for some time. Some nations may not have stagnated completely but their investment and growth rates will be faltering; other nations may be at or beyond the crisis point where the economy is stagnant.

Now in all cases it is clearly in the best interests of capitalists in this model, if they wish to sustain capitalism, to try and keep working-class strength (b) as low as possible. At the same time it is always in workers' best interests, if they wish to maximize their consumption, to increase their strength. This conflict is basic in this simple world and implies strategies on the part of each group to achieve these conflicting ends.

However in this simple caricature other less obvious conflicts and potential strategies are apparent. First in countries where the workers are strong, so that $b > \frac{1}{2}$, and we are approaching stagnation, we would expect to see capitalists attempting to persuade workers that the return on investment *to workers* is high. If this capitalist strategy is successful workers will agree to set aside resources for investment. However there are problems attached to this strategy, for the capitalists, since once stagnation occurs the workers will demand their returns on past abstinence. This will make capitalist restructuring plans more difficult as capitalist command over resources in stagnation will be constrained. At this point we might expect capitalists to point out the necessity of restructuring and to argue that if the workers assist, by freeing resources for investment, the workers will ultimately gain returns from this investment. This amounts to offering the workers an indefinitely postponed splurge, since if the workers continually agree to minimal consumption they will never see the rewards on it. Basically

177

restructuring will be more difficult and more conflict-ridden where workers are strong.

Nevertheless around the point of stagnation we would expect to observe considerable friendly persuasive dialogue on the part of capitalists with the workers if and only if the working class is strong. If the working class is not so strong ($b < \frac{1}{2}$) they will be aiming for maximum consumption plans and will be less amenable to friendly discourse about the gains on investment to workers as a group. They are relatively so weak that they never expect to reap these gains, so friendly dialogue will get nowhere. We might therefore argue that it is no surprise that liberal corporatism, with the state acting as a mediator between capitalists and workers, and the state itself seeking to sustain the system, should only arise in countries where the workers are strong and where they perceive high returns on invesment. If the workers are not strong there is no point in trying to get an agreement to curtail worker consumption since the workers would not agree to it. Furthermore the need for this type of agreement, to curtail consumption, is more pressing as stagnation is approached. Co-operation may not just be a feature when workers' strength is high and their perceived returns on investment are high; it is more necessary as stagnation occurs.

It is also of interest to consider the situation just beyond the stagnation point, t^*. It can be shown (see Lancaster 1973) that for some time period beyond this point the return on investment to workers ($y_1 > 1$) is sufficient for them to curtail their consumption if they are strong ($b > \frac{1}{2}$). However capitalists have stopped investment because the return on investment to capitalists is insufficient ($y_2 < 1$), and as a consequence the workers consume maximally. There is no new investment. If a state decided at this juncture to maximize social welfare, defined as maximizing total consumption, investment would continue until the workers' return on investment had fallen to $y_1 < 1$. This happens at some point beyond t^*, and before T. Thus once the economy has got to t^*, workers in a social welfare state would continue to leave resources aside for investment if such investment would occur. Capitalists will not carry it out however ($y_2 < 1$), and if this social welfare solution is to hold one solution would be for the state to do the investment. The social value of investment is above the capitalists' value of investment immediately beyond t^* so there is a potential consensus here between workers and the state.

There are shades of this behaviour in the Swedish Meidner plan where investment is more socialized and more controlled by the workers. The value to workers of investment is above the value of investment to capitalists and investment continues beyond t^*. Such a strategy shifts the point of economic stagnation, and no new investment, further into

178

the future, but it is hardly a capitalist solution and would obviously be opposed by the capitalists. They lose control over the investment decisions or at least some part of investment decisions. Also this socialization of investment, while perfectly rational, only delays the day when restructuring becomes necessary. At some point, beyond t* but before T, the social value of investment will fall so far that investment ceases. However on the basis of this argument we might expect the pressure for restructuring to be more immediately pressing in those countries where the state does little investment and where investment is less socialized.

Summary

Hence in summary I have suggested that when capitalist economies are nearing stagnation or have reached this crisis point the basic conflict of capitalism is present, as ever. Workers wish to maximize their share of resources and capitalists wish to maximize their share. However in countries where workers are strong there may be a voluntary abstinence in workers' consumption, but this is dependent upon perceived future gains from this sacrifice. In countries where workers have received previous returns from investment we might expect the conflict between workers and capitalists to be less severe even if workers are strong. Restructuring is likely to be carried out with most ease in countries where the working class is weak, *ceteris paribus*, and where previous returns on investment to workers have been high, *ceteris paribus*. These nations will have experienced relatively better past economic growth and be in a better relative income position to restructure. Nations where the working class is weak will find conflict severe. though the worst conflict, and most difficulty in restructuring, will occur in nations where the working class is strong and previous returns on investment have been weak.

These suggestions, derived from the simple dynamic model of capitalism, also provide several insights into the behaviour of the developed economies that we discussed in Chapters 3 and 4. The presence of consensual interest intermediation arrangements can be explained by both institutional and economic determinants. But when we add the economic factors discussed in this chapter it is clear that consensual arrangements may not be stable since they depend on expected future gains for workers. When these cease, conflict will be heightened and the necessity to restructure will pose considerable difficulties for both the state and the capitalists.

If the state is social democratic and the working class is strong, as in Sweden in 1983, we predict a move towards the increased socialization

179

of investment. This democratic road to socialism will of course be opposed by capitalists who will gradually lose their control over investment. It is also not an easy route for the state, since it must replace the old investment technology with a new one. This means acquiring the resources to do so and having the expertise to restructure adequately. But if the working class is both highly mobilized and in political control of the state this option is well within the rationale of this model.

On the other hand the state, in its attempt to maintain and reproduce order once growth has halted, could pursue policies that would aid capitalist restructuring and moves to a new investment technology. Subsidies to industry and moves to limit the claim of workers over resources are both possibilities within this scenario. However this route is more difficult for countries where the working class is strong and where it is pursuing its maximum claim over resources. This suggests that the developed countries which will most successfully cope with the present stagnation and subsequent restructuring will be those where, *ceteris paribus*, the working class is weak. Ireland, Canada, the US and possibly Japan are countries where the working class is weaker than elsewhere. But as we argued in Chapter 3, even these countries now face a stronger working class than has historically been the case. The route out of our present economic difficulties will not be as easy as it has been in the past because the power resources of the workers must now be accommodated.

This leads me to suggest that the economic problems of the 1970s may be difficult to solve and may be very persistent because of the gradual increase this century in the power of workers. While investment and growth was forthcoming, this increase in power was of little economic consequence because workers were moderate in their claims. But now that growth has slackened the consequences of this increase in power on economic outcomes are profound. The persistence of slow growth and slack investment is not principally the result of incorrect economic policies or exogenous events like commodity price rises. The economic problems persist because the developed countries have not yet found a way to increase investment and maintain order simultaneously. In the event order has so far been maintained but investment is still slack, and this is directly related to the powerful and justified claim that workers are now making over resources.

11 The Present Dilemmas of Economic Management

> The last word on how we may live or die
>   Rests today with such quiet
> Men, working too hard in rooms that are too big,
>   Reducing to figures
> What is the matter, what is to be done.
>
> Auden, 'The Managers'

In view of the preceding arguments we are now in a position to examine economic management in developed countries and the broad dilemmas that may currently confront it. My remarks are confined to domestic issues, and the implications of these issues for both the economic theory of policy and the implementation of policy will be discussed. My general conclusions are not optimistic. The particular conjuncture of political and economic circumstances that are now facing the developed democracies are historically new and unique; and the problems they pose for state economic management are particularly challenging. A resolution of these problems is required in order to get a better economic performance than that achieved throughout the dismal 1970s and early 1980s. While we may be in a position to identify these problems we are not necessarily in a position that will lead to their resolution. On this basis it appears that relatively slow growth, low investment, high unemployment and a general underlying tendency towards inflation may well be with us for the immediately foreseeable future.

The Implications of Changes in the Distribution of Power

In Chapter 3 it was argued that the power resources of the workforce in all developed countries had increased gradually and dramatically over this century. This increase in power resources has taken two identified routes. On the one hand the workforce in all developed countries has become more mobilized, in the sense of increasing its unionization. Before World

War I only about 10 per cent of the workforce was unionized in most Western countries. Now, only in Japan, Switzerland, Italy and France is union membership less than 30 per cent of the non-agricultural workforce, and even in those nations the level of unionization is significant.

The other identified shift in the power resources of the workforce was in the extent of their political influence. Universal suffrage has now been introduced in all developed countries and the left share of the vote has gone up rather steadily in all countries except the United States. This increasing left share of the vote has been accompanied by an increased presence of left cabinet representatives, and in many nations the governing political party has frequently identified itself with the interests of the workforce.

Now, neither of these power resource developments have led to the peaceful demise of capitalism as a social and economic system. But they have had a profound influence on the developed economies. The increase in unionization and collective organization by the workforce does appear to be related to the downward stickiness in money wage movements. Money wages no longer automatically fall during economic contractions, and this, along with increased industrial concentration, implies that price movements are also sticky in a downwards direction. The workforce is now sufficiently strong to stop money wages falling if it so desires.

It also seems clear that where political influence had increased this power shift has been accompanied by an increasing size in the public sector. Countries where the left share of the vote has been high and where left representation in government has been stable have developed relatively large public expenditures which are frequently directing benefits towards the working class. Only in countries where the workforce has had little political influence has government expenditure out of GDP been relatively moderate.

These changes in power resources, and their economic consequences, have important implications for both the economic theory of policy and the practice of that policy. On the economic theory front, it must now be recognized that the society we are analyzing has experienced a change in its power distribution. The capitalist economy we are now seeking to understand is not anything like that in the last century, and this change implies that our economic models must also change. Models that implicitly assumed that power was either diffuse in society or concentrated in the hands of an elite few are no longer applicable to the modern world.

This argument is particularly damaging to what we referred to in Chapter 2 as neoclassical macroeconomic theory. Policies that are derived from this particular theoretical position suggest that inflation should be attacked by restrictive fiscal and monetary policies and unemployment should be attacked by lowering real wages. However if the money supply is severely constrained and fiscal expenditure is reduced, it is not necessarily the case that either real wages or prices will fall. One other possibility is that output and employment will be reduced, and this possibility will occur when real wages and prices do not fall in response to the restrictive policy (Gordon, 1981). The managed recession will most certainly have an economic effect, but if the workforce is sufficiently strong to stop real wages falling then the outcome of this restrictive policy will be higher unemployment, lower output, increased bankruptcies and stagnant investment. And this set of undesirable outcomes will be accompanied by virtually no fall in real wages or prices. Hence if the neoclassical model is applied and pursued in a society where the workforce is sufficiently strong to maintain real wages at the prevailing rate, the end result will be catastrophic and the pursuit of neoclassical policy in these circumstances is irresponsible.

Proponents of this theory might suggest that it would eventually achieve its desired objectives because increased unemployment would so weaken the workforce that they would eventually allow real wages to fall. But the problem with this solution is that it would in reality take a long time to happen, and its social cost is enormous, both in terms of unemployed people and corporate bankruptcies. In view of the present strength of the workforce in all developed countries, this policy must rationally be rated as a most undesirable option. It flows from a model that assumes that power is spread diffusely in society, and this assumption is no longer tenable.

In addition an attempt to apply this neoclassical policy in present systems is bound to eventually cause problems of governance. The extent to which a democratic society can put up with ever-increasing unemployment and corporate bankruptcies is not without limit. At some point the social order is likely to be challenged, and/or the government pursuing this particular policy will be replaced by an alternative one. In this respect it is notable that the restrictive policies of the Conservative government in Britain since 1979 have not been accompanied by falls in real wages but by ever-increasing unemployment and stagnant growth and investment. This government is also facing considerable opposition, both within its own Cabinet and without, to further restrictive policies, and its pursuit of this policy option is clearly being politically constrained.

The changes in power that are evident in modern society also have implications for neo-Keynesian theories of policy, though these implications are more complex. The increase in the power of the workforce appears to rule neoclassical theory completely out of rational consideration, but with neo-Keynesian theory the consequences of this change in power can be accommodated to a limited extent. As discussed in Chapter 2, Keynesian theory suggests that unemployment should be tackled by expansionary fiscal and monetary policy and inflation should be controlled through incomes policies. If incomes policies are unsuccessful and cannot be practically implemented, the effect of economic expansion will simply be runaway inflation. Hence in this model of economic policy the route to success depends intimately on whether or not an incomes policy can be successfully mounted. If it cannot be, then there is no Keynesian solution to the dual problems of inflation and unemployment.

Now the very reason we need an incomes policy to restrain money wages and prices is because of the increased strength of the workforce, and in recognizing this the Keynesians are at least one step ahead of their neoclassical colleagues. But where Keynesian theorists appear to have been remiss is in the lack of attention they have paid to the practice and potential stability of incomes polices when the workforce is powerful in a capitalist system. These latter issues have generally been derided as being 'not economic' concerns and economists have rarely focussed on them. The fact that these issues have been studied by sociologists and political theorists has encouraged many economists to avoid them like the plague. The queen of the social sciences must not, apparently, be tainted by social and political matters that are viewed as being outside the more rigorous affairs of economic theory. This amounts to no more than academic snobbery and is a dereliction of duty that in the end makes Keynesian analysis far less helpful than it ought to be.

If we examine the political and sociological studies of economic policy management, as we did in Chapter 4, several facts emerge about the conduct of economic policy that are important in this context. The relative severity of unemployment and inflation in the developed countries throughout the 1970s appeared to be closely related to political arrangements. In nations where liberal corporatism had been practised, the level of unemployment and the rates of wage and price inflation were relatively moderate. On the other hand in countries where no successful attempt had been made at introducing such political arrangements, the extent of unemployment and inflation was severe. The lack of success in dealing with unemployment and inflation has been noted in Italy, Ireland, the United States, Canada, and Britain. On the other hand Japan, Austria, Germany, Switzerland, Norway and Sweden have been more fortunate in coping with both unemployment and inflation.

In this latter corporatist group of countries the implementation of an incomes policy was voluntary and consensual and the institutional reasons for this successful implementation of an incomes policy are important to recognize. In nations where political arrangements appear adequate to cope, the workforce is not necessarily weak; and indeed in Austria, Norway and Sweden it has been suggested that the power resources of the workforce are most strong. But in all these corporatist countries, encompassing interest groups have been formed. Interest groups are not fragmented and they have emerged so that their leaders can negotiate and bargain and ultimately deliver the promises they have made in the negotiations. Because the interest groups are encompassing, they seek economic outcomes that are in the interests of virtually all the society they represent, and because they are powerful, and hierarchical, they can deliver their side of the agreement.

This agreement is thus a powerful and encompassing arrangement, though it is also voluntary and consensual. It is impossible for the workforce in countries like Britain and the USA to behave like this because their collective interest group is fragmented and non-hierarchical. Their peak workforce negotiator in a country like Britain is the Trades Union Congress, but this group does not have controlling power over the rest of the fragmented union movement, and whatever it should agree is not necessarily enforceable on its members. Furthermore its membership is fragmented and, as public choice theory suggests, it will not rationally pursue ends that are in the wider social interest. Each fragment or trades union seeks to further only its particular concern, and this is not necessarily going to be in line with the broader interest of the entire workforce. Hence the only way in which incomes policies can be introduced in a country like Britain is by government imposition. They are not truly voluntary and consensual arrangements, and the chances of such a policy lasting must be slim, as the history of the British Social Contract in the mid-1970s suggests. Hence in nations where the workforce may be strong, but fragmented, the possibility of achieving voluntary, consensual agreements around economic policy is slight. And if some incomes policy is imposed it is likely to break down.

This argument means that countries which have not historically developed encompassing peak-interest groups will find it virtually impossible to enforce an incomes policy. And this in turn means that in these nations a Keynesian expansion is economically out of the question as it will only generate inflation. In terms of historically developed political arrangements, countries like Britain, the United States, Ireland, Italy and Canada, are in a most unfortunate position. The workforce is not weak and neoclassical solutions will not be effective; but Keynesian solutions will also be ineffective. On the other hand this argument means that countries with encompassing peak interest groups (Austria, Norway, Sweden, Japan, Switzerland) can contemplate an expansionary Keynesian solution in response to their current domestic economic difficulties of slow growth and low investment. Such an expansion would not generate inflation since in these countries the prevailing political arrangements make the implementation of an incomes policy possible and there is no reason why this policy could not be long-lasting.

In this view of affairs, which we covered in Chapters 2 and 4, the state is simply concerned with achieving domestic macroeconomic objectives. These objectives were the familiar ones of price stability, full employment and economic growth. We have now argued that when one considers the changes in the power distribution in modern society this century, the neoclassical model and its derived policy implications are not applicable. A managed recession will not decrease real wages and the desired economic objectives are thus not attainable in any developed country. In addition the Keynesian model and its derived policies are only viable in those countries where encompassing peak-interest groups have historically emerged. Whether or not price stability, full employment and economic growth can be achieved in developed nations depends critically on existing institutional arrangements, or alternatively whether suitable institutions can be developed. It is clear that many countries are going to find it well-nigh impossible to achieve their domestic macroeconomic objectives unless they manage to develop suitable institutions.

The Maintenance of Order

This discussion leads directly to the conclusion that where encompassing peak-interest groups do not exist, the state, in its attempt to achieve domestic macroeconomic targets, should encourage the formation and development of such groups. The pursuit of macroeconomic policy should be accompanied by whatever statesmanship is necessary to get these particular institutions formed. But this conclusion rests directly on the premise that the principal objective of the state is to achieve these macroeconomic targets. The state, by implicit assumption, should achieve these targets and it will seek to do so. In reaching price stability, full employment and some level of economic growth the state is now constrained by both its particular economy and its political arrangements, but these economic goals are nevertheless assumed to be the target of state behaviour.

But this assumption about the actual behaviour of a state is naive, as we pointed out in Chapter 5. In reality a state may not wish to pursue these objectives, and even if if does so wish, it is not omnipotent in its position in society. Two types of theories that seek to explain actual state behaviour were explored in Chapters 6 and 7. Mainstream economic theories of the state assume self-interested behaviour on the part of agents in the public sector, and Marxist theories assume that the state will behave in the interests of the capitalist class. Both these approaches were criticized for the lack of attention they pay to the state's pursuit of economic and social order. It was suggested that the fundamental and overriding concern of any state is the maintenance of order, including economic order, and only when this objective is achieved will a state contemplate any other action.

The behaviour of a state that is seeking order was discussed in Chapters 9 and 10, and on the basis of this work we can now recognize the current dilemmas facing the developed countries in their economic management. The new and unique conjuncture of events that confronts all developed countries at the present time is a mixture of both the political and the economic. On the political front the modern state is now faced with a workforce which has more power resources at its disposal than at any time in previous history. All countries have highly unionized labour forces, and in most nations the workforce also exerts a significant degree of political influence. The introduction of universal suffrage and the accompanying increased share of left-of-centre votes is a relatively new phenomenon.

This gradual but dramatic change in the power distribution is now, for the first time, accompanied by economic stagnation. During the 1950s and 1960s the high investment activity and growth in developed countries meant that the workforce were likely to be quiescent and consensual, as the gains from this growth accrued to them in increasing private and public consumption and expectations of rising living standards. However as the return on investment fell in the late 1960s and 1970s, private investment faltered, and growth stagnated or fell to very low levels. We now have, for the first time, a rather powerful workforce and a stagnant economy.

This particular conjuncture of political and economic issues is of particular relevance to the state in its attempt to maintain and reproduce economic order. New investment activity must be increased to stop the economic system stagnating, but channelling resources into new investment necessarily means constraining private and public consumption. Furthermore, in a capitalist system the dominant share of investment is controlled by the private sector, and it is this fact that raises particular difficulties for the state in its pursuit of order and its concurrent conduct of economic policy management. As we saw in Chapter 10, the state has basically two immediate options once the economy has stagnated and the workforce is powerful: it can either socialize investment or it can try and encourage more new private investment. Both these options however are fraught with difficulties.

In a stagnant economy, if the state socializes investment, this will, on the basis of the model in Chapter 10, gain the consent of the workforce. The state undertakes investment activity itself and the workers are agreed to this strategy since the return on this investment to them is adequate. In this scenario the workers will aid investment by forgoing current consumption claims or saving to fund the investment. However private entrepreneurs would clearly oppose such a policy, since their control over investment is directly threatened and their power in capitalism is quite overtly challenged. Recent capitalist opposition in Sweden to a policy that is of this ilk certainly confirms that it is an option which will generate considerable social conflict.

Furthermore, as we saw in Chapter 10, this socialization of investment is only a short-term panacea. Over time the return on investment is falling, and at some point the return on this investment to the workers will not be sufficient for them to curtail their current consumption claims. The only way in which growth can be upheld and stagnation avoided is for a new investment technology to be introduced. This introduction of a new investment technology was referred to as restructuring. Old investment techniques must be replaced by new techniques with higher returns. Hence, even if a social democratic state does undertake investment it must also at some point begin the task of introducing new technology with higher returns. This in turn means that the state, with socialized investment, must be practically capable of efficiently introducing the appropriate new technology, and it must develop ways of managing this restructuring process. This is a task which no democratic state has ever attempted before, and no state institutions exist that can really manage such a process.

Hence if the state socializes investment it faces two problems. One is the opposition to this policy that will be forthcoming from private entrepreneurs and the threat to economic order that this implies. The second problem is a fundamental question of whether or not the state is equipped to manage investment efficiently, and this will be particularly difficult when new technology has to be chosen and put in place.

On the other hand the socialization of investment is not the only option once growth and new private investment has stagnated. The other obvious alternative is for private entrepreneurs to increase their new investment, but for this to happen the return on this investment to them must be adequate. Since return on the prevailing technology has fallen to a point where new investment that incorporates this existing technology is not viable, there must be restructuring. New technology must be introduced that yields a higher return to the private investors. But for this new technology to be introduced, both capitalists and workers must forgo at least some part of current consumption claims to finance the new investment. The workers and capitalists will do so if they can see a future return on it for themselves, but this future return must really be perceived. Workers in countries that have experienced returns on past investment that have been high will be more willing to co-operate than in those countries where previous returns have been low to the workers.

In this sense countries like Japan and West Germany will be in a better position to both generate new investment and maintain economic order than countries like Britain where previous returns on investment, to the workers, have been less favourable. If workers have generated relatively little return on past abstinence, they will not be so prepared to forgo consumption claims and hence aid new investment. Hence the period of stagnating investment and growth could be very long-lived, and this is especially likely to be the case in countries where growth has been less favourable in the past. Introducing policies to increase private investment could generate economic conflict if these policies also constrain private and public consumption. This conclusion, derived from the model in Chapter 10, does mean that economic policy in the stagnant democratic societies of the 1980s could be severely constrained on grounds of political or economic order.

If this argument is right the particular conjuncture of low investment and growth along with a more powerful workforce poses considerable difficulties for economic management. The reason why slow growth persists may not be because there is anything technically or inherently wrong with economic theory or the policies derived from it. The main problem may be that we have not yet found a workable and operational policy. Policies suggested on a purely technical basis may be inoperable because they would generate economic disorder and conflict. If new investment is increased by socializing the investment process then capitalists will object most strongly. On the other hand if increased new investment is sought by encouraging private investment the workforce will object most strongly if their consumption claims are constrained. And no state will rationally implement any policy that it considers to be a threat to order. Hence the democratic developed nations are groping for a workable policy that will both increase investment and maintain order, and this search could continue and persist for a very long time. Economists, in considering policy implementation and recommendations, must focus their attentions on the constraints that the maintenance of order dictates. And if this takes economics into the wider fields of politics and sociology, as it must, then the economics discipline will only became more able to address the very real difficulties now facing developed societies.

Bibliography

Fondly I ponder You all:
without You I couldn't have managed
even my weakest lines.

Auden, 'A Thanksgiving'

Aaronovitch, Sam, 1956. *The Ruling Class*, Lawrence and Wishart, London.

Abraham, David, 1981. *The Collapse of the Weimar Republic*, Princeton University Press, Princeton.

Ahlbrandt, Roger, 1973. 'An Empirical Analysis of Private and Public Ownership and the Supply of Municipal Fire Services', *Public Choice*, Vol.16, Fall.

Alt, James E., and K. Alec Chrystal, 1981. 'Politico-economic models of British fiscal policy', in D.A. Hibbs Jr, H. Fassbender, and R.D. Rivers (eds.), *Contemporary Political Economy*.

Alt, James E., and K. Alec Chrystal, 1983. *Political Economics*, Wheatsheaf, Brighton.

Altvater, Elmar, 1973. 'Notes on some Problems of State Interventionism (I)', *Kapitalistate*, Vol.1, pp.96–108.

Altvater, Elmar, 1973, 'Notes on some Problems of State Interventionism (II)', *Kapitalistate*, Vol.2, pp.76–83.

Altvater, E., 1978. 'Some Problems of State Interventionism', in Holloway, John, and Sol Picciotto (eds.) (1978), *State and Capital*.

Amacher, R.C., R.D. Tollinson and T.D. Willett (eds.), 1976, *The Economic Approach to Public Policy*, Cornell University Press, Ithaca.

Ames, E., 1965. *Soviet Economic Processes*, Homewood, Illinois.

Arrow, K.J., 1951. *Social Choice and Individual Values*, John Wiley and Sons, New York.

Arrow, K.J., 1974. *The Limits of Organization*, W.W. Norton, New York.

Arrow, K.J., and F.H. Hahn, 1971. *General Competitive Analysis*, Oliver and Boyd, Edinburgh.

Ashenfelter, O., and S. Kelley Jr., 1975. 'Determinants of Participation in Presidential Elections', *Journal of Law and Economics*, December, Vol.18.

Atkinson, A.B., and J.E. Stiglitz, 1980. *Lectures on Public Economics*, McGraw Hill, Maidenhead.

Bachrach, Peter, and Morton S. Baratz, 1962. 'The Two Faces of Power', *American Political Science Review*, Vol.52

Bachrach, Peter, and Morton S. Baratz, 1970. *Power and Poverty: Theory and Practice*, Oxford University Press, New York.

Bacon, Robert, *et al.*, 1976. *The Dilemmas of Government Expenditure*, Institute of Economic Affairs, London.

Barry, Brian, 1970. *Sociologists, Economists and Democracy*, University of Chicago Press, Chicago.

Barry, Brian, 1983. 'Some Questions About Explanations', *International Studies Quarterly*, Vol.27.

Baumol, W.J., 1965. *Welfare Economics and the Theory of the State*, Prentice Hall, London.

Baumol, W.J., P.A. Samuelson and Michio Morishima, 1974. 'On Marx, the Transformation Problem and Opacity', *Journal of Economic Literature*.

Bell, Daniel, and Irving Kristol (eds.), 1981. *The Crisis in Economic Theory*, Basic Books, New York.

Bentham, Jeremy, 1830. *The Constitutional Code*, in F. Rosen and J.H. Burns (eds.), *Collected Works of Jeremy Bentham*, Oxford University Press, Oxford.

Beyme, K. von, 1977. *Gewerkschaften und Arbeitsbeziehungen in Kapitalistischen Ländern*, Piper, Munich.

Blinder, A.S., and R. Solow, 1973. 'Does Fiscal Policy Matter?', *Journal of Public Economics*, Vol.2.

Borcheding, Thomas E. (ed.), 1977. *Budgets and Bureaucrats: The Sources of Government Growth*, Duke University Press, Durham, North Carolina.

Bradford, D.F., R.A. Malt and W.E. Oates, 1969. 'The Rising Cost of Local Public Services: Some Evidence and Reflection', *National Tax Journal*, June, Vol.22.

Braybrooke, David, and Charles E. Lindblom, 1963. *A Strategy of Decision*, Free Press, New York.

Brennan, H.G., and James M. Buchanan, 1981. *Monopoly in Money and Inflation*, Institute for Economic Affairs, London.

Breton, A., 1974. *The Economic Theory of Representative Government*, Aldine, Chicago.

Breton, A., and R. Wintrobe, 1975. 'The Equilibrium Size of a Budget Maximizing Bureau', *Journal of Political Economy*, February, Vol.83.

Brittan, Samuel, 1977. *The Economic Consequences of Democracy*, Temple Smith, London.

Brown, C.V., and P.M. Jackson, 1978. *Public Sector Economics*, Martin Robertson, Oxford.

Brunner, Karl, and William H. Meckling, 1977. 'The Perception of Man and the Conception of Government', *Journal of Money, Credit and Banking*, Vol.9.

Buchanan, J.M., 1975. *The Limits of Liberty*, University of Chicago Press, Chicago.

Buchanan, James M., *et al.*, 1978. *The Economics of Politics*, Institute of Economic Affairs, London.

Buchanan, James M., and M.R. Flowers, 1975. *The Public Finances*, Richard D. Irwin, Homewood, Illinois.

Buchanan, James M., and Gordon Tullock, 1962. *The Calculus of Consent*, University of Michigan Press, Ann Arbor.

Buchanan, James and R.E. Wagner, 1977. *Democracy in Deficit*, Academic Press, New York.

Bull, Hedley, 1977, *The Anarchical Society*, Macmillan, London.

Bush, W.C., 1972. 'Individual Welfare in Anarchy', in G. Tullock (ed.), 1972, *Explorations in the Theory of Anarchy*.

191

Bush, W., and A. Denzau, 1977. 'The Voting Behaviour of Bureaucrats and Public Sector Growth', in Borcheding, Thomas E. (ed.), 1977, *Budgets and Bureaucrats*.

Bush, W.C. and L.S. Mayer, 1974. 'Some Implications of Anarchy for the Distribution of Property', *Journal of Economic Theory*, Vol.8, August.

Cagan, P., 1975. 'Changes in the Recession Behaviour of Wholesale Prices in the 1920s and Post World War II', *Explorations in Economic Research*, Winter, Vol.2.

Cameron, David R., 1982. 'On the Limits of the Public Economy', *Stato e Mercato*, Vol.2, April.

Cameron, David, 1983. *Social Democracy, Corporatism, Labour Quiescence, and the Representation of Economic Interest in Advanced Capitalist Society*. Forthcoming in John Goldthorpe (ed.), *Order and Conflict in Contemporary Capitalism*.

Catephores, George, 1979a. 'The Labour Theory of Value: Myth or Reality?', *Economic Bulletin*, No.5, Central Books, London.

Catephores, George, 1979b. Review: 'Marx After Sraffa', *Journal of Political Economy*, October, Vol.87.

Cheprakov, V. (ed.), 1969. *State Monopoly Capitalism*, Progress Press, Moscow.

Chrystal, K.A., 1979. *Controversies in British Macroeconomics*, Philip Alan, London, first edition.

Chrystal, K.A., and J. Alt, 1979. *Public Sector Behaviour: The Status of the Political Business Cycle*, Presented at the Annual Conference of the A.U.T.E., Exeter, March.

Coase, R., 1960. 'The Problem of Social Cost', *Journal of Law and Economics*, October.

Cockburn, Cynthia, 1978. *The Local State*, Pluto Press, London.

Communist Party of Great Britain, 1977. *The British Road to Socialism*, draft, Communist Party of Great Britain, London.

Coombes, David, 1982. *Representative Government and Economic Power*, Heinemann, London.

Cornwall, John, 1977. *Modern Capitalism*, Martin Robertson, Oxford.

Crain, M., and R. Tollinson, 1976. 'Campaign Expenditure and Political Competition', *Journal of Law and Economics*, Vol.19, April.

Crouch, Colin (ed.), 1979. *State and Economy in Contemporary Capitalism*, Croom Helm, London.

Crouch, Colin, 1982. *Trade Unions: the Logic of Collective Action*, Fontana, London.

Crozier, Michael J., Samuel P. Huntington and Josi Watanuki, 1975. *The Crisis of Democracy: report on the governability of democracies to the Trilateral Commission*, New York.

Dahl, Robert A., 1957. 'The Concept of Power', *Behavioural Science*, Vol.2.

Dahrendorf, Ralf, 1980. 'Effectiveness and Legitimacy: on the "governability" of democracies', *Political Quarterly*, Vol.51, No.4.

Davies, D.G., 1971. 'The Efficiency of Public Versus Private Firms', *Journal of Law and Economics*, Vol.14, April.

Davis, Horace B., 1978. *Toward a Marxist Theory of Nationalism*, Monthly Review Press, New York.

Desai, M., 1979. *Marxian Economics*, Blackwells, Oxford.

Desai, M., 1981. *Testing Monetarism*, Frances Pinter. London.

Di Stefano, J.J., A.R. Stubberud and I.J. Williams, 1976. *Feedback and Control Systems*, Schaum's Outline Series, McGraw Hill, New York.

Dixit, A.K., 1976. 'Public finance in a Keynesian temporary disequilibrium', *Journal of Economic Theory*, Vol.12.

Dobb, M.H., 1973. *Theories of Value and Distribution*, Cambridge University Press, Cambridge.

van den Doel, Hans, 1974. *Democracy and Welfare Economics*, Cambridge University Press, Cambridge.

Downs, A., 1957. *An Economic Theory of Democracy*, Harper and Row, New York.

Downs, A., 1960. 'Why the Government Budget is Too Small in a Democracy', *World Politics*, July, Vol.12.

Dyson, Kenneth, 1980. *The State Tradition in Western Europe*, Martin Robertson, Oxford.

Fair, Ray C., 1978. 'The Sensitivity of Fiscal Policy Effects to Assumptions about the Behaviour of the Federal Reserve', *Econometrica*, Vol.46, September.

Fine, Ben, and Laurence Harris, 1976a. 'Controversial Issues in Marxist Economic Theory', *Socialist Register*, Merlin Press, London.

Fine, Ben and Laurence Harris, 1976b, 'State Expenditure in Advanced Capitalism: A Critique', *New Left Review*, Vol.98, July/August.

Foley, D.K., 1978. 'State Expenditure from a Marxist Perspective', *Journal of Public Economics*, Vol.9, April.

Frankel, Joseph, 1970. *National Interest*, Macmillan, London.

Frey, B., 1978. *Modern Political Economy*, Martin Robertson, Oxford.

Frey, Bruno, and L.J. Lau, 1968. 'Towards A Mathematical Model of Government Behaviour', *Zeitschrift für Nationalökonomie*, Vol.28.

Frey, B.S., and F. Schneider, 1978. 'An Empirical Study of Politico-Economic Interaction in the United States', *Review of Economics and Statistics*, Vol.60.

Frey, B.S., and F. Schneider, 1978. 'A Politico-Economic Model of the United Kingdom', *Economic Journal*, Vol.88.

Frey, B., and F. Schneider, 1979. 'An Econometric Model with An Endogenous Government Sector', *Public Choice*, Vol.34.

Friedman, Benjamin M., 1978. 'Crowding Out or Crowding In? Economic Consequences of Financing Government Deficits', *Brookings Papers on Economic Activity*, No.3.

Friedman, Milton, 1948. 'A monetary and fiscal framework for economic stability', *American Economic Review*, Vol.38.

Friedman, Milton, 1959. *A Program for Monetary Stability*, Fordham University Press, New York.

Friedman, Milton, 1977. Nobel Lecture: 'Inflation and Unemployment', *Journal of Political Economy*, June.

Galbraith, J.K., 1967. *The New Industrial State*, Penguin, London.

Gilpin, Robert, 1981. *War and Change in World Politics*, Cambridge University Press, Cambridge.

Glyn, A., and Bob Sutcliffe, 1972. *British Capitalism, Workers and the Profit Squeeze*, Penguin, London.

Goldfeld, S.M., and A.S. Blinder, 1972. 'Some Implications of Endogenous Stabilization Policy', *Brookings Papers on Economic Activity*, Vol.3.

Goldthorpe, John (ed.), forthcoming. *Order and Conflict in Contemporary Capitalism*, Oxford University Press, Oxford.

Goodhardt, C.A.E., and R.J. Bhansali, 1970. 'Political economy', *Political Studies*, Vol.18.

Gordon, D.M., 1972. 'Taxation of the poor and the normative theory of tax incidence', *American Economic Review, Papers and Proceedings*, Vol.62.

193

Gordon, R.J., 1975. 'The demand for and supply of inflation', *Journal of Law and Economics*, Vol.18.

Gordon, R.J., 1981, 'Output Fluctuations and Gradual Price Adjustment', *Journal of Economic Literature*.

Gough, Ian, 1975. Review of *The Fiscal Crisis of the State* by James O'Connor. *Bulletin of the Conference of Socialist Economists*, Vol.4.

Gough, Ian, 1975. 'State Expenditure in Advanced Capitalism', *New Left Review*, Vol. 92. July/August.

Gough, Ian, 1979. *The Political Economy of the Welfare State*, Macmillan, London.

Green, J., and E. Sheshinkski, 1976. 'Direct versus Indirect Remedies for Externalities', *Journal of Political Economy*, Vol.84.

Hampshire, Stuart (ed.), 1975. *Public and Private Morality*, Cambridge University Press, Cambridge.

Hardin, Russell, 1982. *Collective Action*, Johns Hopkins University Press, Baltimore.

Harsanyi, John C., 1977. *Rational Behaviour and Bargaining Equilibrium in Games and Social Situations*, Cambridge University Press, Cambridge.

Hawtrey, R.G., 1930. *Economic Aspects of Sovereignty*, Longmans, Green and Co., London.

Hayek, F.A., 1944. *The Road to Serfdom*, Routledge and Kegan Paul, London.

Hayek, F.A., 1960. *The Constitution of Liberty*, Routledge and Kegan Paul, London.

Heclo, Hugh and Aaron Wildavsky, 1981. *The Private Government of Public Money*, Macmillan, London. Second edition.

Hibbs, Douglas, 1977. 'Political Parties and Macroeconomic Policy', *American Political Science Review*, Vol.71.

Hibbs, D.A., Jr., H. Fassbender and R. Douglas Rivers (eds.), 1981. *Contemporary Political Economy*, North Holland, Amsterdam.

Hicks, J.R., 1932. *The Theory of Wages*, Macmillan, London.

Hicks, J.R., 1937. 'Mr Keynes and the Classics; A Suggested Interpretation', *Econometrica*, Vol.5, April.

Hicks, J.R., 1976. '"Revolutions" in Economics', in Spiro Latsis (ed.), *Method and Appraisal in Economics*, 1976, Cambridge University Press, Cambridge.

Hirsch, Fred, and John H. Goldthorpe (eds.), 1978. *The Political Economy of Inflation*, Martin Robertson, Oxford.

Hirsch, Joachim, 1978. 'The State Apparatus and Social Reproduction: Elements of a Bourgeois State', in Holloway, John, and Sol Picciotto (eds.), 1978, *State and Capital*.

Hirschman, Albert O., 1945. *National Power and the Structure of Foreign Trade*, University of California Press, Berkeley.

Hirschman, Albert O., 1970. *Exit, Voice and Loyalty*, Harvard University Press, Cambridge.

Hirschman, Albert O., 1977. *The Passions and the Interests: Political Arguments for Capitalism before its Triumph*, Princeton University Press, Princeton.

Hobbes, T., 1651. *Leviathan*, Basil Blackwell, Oxford (1946 edition).

Holloway, John, and Sol Picciotto, 1977. 'Capital, Crisis and the State', *Capital and Class*, Vol.2, Summer.

Holloway, John, and Sol Picciotto (eds.), 1978. *State and Capital, A Marxist Debate*, Edward Arnold, London.

Hotelling, H., 1929, 'Stability in Competition', *Economic Journal*, March, Vol.39.

Hunt, Alan (ed.), 1980. *Marxism and Democracy*, Lawrence and Wishart, London.

Hutchison, T.W., 1966. *Markets and the Franchise*, Institute of Economic Affairs, London.

Intriligator, Michael D., 1971. *Mathematical Optimization and Economic Theory*, Prentice Hall, Englewood Cliffs, N.J.

Ionescu, Ghita, 1975. *Centripetal Politics*, London.

Jackson, P.M., 1982. *The Political Economy of Bureaucracy*, Philip Alan, Oxford.

Jessop, Bob, 1977. 'Recent theories of the Capitalist State', *Cambridge Journal of Economics*, Vol.1, December.

Jessop, Bob, 1979. 'Corporatism, Parliamentarism and Social Democracy', in P.D. Schmitter and G. Lehmbruch (eds.), *Trends Towards Corporatist Intermediation*.

Jessop, Bob, 1982, *The Capitalist State*, Martin Robertson, Oxford.

Jevons, W.S., 1871. *Theory of Political Economy*, Macmillan, London.

Kalecki, Michal, 1943. 'Political Aspects of Full Employment', *Political Quarterly*.

Kindleberger, Charles P., 1970. *Power and Money*, Macmillan, London.

Kindleberger, Charles, 1983. 'On the Rise and Decline of Nations', *International Studies Quarterly*, Vol.27.

King, Anthony, 1975. 'Overload: problems of governing in the 1970s', *Political Studies*, Vol.XXIII, No.3.

King, M.A., 1975. 'The UK Profits Crisis: Myth or Reality?', *Economic Journal*, Vol.85, March.

Korpi, Walter, 1983. *The Democratic Class Struggle*, Routledge and Kegan Paul, London.

Korpi, Walter and Michael Shalev, 1980. 'Strikes, Power and Politics in the Western Nations, 1900–1976', in Maurice Zeitlin (ed.), *Political Power and Social Theory*, Vol.I, JAI Press, New York.

Kramer, G.H., 1971. 'Short term fluctuations in U.S. Voting Behaviour', 1896–1964', *American Political Science Review*, Vol.65.

Kreisi, Hanspeter, 1982. 'The Structure of the Swiss Political System', in G. Lehmbruch and P.C. Schmitter (eds.), 1982, *Patterns of Corporatist Policy Making*.

Laclau, Ernesto, 1975. Review article: 'The Specificity of the Political: the Poulantzas – Miliband debate', *Economy and Society*, Vol.4, February, pp.87–110.

Laidler, David, 1981. 'Monetarism: An Interpretation and An Assessment', *Economic Journal*, March, Vol.91.

Lancaster, Kelvin, 1973. 'The Dynamic Inefficiency of Capitalism', *Journal of Political Economy*, Vol.81, July–Dec.

Lange, Peter, 1984. 'Unions, Workers and Wage Regulation in Advanced Industrial Democracies: The Rational Bases of Consent'. Forthcoming in John Goldthorpe (ed.), *Order and Conflict in Contemporary Capitalism*.

Laski, Harold, 1931. *Introduction to Politics*, George Allen and Unwin, London.

Lehmbruch, G., 1977. 'Liberal Corporatism and Party Government', *Comparative Political Studies*, Vol.10.

Lehmbruch, G., and P.C. Schmitter (eds.), 1982. *Patterns in Corporatist Policy Making*, Sage, London.

Lenin, V.I., 1965. *The State and Revolution*, Foreign Languages Press, Peking.

Lindbeck, Assar, 1976. 'Stabilization Policy in Open Economics with Endogenous Politicians', *American Economic Review, Papers and Proceedings*.

Lindblom, Charles E., 1977. *Politics and Markets*, Basic Books, New York.

Locke, J., 1939. 'An Essay Concerning the True Original Extent and End of Civil Government', reprinted in *The English Philosophers*, Random House, New York.

Lucas, R.E., 1976. 'Econometric Policy Evaluation: A Critique', in K. Brunner and A.H. Meltzer (eds.), *The Phillips Curve and the Labour Market*, North Holland, Amsterdam.

Luce, R. Duncan, and Howard Raiffa, 1957. *Games and Decisions*, John Wiley, New York.

Lukes, Stephen, 1974. *Power: A Radical View*, Macmillan, London.

Machiavelli, Niccolo, 1520. *The Prince*, 1982 edition, Penguin, Harmondsworth.

MacPherson, C.B., 1962. *The Political Theory of Possessive Individualism*, Oxford University Press, Oxford.

MacRae, G.D., 1977. 'A Political Model of the Business Cycle', *Journal of Political Economy*, Vol.85.

Malinvaud, E., 1972. *Lectures on Microeconomic Theory*, North Holland, Amsterdam.

Mandel, Ernest, 1962. *Marxist Economic Theory*, Merlin, London.

Marx, Karl, 1973. *Grundrisse*, Penguin, London.

Marx, Karl, 1974. *Capital*, Vol.1, Penguin, London.

Meidner, Rudolf, *et al.*, 1978. *Employee Investment Funds*, Allen and Unwin, London.

Migue, J.L., and G. Belanger, 1974. 'Towards a General Theory of Managerial Discretion', *Public Choice*, Vol.17, Spring.

Miliband, Ralph, 1973. *The State in Capitalist Society*, Quartet, London.

Miliband, Ralph, 1977. *Marxism and Politics*, Oxford University Press, Oxford.

Miliband, Ralph, 1982. *Capitalist Democracy in Britain*, Oxford University Press, Oxford.

Mill, J.S., 1962. *Considerations on Representative Government*, Gateway, New York. Original edition London 1861.

Mill, J.S., 1965. *Principles of Political Economy*, Toronto University Press, Toronto. Original edition London 1848.

Mises, L. von, 1944. *Bureaucracy*, Yale University Press, New Haven.

Modigliani, F., 1977. 'The Monetarist Controversy, or Should We Forsake Stabilization Policies', *American Economic Review*, March, Vol.67.

Moore, Barrington, Jr., 1967. *Social Origins of Dictatorship and Democracy*, Penguin, Harmondsworth.

Morgan, Brian, 1980. *Monetarists and Keynesians*, Macmillan, London.

Morishima, Michio, 1973. *Marx's Economics*, Cambridge University Press, Cambridge.

Morishima, Michio, 1974. 'Marx in the Light of Modern Economic Theory', *Econometrica*, July, Vol.42.

Morishima, Michio, and George Catephores, 1978. *Value, Exploitation and Growth*, McGraw Hill, London.

Mosley, Hugh, 1978. 'Is There a Fiscal Crisis of the State?', *Monthly Review*, Vol.30, May.

Mueller, Dennis C., 1979. *Public Choice*, Cambridge University Press, Cambridge.

Musgrave, Richard A., 1959. *The Theory of Public Finance*, McGraw Hill, New York.

Nash, John F., 1950. 'The Bargaining Problem', *Econometrica*, Vol.18.

Nash, John F., 1953. 'Two Person Co-operative Games', *Econometrica*, Vol.21.

Newbery, D.M.G., and J.E. Stiglitz, 1979. 'Pareto-inferior trade', *Oxford University Discussion Paper*.

Niskanen, William A., 1968. 'The Peculiar Economics of Bureaucracy', *American Economic Review*, May.

Niskanen, William A., 1971. *Bureaucracy and Representative Government*, Aldine Atherton, Chicago.

Niskanen, William A., 1979. Review of Susan Rose-Ackerman, 1978, *Corruption: A Study in Political Economy*, Academic Press, London, in *Journal of Economic Literature*, June, Vol.17.

Nordhaus, W., 1975. 'The Political Business Cycle', *Review of Economic Studies*, Vol.42.

Nozick, Robert, 1974. *Anarchy, State and Utopia*, Basil Blackwell, Oxford.

Nutter, G., 1978. *Growth of Government in the West*, American Enterprise Institute, Washington.

Oates, W.E., 1972. *Fiscal Federalism*, Harcourt Brace Jovanovich, New York.

O'Connor, James, 1973. *The Fiscal Crisis of the State*, St. Martin's Press, New York.

Olson, M., 1965. *The Logic of Collective Action*, Harvard University Press, Cambridge.

Olson, M., 1982. *The Rise and Decline of Nations*, Yale University Press, New Haven.

Orzechowski, William, 1977. 'Economic Models of Bureaucracy', in Borcheding, Thomas E. (ed.), 1977, *Budgets and Bureaucrats*.

Panitch, Leo, 1975. *Social Democracy and Industrial Militancy*, Cambridge University Press, Cambridge.

Parkin, Frank, 1979. *Marxism and Class Theory*, Tavistock, London.

Parsons, T., 1937. *The Structure of Social Action*, Free Press, Glencoe, Illinois.

Payne, J., 1979. 'Inflation, Unemployment and Left Wing Parties: A Re-analysis', *American Political Science Review*, Vol.73.

Peacock, Alan, 1979. *The Economic Analysis of Government*, Martin Robertson, Oxford.

Peacock, Alan T., and Jack Wiseman, 1967. *The Growth of Public Expenditure in the U.K.*, George Allen and Unwin, London.

Pempel, T.J., and Keüchi Tsunekawa, 1979. 'Corporatism without Labour? The Japanese Anomaly', in P.C. Schmitter and G. Lehmbruch (eds.), 1979, *Trends in Corporatist Intermediation*.

Perez-Diaz, Victor M., 1978. *State, Bureaucracy and Civil Service*, Macmillan, London.

Pontryagin, L.S., *et al.*, 1962. *The Mathematical Theory of Optimal Processes*, John Wiley, New York.

Poulantzas, N., 1972. 'The Problem of the Capitalist State', in Robin Blackburn (ed.), *Ideology in Social Science: Readings in Critical Social Theory*, Fontana, London, 1972.

Poulantzas, N., 1975. *Political Power and Social Classes*, New Left Books, London.

Przeworski, Adam, and Michael Wallerstein, 1982. 'The Structure of Class Conflict in Democratic Capitalist Societies', *American Political Science Review*, June, Vol.76.

Rapoport, Anatol, 1960. *Fights, Games and Debates*, The University of Michigan Press, Ann Arbor.

Rawls, J.A., 1971. *A Theory of Justice*, Harvard University Press, Harvard.

Robbins, Lord, 1978. *The Theory of Economic Policy in English Classical Political Economy*, 2nd edition, Macmillan, London.

Robinson, Joan, 1942. *An Essay in Marxian Economics*, Macmillan, London.

Robinson, Joan, 1962. *Economic Philosophy*, Penguin, Harmondsworth.

Robinson, Joan, 1965. 'What Remains of Marxism', *Collected Economic Papers*, Blackwells, Oxford.

Rosen, F., 1983. *Jeremy Bentham and Representative Democracy: A Study of the Constitutional Code*, Clarendon Press, Oxford.

Rostow, W.W., 1960. *The Stages of Economic Growth*, Cambridge University Press, Cambridge.

Rowthorn, Bob, 1980. *Conflict and Inflation*, Lawrence and Wishart, London.

Sachs, J., 1980. 'The Changing Cyclical Behaviour of Wages and Prices, 1890–1976', *American Economic Review*, March.

Samuelson, P.A., 1971. 'Understanding the Marxian Notion of Exploitation', *Journal of Economic Literature*, June, Vol.9.

Sargent, Thomas J., 1976. 'A Classical Macroeconomic Model of the United States', *Journal of Political Economy*, Vol.84.

Sargent, Thomas J., 1979. *Macroeconomic Theory*, Academic Press, New York.

Sargent, Thomas J., and N. Wallace, 1975. 'Rational expectations, the optimal monetary instrument and the optimal money supply rule', *Journal of Political Economy*, Vol.83.

Sbodnikov, Y. (ed.), 1971. *Socialism and Capitalism: Score and Prospects*, Progress Press, Moscow.

Scharpf, Fritz W., 1981. *The Political Economy of Inflation and Unemployment in Western Europe: An Outline*, Discussion Paper, IIM/Labour Market Policy, Wissenschaftszentrum, Berlin.

Schelling, Thomas C., 1960. *The Strategy of Conflict*, Harvard University Press, Cambridge.

Schmidt, Manfred G., 1982. 'Does Corporatism Matter? Economic Crisis, Politics and Rates of Unemployment in Capitalist Democracies in the 1970s', in G. Lehmbruch and P.C. Schmitter (eds.), 1982, *Patterns of Corporatist Policy Making*.

Schmitter, P.C. and G. Lehmbruch (eds.), 1979. *Trends Towards Corporatist Intermediation*, Sage, London.

Schott, Kerry, 1982. 'The Rise of Keynesian Economics', *Economy and Society*, Vol.11.

Schott, Kerry, 1984. 'Investment, Order and Conflict in a Simple Dynamic Model of Capitalism'. Forthcoming in John Goldthorpe (ed.), *Order and Conflict in Contemporary Capitalism*.

Schumacher, E.F., 1973. *Small is Beautiful*, Abacus, London.

Schumpeter, Joseph A., 1943. *Capitalism, Socialism and Democracy*, George Allen and Unwin, London.

Sen, Amartya K., 1974. 'Choice, Orderings, and Morality', in S. Körner (ed.), 1974, *Practical Reason*, Yale University Press, New Haven and London.

Sen, Amartya K., 1977. 'Rational Fools: A Critique of the Behavioural Foundations of Economic Theory', *Philosophy and Public Affairs*, Vol.6.

Seton, F., 1957. 'The Transformation Problem', *Review of Economic Studies*, June.

Sherman, R., 1971. 'Experimental Oligopoly', *Kyklos*, Vol.24.

Shonfield, Andrew, 1969. *Modern Capitalism*, Oxford University Press, Oxford.

Shonfield, Andrew, 1982. *The Use of Public Power*, Oxford University Press, Oxford.

Siegel, S., and L.E. Fouraker, 1960. *Bargaining and Group Decision Making*, McGraw Hill, New York.

Spann, R.M, 1977. 'Rates of Productivity Change and the Growth of Local Government Expenditure', in Borcheding, Thomas E. (ed.), 1977, *Budgets and Bureaucrats*.

Steedman, Ian, 1977. *Marx After Sraffa*, New Left Books, London.

Stiglitz, J.E., 1980. *Information and Economic Analysis*, Oxford University Press, Oxford.

Stokes, D.E., 1963. 'Spatial Models of Party Competition', *American Political Science Review*, June, Vol.57.

Stone, R., and Company, 1973. 'Survey of 85 Municipal Governments', *Municipal Yearbook*, 1973 volume, U.S.A.

Sweezy, Paul, 1942. *The Theory of Capitalist Economy*, Monthly Review Press, New York.

Taylor, M., 1976. *Anarchy and Cooperation*, John Wiley, New York.

Therborn, Goran, 1977. 'Capital and Suffrage', *New Left Review*, Vol.103, May/June.

Therborn, Goran, 1978. *What Does the Ruling Class Do When It Rules?*, New Left Books, London.

Thompson, Dennis F., 1976. *John Stuart Mill and Representative Democracy*, Princeton University Press, Princeton.

Tollinson, R.D., M. Crain and P. Paulter, 1975. 'Information and Voting', *Public Choice*, Winter, Vol.24.

Tufte, E., 1978. *The Political Control of the Economy*, Princeton University Press, Princeton.

Tullock, G., 1965. 'Entry Barriers in Politics', *American Economic Review, Papers and Proceedings*, May.

Tullock, G., (ed.), 1972. *Explorations in the Theory of Anarchy*, Center for the Study of Public Choice, Blacksberg, Virginia.

Turnovsky, Stephen J., 1976. 'On the Scope of Optimal and Discretionary Policies in the Stabilization of Stochastic Linear Systems', in J.D. Pitchford and S.J. Turnovsky (eds.), *Applications of Control Theory to Economic Analysis*, North Holland, Amsterdam, 1976.

Turnovsky, Stephen J., 1977. *Macroeconomic Analysis and Stabilization Policy*, Cambridge University Press, Cambridge.

Usher, Dan, 1981. *The Economic Prerequisite to Democracy*, Basil Blackwell, Oxford.

de Vries, Jan, 1983. 'The Rise and Decline of Nations in Historical Perspective', *International Studies Quarterly*, Vol.27.

Weber, M., 1947. *The Theory of Social and Economic Organisation*, Oxford University Press, Oxford.

Weintraub, E. Roy. 1975. *Conflict and Co-operation in Economics*, Macmillan, London.

Whynes, D.K., and R.A. Bowles, 1981. *The Economic Theory of the State*, Martin Robertson, Oxford.

Wildavsky, Aaron, 1979. *The Politics of the Budgetary Process*, Little Brown, Boston.

Williamson, Oliver E., 1964. *The Economics of Discretionary Behaviour: Managerial Objectives in a Theory of the Firm*, Prentice Hall, Englewood Cliffs, N.J.

Wilson, Woodrow, 1887. 'The Study of Administration', *Political Science Quarterly*, Vol.2 (reprinted Vol.56, 1941).

Wolfe, Alan, 1977. *The Limits of Legitimacy*, Free Press, New York.

Wright, Erik Olin, 1978. *Class, Crisis and the State*, New Left Books, London.

Index